PENGUIN BOOKS

EATING THE PRESENT, TASTING THE FUTURE

Charmaine O'Brien has been researching and writing on the history and culture of food and eating for more than two decades, specifically Indian and Australian food and is internationally recognized for her work on both. Her publications include *The Penguin Food Guide to India*, the first comprehensive guide to Indian regional food. Her work won the Best National Food Writing award and the Gourmand World Cookbook Awards in 2017. She also holds a PhD in creative writing, with a focus on the psychology of creativity and creative development.

Celebrating 35 Years of
Penguin Random House India

ALSO BY THE AUTHOR

The Penguin Food Guide to India
Flavours of Delhi: A Food Lover's Guide

Eating the Present

Present

TASTING the FUTURE

EXPLORING INDIA
THROUGH HER
CHANGING FOOD

CHARMAINE O'BRIEN

PENGUIN BOOKS

An imprint of Penguin Random House

PENGUIN BOOKS

USA | Canada | UK | Ireland | Australia
New Zealand | India | South Africa | China

Penguin Books is part of the Penguin Random House group of companies
whose addresses can be found at global.penguinrandomhouse.com

Published by Penguin Random House India Pvt. Ltd
4th Floor, Capital Tower 1, MG Road,
Gurugram 122 002, Haryana, India

Penguin
Random House
India

First published in Penguin Books by Penguin Random House India 2023

ISBN 9780143450238

Typeset in Adobe Caslon Pro by Manipal Technologies Limited, Manipal

www.penguin.co.in

Contents

Introduction

In December 1995, the year I first travelled to the subcontinent, this is what I thought I knew about India when I landed at Delhi's Indira Gandhi Airport:

1. India had a national cuisine called curry. I knew this because all the Indian restaurants I had been to in Australia served a menu of similar, if not the same, dishes.
2. India had a national cricket team. I knew this because my father watched the World Cup on television. I noticed Kapil Dev was a very handsome Indian cricketer.
3. India had Indian elephants, different from African elephants, and the Taj Mahal was one of the seven modern wonders of the world. These were general facts learnt at school.
4. When Indians were not eating curry, they were starving. This was learnt from the brief mention of India in our school history books.

5. When Indians were not playing cricket, they were struggling with some sort of natural disaster. This was learnt from the Australian media.

6. Indians were one homogenized race of people with a homogenized culture, a notion bred by all of the above.

By February 1996, I had visited the Taj Mahal, where I was so besieged by touts, randy teenage boys, and families insistent, no matter my reluctance, that I posed for a photograph with them. There was little opportunity for me to enjoy the 'wonder' of the country's most famous monument; I had seen a few elephants here and there, noticed boys playing cricket on any available flat open ground, and learnt Kapil Dev was not only good-looking, but he was also close to being a deity. Everything else I thought I knew about India and Indians was wrong, especially about what they ate: There was no generic 'Indian food' such as what was represented in restaurants in the West.

Not Love at First Sight: Falling for India

I had wanted to leave India after my first week there: Delhi's swirling urban chaos of people and cars, the gritty air, and men expectorating streams of red saliva everywhere (Was it blood? Was there a plague?) put me on my defence from the outset. Travelling on to Agra to see the world's most famed monument to love only heightened this apprehension. There I was pursued by a pack of excited local teenage boys—possibly passion fuelled by living close to said romantic edifice—around that city's Red Fort and when I was woken in my hotel room at some pre-dawn hour by the sound of several other guests practising a vigorous phlegm-cleansing routine that reverberated through the flimsy walls, I fled to Rishikesh. There, I picked up a pernicious, lingering, stomach bug after eating a thali at a popular tourist restaurant. The only thing that prevented me from packing up and taking a flight home at this point was the necessity of staying within metres of a bathroom. I waited out the worst of my malady in a riverside ashram, decided to persist with the journey I had started, and spent the next eight weeks travelling the country in lumbering local buses and third-class railway carriages, sleeping on brutally hard beds in cheap hotels. Walking alone anywhere meant being the target of a barrage of verbal harassment from men. I was so frazzled by this in Jaipur that I had to hole up in my hotel room for 24 hours, concerned that if I went out sightseeing, I might snap and physically assault the next person who troubled me. By the time this trip wound up, I had had enough and could hardly wait to get on my departing flight, but it was not a terminal end to the relationship. I had connected to something in India. Two weeks after arriving home, I booked a flight to Delhi for November of that year. I have been a regular visitor, sometimes resident, and a perpetual student of India since then.

The digestive gremlin I picked up in Rishikesh proved a persistent companion on my first Indian journey, limiting my diet to toast, pancakes, finger chips, and bananas for many weeks. Despite being unable to eat any local cuisine until the latter part of this adventure, I was keenly observing India's food life all along, which I will write more on in Chapter 1. Suffice to say here, I found myself with an ambition to write a book about India's regional cuisine, not a recipe book, but a unique concept of a historical, sociocultural, and practical guide to exploring the country's diverse food cultures. Even though I can now give a comprehensive account of what inspired this notion, at the time, it was merely a gathering of glimpses that indicated how India's social and cultural fabric, interwoven with diverse ethnicities, languages, religious faiths, castes, and classes, her ancient history of trade, and a varied geography—encompassing soaring mountain peaks, deserts, a network of mighty rivers, 6000 kilometres of coastline, evergreen, tropical, and alpine forests—as well as some of the richest agricultural lands in the world, were all, people and place, mirrored in the multiplicity of her food production, cooking practices, cuisines, and eating habits. Regardless of all the challenges, I wanted to know more about India, and food was going to be my way into understanding her.

The turning of the twenty-first century did not unleash the dramatic events many imagined, but 2000 seemed like a time to pack up my life in Australia and head off to India to pursue my book idea, only to realize once I was there that I lacked the experience and resources to take on the entire country—yet. Instead, I wrote a book about the history of food in Delhi and then another about a singular food culture of that city. Researching India's food inspired me to look into my own backyard, and I started writing on Australia's food history. After all of this, I finally felt ready to take on all of India. Several years of travel, conversation, cooking, eating, and scholarly research followed to finally produce *The Penguin Food Guide to India* in 2013.

For fifteen years, my focus had been on India's 'traditional' food system, the established production and processing practices and cuisines distinctive of different regions and communities, retained through generations of replication and incrementally evolving through the absorption of new foods and influences. Still, over this time, I also noticed how the country was changing at a swift pace. The liberalization of the Indian economy had unleashed concurrent forces of globalization, capitalism, and rapid urbanization, turning India's metropolitan areas into megacities and a much larger segment of her population into enthusiastic consumers. As soon as the *Guide* was done, I turned my attention from India's living food heritage to the idea of documenting the pulsating transformation of her contemporary foodscape, what was influencing this change, and what it might augur for the future. History was not out of the picture though.

What We Eat Is More Than What Is on the Plate

Every one of us eats, albeit to our own preferences and circumstances. Exploring changes in what and how India is eating offers a bigger story of a nation: Food uniquely connects Indians with each other in many ways. Food is identity: It variably signifies community, culture, religion, ethnicity, location, caste, and class. It is political and economic: Food production ensures food security and is one of India's most important market sectors, a critical contributor to national prosperity and citizen well-being. Food is also a marker of contemporality in India, expressed through a boom in restaurant dining, commercial food production, and food media, and an emerging emphasis on individuality—experimenting with novel foods and developing new taste preferences can make a statement about one's distinctiveness outside of inherited identity. When noted journalist Vir Sanghvi delivered the keynote speech at a food writing conference, which I attended in Bengaluru in 2019, he began by declaring that India had experienced a 'food explosion' and went on to list economic development, technology, political agendas, government policy, social and material aspirations, changing family structure, environmental concerns, and globalized media as elemental in detonating new Indian food habits. It is the shifts in these areas that transform food, rarely the other way around; however, exploring changing food practices offers a way to see how this transformation is playing out in everyday life in India. The significant changes in the ways Indians produce, collect, buy, prepare, eat, and sell their food are exciting to observe. While these have eased some women's domestic labour, they have also raised concerns about potential negative environmental and health impacts, increasing social division and equitable access to food, homogenization of foodways, and diminishing of culinary diversity and traditional food cultures.

This book is part memoir as I use my personal experiences throughout as a marker of change in India's food as I have seen it, but it is not solely drawn from my idiosyncratic experiences and observations. I am acutely aware that I am an outsider in India, an ardent observer of life here but not a daily participant in it. Being an onlooker has advantages as one might more readily notice change than those immersed in it, potentially affording useful insights. Conversely, it can also result in misinterpretation or misunderstanding because the nuances and unspoken rules of social and cultural interactions are not fully understood. I wanted this work to be inclusive of the views of Indians across the food system, and I conducted formal interviews and informal conversations with chefs, professional and domestic cooks, restaurateurs, farmers, hospitality and hotel professionals, academics, food producers, writers and journalists, retailers, event and media creators, tourism operators, even a food architect, winemakers, workaday cooks, and consumers across the country. I have used direct quotes and the collective opinions of these individuals in this book.[1] In addition, I have drawn on research, print and social media, by Indians about food, general commentary on India's changing material, economic, and social environment as well as international sources to contextualize the global influences, particularly so-called 'well-being' concepts shaping what contemporary Indians are choosing to eat.

The Future Is Here

Stuck in a Delhi traffic gridlock circa 2016, the thought occurred to me that rather than being a so-called 'developing' nation, India had reached the future in her metropolises.[2] It was a playful speculation, but perhaps I wasn't far off the mark: Amongst those whose business it is to predict how we might live in the future, the clear consensus is that 80–90 per cent of the world's population will live in cities, swelling more and more of these to megacities, and Delhi is on a trajectory to be the biggest urban agglomeration in the world by 2030, with an estimated population of 36 million (or maybe not in the post-pandemic world, but I will get to that). The idea that the citizens of Delhi and India's other megacities—Mumbai, Bengaluru, Kolkata, and Chennai—are potentially living in the way most of the world will in the future, as well as the general population transition from rural to urban living swelling cities such as Hyderabad and Ahmedabad towards megacity status, influenced my decision to focus on food in urban India in this book. After I had settled on this idea, the COVID-19 pandemic sparked off a massive reverse rural migration from India's cities. Only time will tell if this is a more permanent volte-face from rural to urban migration—there have been mixed reports on the number of migrant workers who have returned to cities—but even if growth slows in India's megacities, urbanization has played a significant role in changing India's foodscape and is likely to continue doing so: The outbreak of the bubonic plague in Bombay in 1896 triggered a massive reverse migration and a drastic fall in the population at that time: You can see how that turned out in the long run!

Same Same

Discovering that India was home to a multitude of distinctive culinary cultures had got me interested in her regional cuisines. While the country's contemporary food landscape remains inimitable, one of the key themes explored in this work is quite the opposite: The growing uniformity of food in India's metropolises, particularly the emergence of a type of globalized style found in eateries in western, or westernized, cities around the world. Increasingly, I find myself in cafés in Delhi where I lose sight of where I am because the menu and design of the place are so faithful to this global pattern that I could just as well be in Sydney. Delhi is the city that comes into focus the most in this book because I have had the most experience of everyday Indian food life there. However, I have spent time in other Indian cities over the years, travelling to these again as time, resources, and prevailing circumstances allowed, specifically for this book, to know this international food style is common to all, such that when I give an example of a trend noticed and explored in Bengaluru, in most cases, the same change will be mirrored in other metropoles. A major factor in this growing homogeneity of food and product trends is the connection internet technology has given Indians to hyper-globalized mass media as much as local considerations. The changes in India's foodscape have certainly not occurred solely under the stimuli of global forces or ideas: Indians are actively influencing change in their food system in distinctive ways.

Who Is This Book About?

As I worked on this book and wrote general statements such as 'Indians are buying more flavoured yoghurt' or 'Indians are drinking more wine', I was aware such pronouncements were not true of the collective population in the way the unqualified use of 'Indians' might suggest. I want to qualify then that this book is predominantly concerned with the food habits of people living in metropolitan India who have the means and the inclination to take on new taste concepts and dietary practices.

Even then, this is more categorical than necessary as many Indians who live outside of big cities are just as keenly adopting novel foods and ways of eating.

Convenience

In launching the Godrej Food Trends Report 2020, its author, food writer, researcher, and consultant, Rushina Munshaw Ghildiyal, announced that 'convenience is what Indians will most look for in food' into the future. The 2021 report again cited convenience as a key influence on Indians' food choices, despite predictions that they would return to home cooking because of the pandemic. If we inquire as to why convenience has come to reign over food, a comprehensive answer will have to address the role that economic prosperity, urbanization, the increased participation of women in the workforce, development in food retail, technology, and media play; the influence of any one of these factors, although variable, is inseparable from the other. Nevertheless, I have parsed out these interconnected factors more singularly in the various chapters to minimize repetition, emphasizing here that there is no one story in this book about contemporary food in India that is not connected to another. The following universal influences also serve as a framework for reading the subsequent chapters.

Urbanization: Food in Cities

Urbanization impacts people's food habits in numerous ways. There is a greater choice of food available, and it is easier to access. With more places selling food, vendors often compete on price and/or service, such as longer hours of operation and/or delivery. Corporate food retail chains set up stores in urban areas because the size of the population there makes their business model feasible, bringing an increased variety of food into one place, usually at lower prices, which can 'pull' people to shop at supermarkets and away from small local vendors. Distribution infrastructure is better in urban areas, facilitating more effortless access to food. There are more restaurants in urban places, which can encourage people to experiment with new foods, to cook less, and to eat out more. Easy access to a wide variety of choices can also encourage people to eat more and expend less effort to get their food. Lifestyle diseases associated with an imbalanced diet, such as obesity and diabetes, are more prevalent in urban India. Urban Indians generally have higher incomes, and money plays a major role in shaping eating habits and food systems.

Eating Prosperity

Cultural tastes, including food, change because of economics. For example, if enough people spend money on online food delivery, more players enter the market, competition lowers prices, which encourages consumers to utilize the service more often, the availability of the service expands, even more people use it, and what was once new, an outlier, becomes embedded, normalized, and changes the shape of the food system.

When people have more disposable income, they are also more inclined to try new foods because if they chose something they do not like, they have the means to get something else, i.e., they won't go hungry—money affords them the confidence to take risks.

> The nearness of hunger breeds conservatism. Only the well fed can afford to try something new, because only they can afford to leave it on the plate if they dislike it.[3]

Prosperity also inspires novelty seeking in food because there is status in the new and in being part of the zeitgeist.

Globalization

Globalization is the process through which the world is becoming increasingly interconnected through trade and cultural exchanges, but in the twenty-first century, it is often used to mean Americanization.[4] What this book is concerned with in relation to globalization is the significant influence of Euro–American, or western, concepts of food and food trends on domestic cooking and eating, on restaurant menus and retailing, and on shaping the understanding of health and well-being with respect to food in India, all of which seems to be leading to 'a standardization of food and tastes in urban areas [stimulating] a flattening of the food terrain [towards a westernized] global cuisine'.[5] I notice the globalization of food in India showing up in two key ways: First, the industrialization of consumer food in which homogenization and 'standardization' are critical, such as in large chain supermarkets and in packaged and processed convenience foods. Second, the ardent pursuit of the more privileged in the western world to attain well-being or 'healthism' by consuming a diet of typically expensive, organic and 'superfoods' and/or regimented eating regimens that exclude certain items or categories, such as gluten-free and keto, is significantly shaping the dietary preferences of the more privileged in India. As someone who is psychology minded as well as and historically minded, I also see two universal and enduring aspects of human nature at work here: The psychological aspects of prosperity and the appeal of novel foods and the drive for status and distinction.

Status and Distinction

The privileged classes in any society commonly use financial prosperity to distinguish themselves through purchasing items that are regarded as status symbols, including edible ones, and food practices can be used as markers of social status. There is a historical pattern of long-term changes in food systems starting at 'the top'—the wealthier sections of society. When I first came to India in the late 1990s, imported western-style food—good quality chocolate, cheese, wine, olive oil, olives, vinegar, and cured and processed meats—were the purview of the country's 'westernized elite', who had had opportunities to develop a taste for such food and drinks, through travel, overseas education, and exposure to international magazines and media, and the means to afford them. There were less expensive local versions of some of these items, but it was the imported, more costly foods that held cachet because access to these was limited. Foreign food styles were generally offered in expensive restaurants, usually in five-star hotels, but dining out in such places was only enjoyed on special occasions for all but a small number of people who could both afford to eat out regularly and were inclined to it. However, stand-alone and more casual restaurants were beginning to blossom in Indian cities in response to the increasing prosperity triggered by economic liberalization.

One of the things that turned my attention to how food was changing in India was the broader availability, consumption, and production of western-style foods, and that the production, quality, and diversity of locally made varieties of these foods had significantly increased. The growth of the Indian economy over the past three decades has improved the incomes of many Indians, and once people had the means, they wanted the type of consumer goods, such as western-style foods, enjoyed by India's elite. The increasing demand for these novel foods, matched by the capacity of consumers to pay for them, encourages expanded production, making these items less expensive and more accessible, eventually bringing them into the mainstream. In this process, the status value of these items is diminished for the upper classes, who then move on to seeking distinction with food in new areas, such as regional and health-related foods.

> Classed associations with food and foodways are not new . . . shifts in 'tastes' across class lines [have taken place] from medieval times when it was prestigious to eat white bread amongst the upper classes, whilst the lower classes could only afford to eat unrefined brown bread . . . followed by a reaction to the [later] excessive industrialisation of food [which made white bread available to all classes] and a movement away from refined products towards 'healthier' foods amongst the upper classes.[6]

Inside to Outside

For most of her history, India's food has been kept to her domestic kitchens and dining spaces, that is, inside the home. Eating home-cooked meals was a source of pride. Public eating was 'confined to religious and royal milieus, where traditional, social, and religious boundaries could be maintained'.[7] Early on, when I mentioned to an Indian acquaintance that I was interested in their country's cuisine, they would often advise me: 'The best food in India is in people's homes'. It surprised me to discover that domestic food was more highly valued in India than that obtained from a commercial provider as the situation was the opposite in Australia in the late 1990s: Restaurants were venerated, and food prepared by a professional cook or chef was generally considered superior to home cookery. I learnt the Indian preference for home food was grounded in distinctive 'cultural logistics' that demarked edibles as 'inside food' or 'outside food'. Inside food, *ghar ka khana*, was food prepared inside the home and was considered 'pure and controlled'.[8] Outside food, *bahar ka khana*, was food prepared outside the home in circumstances unknown and uncontrollable to the consumer, holding the 'danger and the possibility of ritual pollution'.[9] Home-cooked, or 'inside', food was considered natural and nutritive, while food from 'outside' might be adulterated by the caste, habits, and techniques of the cook and/or the quality of ingredients. Long-held beliefs imbuing consumable foodstuff with moral and spiritual qualities that might have been, as my friend Bhuvan suggests, a disguised understanding of food hygiene, shaped this inside–outside paradigm. Of course, other factors may have been at play. Perhaps people did not value outside food because the cooking in their homes was of such high quality and was exclusively formulated to their tastes and principles; it was also less costly to eat meals prepared at home. As I set about researching for and writing this book, one of the patterns of change that clearly emerged was the movement of food in India from 'inside to outside' with domestic food production being displaced, to varying degrees, by food made outside the home. This change in the site of food production is particularly evident in respect to regional food (Chapter 1) and the role Indian women play as domestic food provisioners (Chapter 3).

1

The Rise of Regionalism

The Best Indian Restaurant in the World

It was a Monday when I met restaurant entrepreneur Rohit Khattar for lunch at Indian Accent, the pre-eminent eatery in his Delhi portfolio, esteemed for its menu of contemporary interpretations of classic Indian dishes and regional specialities served in chic surroundings. The elegant dining room was respectably patronized on what is the quietest day of the week for the hospitality industry, and with the socially fabulous (usually prominent here) at home recovering from the weekend, this left Khattar free to give our conversation his undivided attention. Only occasionally did he inquire of passing staff how things were proceeding with the politician and his party sequestered away in a private dining room. While Indian Accent is swanky, its patrons are not limited to the elite and Khattar keenly enunciated the diversity of people who come to enjoy themselves there: Parents bring their children to celebrate educational achievements; children bring their parents to celebrate their first job; couples come to honour special occasions; and for people from around the country, dining here is often the high point of a visit to the capital. A meal at Indian Accent has become a pivotal dining experience, and it has been described as 'the best Indian restaurant in the world'. Yet, it had hardly received such accolades when it first opened.

Indian Accent is the brainchild of Chef Manish Mehrotra; it is his skill and creativity that drives the development of its food, and he has been described as 'India's greatest modern chef'.[1] When I met Mehrotra in Delhi to talk about India's changing foodscape, he took the conversation all the way back to August 1947, citing the events of Partition not only as a pivotal point of change for the country, but for India's urban food culture.[2]

Amongst the hundreds of thousands of people who fled to Delhi from the newly created Pakistan in 1947, some set up small food stalls to earn a living and survive their forced migration. One of these makeshift stalls morphed into Delhi's famed Moti Mahal restaurant, which became a popular haunt of the city's well-to-do. Most social dining still took place in people's homes then, which would remain the case for decades to come, but this was the genesis of sophisticated restaurant culture in India. It was also where the blend of Punjabi, Mughlai, and North-West Frontier dishes—now commonly known as 'North Indian'—emerged. Moti Mahal became the model for what Mehrotra called 'white table cloth' restaurants serving this style of Indian cuisine across India, almost all of which operated in five-star hotels, their menus 'much the same all over', with India's catering colleges focused on training chefs to this standard repertoire.[3] What was offered as 'Indian food' in a restaurant fossilized into this style for decades. There was some experimentation with regional cuisine in the form of the 'food festival', whereby a hotel would offer patrons a limited-time menu of select regional dishes—a 'pop-up' before this term was invented for the concept. This offered Indians who could afford to eat in fancy hotels the opportunity to explore their country's diverse food culture; but as Mehrotra describes it, 'prevailing cultural stereotypes' and unappetizing notions of food of unfamiliar communities curtailed broader interest in regional food—restaurant patrons were, largely, reluctant to pay for it, and restaurateurs focused on what people would buy. If Indians wanted something different when they dined out, international styles such as Chinese, Italian, and Thai were more popular.

Mehrotra first came to note cooking Thai food at a popular Delhi restaurant. But when he opened Indian Accent in 2009, the cuisine was all about his native country; an innovative menu of regional specialities intended to showcase the diverse possibilities of India's food and excite diners about it. The place was not an immediate success. Guests did not understand the novel concept and would say things like 'this is not an Indian restaurant' or 'I know Indian food, and what you are serving is not this', all the while complaining about its cost. Over time, the restaurant gained critical acclaim and, ultimately, more popular acceptance. Nonetheless, the fact that it stayed open long enough to establish an appreciative clientele was due to Mehrotra's and Khattar's steadfast faith in it. The success of Indian Accent undoubtedly exerted influence on what Mehrotra defined, when the trajectory of our conversation moved from the past to the present, as the recent 'broader awakening around regional food' in India. Chefs around the country are extending the boundaries of Indian cuisine by sophisticating traditional regional recipes and drawing on indigenous ingredients and local cooking styles to create new dishes. Restaurateurs are opening smart eateries specializing in singular regional cuisines and incorporating more regional dishes into the menus of established places, alongside a slew of regional-food-focused pop-ups and events. And all of these eats are being met with enthusiastic appreciation by customers. The ascendence of regional food in India was something many of my other interviewees spoke of. Before exploring the broader elements influencing this contemporary trend, I am going to follow Mehrotra's lead and go back in time a couple of decades to when my own particular interest in India's regional food began.

I am not sure if Chef Mehrotra understood that I was nodding my head in recognition when he spoke of the prejudices existing amongst Indians about the food of regions different to their own. Up until the early 2010s, I often met Indians who were genuinely perplexed as to why I would bother researching their country's regional food, sharing with me their store of unappetizing cameos of the food of other states or communities as proof of the futility of my undertaking:

> 'I am not sure whether you will find much to interest you in the south . . . Too much rice and coconut, and the food is all soft.'
>
> 'Isn't the food in the south just idli, dosa?'
>
> 'Gujarati food is all too sweet.'
>
> 'Oh, why go to Nagaland? They just eat anything there.'
>
> 'Punjabi food is so heavy; it just makes you sleepy.'

From my perspective, I was surprised that Indians were not more interested in their country's vast storehouse of regional cuisines.

If I gave any thought to the culinary possibilities of India before I embarked on my first visit in 1995, I do not recall it. I was going to India to walk in the mountains, marvel at ancient monuments, ride elephants in the jungle, and check out the party scene in Goa. As far as I understood it, Indian food was singularly made up of gravy-based dishes explosive with chilli all called 'curry', along with pakoras, samosa, poppadums, and tandoori chicken. There was nothing in this lot that excited me, but I also wasn't concerned about what I would eat when I was on the subcontient; it was just neutral territory. This wasn't due to my lack of interest in food, though; quite the opposite: I had completed a professional cookery education, ran a small catering business specializing in robust Middle Eastern and

Spanish food, and possessed a nascent desire to write about food history, although the history of which food was not yet apparent. If nothing else, I was primed to observe food when I arrived in India, and in retrospect, I think coming with such low expectations of her food played a part in igniting what was to follow.

Illness might have left me unable to tolerate Indian food for many weeks on my first Indian adventure, but it did not inhibit my observation of the food I saw around me. Travelling on long-distance trains, I was intrigued that the type of snacks and light meals sold by food vendors could be quite different a few hundred kilometres down the line. Travelling by bus from Hospet, Karnataka, all the way back to Delhi, I made a sport of noticing all the different foods on offer at streetside stalls throughout the journey. I had landed up in Hospet from Hampi (where I had been marvelling at the ruins of the Vijayanagara empire) to begin the first stage of my long northward road trip. It was early evening when I arrived and having several hours to kill until my bus departed, I decided to take a walk around the town to find something for dinner. As I had regained my full digestive capabilities by this time, I was ready to give reign to my culinary curiosity. A busy restaurant caught my eye; its signage was in Kannada, giving me no idea what type of food was on offer, but I went in and sat down at a table regardless. There was no menu and no mutual language to ask questions: A waiter put down a thali in front of me and lined up a series of katoris around its perimeter, another put a small mound of rice on the plate, while others decanted various sauces into the small bowls and dolloped pickles, chutney, crunchy savoury titbits, and a little pile of salt onto the space around the rice. Then I was left to it. There was no cutlery. How was I going to pick up the rice and the sauce? I had never eaten a soft combination of food like that with my hands before. I looked around and noticed how the other patrons were eating: Mashing the other items into the rice and shaping it into small balls, picking these up with the very tips of their fingers, and deftly flicking them into their mouths. I copied this process. I was quite impressed with myself when I successfully conveyed a rice ball into my mouth without spilling it. Then, the food totally surprised my tongue: The combinations of sweet, sour, tangy, and spicy flavours were fresh and light, almost effervescent. I had never tasted anything like that. I have written about this meal before because it was revelatory for me—it not only changed my mind about Indian food, but it also changed my life. The flavours offered by that meal caused an upheaval of my narrow assessment of the culinary possibilities of India: I remember it as the moment I found the subject of my writing.

Decreeing this one meal as my inspiration to write about Indian food culture and food history is not entirely accurate. The seed of it was there by the time I had landed up in Hospet, sown by all the different food I had seen as I travelled around. When I arrived back in Delhi, I ate a plate of paapdi chaat from a roadside stall: The textural and flavour combinations in this inexpensive commonplace street eat astounded me. I did not have a sheltered palate.

I was an adventurous eater. But here was something else I had never tasted the like of. This experience affirmed that India's food was something to know more about. I then went to stay with friends in Uttarakhand, where my experience of domestic food culture settled the deal: What people ate in their homes little resembled what I had understood India's cuisine to be only two months earlier; her culinary culture was significantly misrepresented in the West, and I was going to do something about that by writing a book on India's diverse food cultures. It wasn't just the material aspect of food that inspired me. I realized India's ancient, complex, and fascinating history was embedded in her food and that exploring her cookery would be my route to understanding her complex social operations—to whatever extent that might be possible for an outsider.

I was captivated by India's food because Australia, my native place, does not have regional food.[4] No matter where we live on our vast island continent, we fundamentally eat the same things. With few exceptions, every fruit, vegetable, spice, herb, meat, and cereal that Australians eat has been transplanted from elsewhere, circumstances resulting from British colonization in the late eighteenth century. More recent infrastructure and technological developments, and the capture of the nation's food supply by a supermarket duopoly, have made any vestige of local seasonality in our food almost disappear. Much is made of the multiplicity of ethnic eateries that can be frequented in urban Australia, thanks to the diverse cultural backgrounds of the contemporary population, but these, too, are imports. The absence of a deeply rooted food culture in my own country made me appreciate that India had one; I thought it was a wonder, a magnificent living heritage. The ambivalence I encountered amongst Indians about their own varied foodways perplexed me: How could one not be fascinated by this? And their dismissive judgements of the food of regions or communities other than their own that they expressed to me were often based on little or no experience of the food in question.

It is human nature to be wary of unknown food; perhaps we might find its material qualities unappetizing, the flavour or texture might be unpleasant, foul, even poisonous, or not acceptable to our religious or ethical sensibilities. We also imbue food with non-material properties: Beliefs that eating certain types of foods can imbue spiritual profit while ingesting others can cause one's very nature to turn malignant, or result in caste pollution, run deep in India, feeding prejudices around the food of other communities and cultures and influencing the idea of how something might 'taste' before it even hits the tongue. What might have been at issue then was a lack of social gratification, or approval, around trying the food of unfamiliar others, and having 'safe' opportunities to do so. As we shall see, exposure to wider cultural influences and a boom in travel have played a role in shifting Indian attitudes to their regional food.

Regional, Traditional, and at Home

Before I proceed with my story, I want to emphasize that there were, of course, Indians keenly interested in their own food culture, and that too well-before I ever ate that chaat on a Delhi kerbside. Still, the publicly demonstrative level of interest in regional food, for example, in published writing and restaurants, was not like it is now. But Indians have been eating 'regional cuisines' for a very, very long time. At this point, a brief segue into some definition is required.

A *regional cuisine* is one distinctive of a place, its characteristics shaped by the geography, climate, economics, cultural and social practices of that locale, and recognizable as being of that region because it has been commonly practised there over time—acknowledging that there will be household-specific variations on the canon and that regional food styles have evolved over time and will continue to do so. Regional food styles might be categorized broadly at a state level, such as Rajasthani or Bengali, or of an area within a state, such as Kutchi or Garhwali.

Traditional food styles retain coherent characteristics wherever they are practised, notwithstanding foods and techniques of a local region making their way into these to produce distinctive sub-cuisines. An example is the Moplah cuisine of Northern Kerala, which is Indo-Muslim in form and incorporates ingredients and techniques belonging to this tropical-coastal environment.

Whilst the food eaten at home by the people of a region is what someone outside of that place would experience as 'regional' cuisine, for the people of that region, it is their 'home food'. Regional food might also be thought of as 'traditional' food by people who have eaten it all their life. In practice, the distinctions between which food is from which region are not as categorical as these definitions suggest, and I am mindful of writer Anoothi Vishal's comment that she feels a 'distinct discomfort as more and more food writers focus on these fissures, oblivious to deeper connections that in fact exist between different cuisines of the subcontinent'.[5] I am aware of the complex interconnectedness of India's food, but in the context of this work, I am going to use the terms 'regional food/cuisine', 'traditional food', and 'home food' interchangeably in this chapter and throughout this book.[6]

Fulfilling my ambition to know more about India's food meant immersing myself in it (not literally). I sought out every possible source of information that I could. In urban areas, I would spend my days walking around taking note of streetside food and what type of eateries were operating. If a place was popular, I would go in and see what was drawing the crowd, and if I found regional specialities on offer, I would sample them. I kept an eye out for canteens serving inexpensive meals to workers as these were a reliable source of decent everyday local food. (I have eaten some memorable, and educative, meals in such places, including one in Puri, Orissa, where out on an exploratory walk, a busy rudimentary open-fronted eatery caught my attention. I stepped in and took a seat at one of its rough wooden tables. A stainless thali was placed in front of me onto which was ladled the local everyday fare, which as a visitor I would describe as 'regional'. Here, I was introduced to the complex vegetable stew called dalma and the dense, slightly sweet cheesecake, chhennapoda, which was eaten with it). The people working in these places were generous with me too; they took lids off cooking pots to show me what was going on inside and answered my questions as best as they could even when we had no shared language.

I visited markets to discover what fresh foods people bought; I inspected the shelves of food stores; I noticed what crops were being grown as I travelled through rural places; I visited farms and food producers; I talked to chefs and cooks. Back home in Australia, I cooked from the regional cookbooks of India that I had collected, a practice that deepened my understanding of the patterns in a particular cuisine—when I invited Australian friends to eat the dishes I made, they almost always exclaimed: 'I had no idea India had food like this', unless they were fellow Indophiles themselves. One exception was the friend who expressed disappointment that the vindaloo I served him, made following a Goan recipe, did not taste like the one he got from his local (Australian) 'curry joint', i.e., it was not mouth-burning with chilli. (He did not receive a return invitation.)

India's streets, stores, and fields were a rich source of information, but my most significant learning about the distinctive food practices of regional communities came from the 'inside', from cooking and conversing with women, and occasionally men, of all castes, creeds, and classes, in their domestic kitchens and dining rooms all over India. I have been inside home kitchens in all but three of India's states and territories and all her major cities;[7] in erstwhile-royal, rural, urban, village, elite, and modest households of Hindu, Muslim, Sikh, Christian, Parsi, Jain, and Buddhist families, in coastal, mountain, and desert regions, in dry, hot, cold, tropical, and moderate climates, across each season of the year. I was humbled by how willing people were to invite me into their kitchens, even though some of the women were perplexed as to why a foreigner wanted to know about their everyday food. Producing meals for their families was routine work for them, and they could see nothing 'special' in it. It seemed to me that the 'inside' nature of regional cuisines played a role in limiting the understanding of these because domestic cookery was women's work and, as such, was hidden away in homes. From here, this chapter will focus on the factors that have influenced the movement of India's regional food from unremarked domestic consumption to broad social acclaim and flourishing commerciality, a process that offers a quintessential example of the migration of food in India from 'inside' to 'outside'.

From the Top

In the 1970s, the luxury ITC hotel chain decided to specialize in serving traditional Indian cuisine in its restaurants and hired Imitiaz Qureshi to create Dum Pukht focused on Awadhi cuisine, and Chef Madan

Jaiswal, who created the North-Frontier-style food for the iconic Bukhara restaurant. They later added Dakshin, which brought together cuisines from various regions of Peninsular India. By the time I arrived in India, there were many upmarket hotels operating regional speciality restaurants, and in my experience, the chefs developing the menus for these places had been deeply interested in India's regional cuisines. Still, these places were luxury experiences available only to a small segment of Indian society. At the other end of the scale, I found regional food in India's metros in the so-called 'Mom and Pop' places small, inexpensive, perfunctory, family-run eateries. These places were affordable, but typically situated in neighbourhoods where a particular community had established itself, and it was these people, for whom the food on offer was their familiar 'home food', who were the regular clientele. I can recall quite a few independent mid-scale regional restaurants, just in Delhi, that opened and did not survive. Regional cuisine seemed to be of more sustainable interest to people for whom it was novel, at the top end of town. Of course, big hotels are better resourced to keep a restaurant operating; nonetheless, they will change it if the concept is not working. But many regional-food-focused restaurants in five-star hotels have stayed the course.

Reading all the writing currently pouring out about India's regional food and food history, let alone that on restaurants, chefs, and other food businesses, would require the dedication of a significant amount of time to this task each week. But twenty years ago, India's food writers were a small contingent, predominantly penning restaurant reviews and longer pieces about food and wine aimed at educating their Indian readers on current, often international, trends and products. Any writing on India's regional food, at least in English—the only language I can read in—was mainly published in cookbooks. In 2000, a dedicated Indian food and lifestyle magazine called *Upper Crust* was launched, the name clearly indicating its intended subject and readership, the elite of Indian society and perhaps those who aspired to emulate them. The content focused on stories about the food and travel habits of celebrated and wealthy Indians, but each edition included a feature piece on some aspect of India's regional food culture—I still have some of these articles filed away. I saw the inclusion of these in this upmarket publication presaging the development of a broader interest in Indians about their own food because, as remarked, what becomes a popular trend, in food as much as anything, often begins with the 'approval', the use, or practice of something at the top of any society, and regional food was now in India's upmarket hotels as well as a glossy magazine about her 'upper crust'. There was something else going on as well. India's wealthier citizens were being influenced towards 'unheard of criteria . . . such as sourcing (the more local, the better), artisanality (the smaller the run, the better), taste (organic methods favoured), sustainability and healthiness', and the nature of much of India's regional food fits very well with such criteria.[8] (See Chapter 5).

Technology-Powered Words

In 2019, popular Mumbai-based food writer and blogger Kalyan Karmakar proposed that the city 'should consider positioning itself as a hub for regional Indian food'.[9] A proposition that could easily be acted upon—the place is richly endowed with regional food enclaves catering to the polyglot communities of this megacity—but what caught my attention was the timing of the idea itself. As Kalyan pointed out, many of these eateries have been operating for decades. So what has changed, or is changing, such that his proposition has been made now? I think the medium Kalyan works in, words transferred through the Internet, particularly blogs and social media, has played an influential role in this.

In his classic essay 'How to Make a National Cuisine: Cookbooks in Contemporary India', renowned scholar Arjun Appadurai explores how the idea of a national Indian cuisine was constructed post-Independence through cookbooks, predominantly written by women.[10] As the traditional holders of domestic cookery knowledge, Indian women have been the primary source of recipes and culinary advice and have ensured that family, community, and regional cookery practices are passed down through the generations—a process customarily done 'in-house' between family members, contributing to what I suggest has been the 'inside' nature of regional cuisines. Without access to homes in different regions of the country, opportunities to learn about regional cuisines were historically limited.

By the early 2000s, internet technology had made it easy for individuals to 'publish' their writing via blogs. Indian women took to blogging with aplomb to share recipes, information on ingredients, tips on cookery, and, later, videos on the same as technology sophisticated: It was an outlet they seemed to have been waiting for.

> Food in India has been virtually absent from the academic discourse because of the diversity and spread of the gastronomic landscape. Things are different on the Internet. In response to the forces of globalization, Indian food blogs both teaching cookery and commenting on food, are mushrooming in cyberspace.[11]

Blogging enabled a boundary-less network of connections and learning. In sharing recipes and stories about their domestic food lives, women across India started creating digital archives of regional food and educating each other on these—Odia recipes posted by a housewife in Puri could easily be accessed by a woman in Bikaner. Blogs offered women a way to look inside the kitchens of other women around India, taking down the walls of the homes that kept women's domestic cookery private. This aroused curiosity about the food lives of others along with the confidence and inspiration to try new dishes because they were now seeing these through words and pictures. Listings of the 'most popular food blogs' in India constantly change, but two things remain constant: The most highly ranked blogs are usually created by women and are focused on recipes and/or their advice about what to eat or not eat. A notable exception to this gender domination in the field is the consistently high rating of the blog run by Anubhav Sapra about the distinctive 'regional' food culture of Old Delhi. The popularity of his work speaks to the interest Indians have developed in their country's distinctive foodways.

Nearly two decades ago, I lived for some time in a south Delhi suburb adjacent to Chittaranjan Park, a locale with a large Bengali community and home to the CR Park Market No. 3. This place was a microcosm of Bengali food culture. There were several fishmongers selling superlative seafood to cater to the Bengali penchant for the 'fruit of the sea'; the subziwallahs sold tropical vegetables specific to their regional tastes; and the confectioners' refrigerated cabinets were filled with small clay pots of nolen gurer mishti doi—date-palm-sweetened yoghurt that I tried here for the first time. I sometimes had a meal at the nearby Bengali restaurant, Baboo Moshai. I was not the only non-Bengali who shopped at the market or ate at this restaurant, but these food places catered primarily to the Bengali community, allowing them to cook and eat their familiar, or regional, food, and they were the predominant clientele. Returning to Chittaranjan Park recently, the market looked much the same, but there were more speciality food stalls, selling distinctive Bengali snacks such as kathi rolls and fish cutlets, operating in the market, and several new Bengali restaurants had opened in the locale. The patrons of these eateries predominantly remain the local community; however, many more Delhiites, of all backgrounds, have started coming here to explore Bengali food, encouraged along by bloggers and social media influencers.

The *MasterChef* Effect

While I was physically getting 'inside' India in her domestic kitchens, making connections with Indian cooks across bubbling pots of dal, sauteed greens, spiced seafood, and slow simmering reductions of milk-based desserts, some other Australians were also getting into India's kitchens, albeit in a more remote fashion. When I asked food writer Phorum Dalal what she thought was influencing the growing interest in regional food in India, she replied that 'much of the credit could be slated to Australian MasterChef (*MasterChef*)'. Chef Abhijit Saha also described *MasterChef* as having 'an amazing influence across the board', including inspiring interest in regional food. Perhaps they were saying this because of my nationality, but since it first appeared on Indian television in 2010, *MasterChef* topped the ratings in its timeslot for each of its subsequent ten seasons. Such has been the impact of this show that it was cited as a notable influence on the contemporary Indian foodscape by many others I interviewed. The premise of *MasterChef* is that a passionate amateur cook can be transformed over the course of a programme season into an expert chef. While the 'action' of the show is focused on this process, Phorum described it as imbuing home cookery with more 'glamour in India, and making India's home cooks [i.e., women] realize professional chefs were not the only ones playing an important role in food'. Abhijit also said that the show had helped domestic cooks see the skills they had and re-evaluate these, as well as gain new, more global, ideals around the presentation of food.

I think the show influenced an interest in regional cuisine amongst its Indian audience in another way: Australia has a multicultural population, and the contestants have been a representative sample of this cultural diversity. Competitors from Indonesian, Egyptian, Chinese, Japanese, Thai, Lebanese, Turkish, Georgian, Malaysian, Singaporean, Bangladeshi, and Indian backgrounds have all appeared on the show—in 2021, two of the three grand finalists had Indian origins—and all were encouraged to look to their culinary heritage and cook dishes reflective of the 'home', or traditional food, of their respective communities. Indians watching the show must have been inspired to think about their cookery skills and food knowledge of their own regions, communities, and homes in a very different way—that they held something unique, something others would be interested in, perhaps even be willing to pay for—inspiring a swathe of women to take their unique regional cookery outside their private kitchens and bring it into an arena of greater visibility.

Travelling to Eat

In 2007, several years before *MasterChef* was televised in India, Rocky Singh and Mayur Sharma were driving around India exploring roadside eateries and filming their experiences for the television series *Highway on My Plate*. The programme's focus was ostensibly on places to eat good inexpensive food along the country's roadways with its affable hosts describing and scoring the food on offer, but it was much more than that. In travelling around the country to eat, Singh and Sharma inevitably discovered regional specialities, taking their viewers into domestic kitchens as well to learn more about local cookery along the way. The enthusiasm, curiosity, and humour the two men brought to the process charmed and engaged audiences, and it remains one of the highest-rated food shows in India. It was also groundbreaking in creating a popular media vehicle (no pun intended, but there it is) through which Indians could discover, or get inside, the rich food cultures of their nation.

Without question, I got to learn about India's regional food because I had the resources, and endurance, to travel the country in search of it. Circa 1988, I looked into flying from Delhi to Chennai. When I discovered that it was going to be $200 one way, I looked elsewhere—at the railway timetable—and took a train instead, journeying for close to forty hours. I had to do the same to come back. It was a lot of time to spend getting somewhere, but I had the time for it. If Indians had held parochial understanding about the food eaten in other parts of their country, perhaps it was, in part, because the financial and temporal challenges of travel limited the possibilities for them to explore it. I suggest this because the more recent boom in domestic tourism, spurred by a combination of increased incomes and affordability and accessibility of internal air travel, has contributed to the groundswell of interest in regional food. Sampling local cuisine has become a key 'must do', if not the primary driver, of travel for many Indians, who enthusiastically post about their culinary experiences on social media, fuelling their 'followers' with ambition to do the same.

The Other Best Indian Restaurant

Mumbai's The Bombay Canteen (often referred to as 'Bombay Canteen') is one of the most popular contemporary restaurants in this city; however, its renown is national. In 2018, it was nominated as the best restaurant in India by *Condé Nast*, coming second to Indian Accent the following year, gaining top ranking on the *Hotelier India* list of the best stand-alone restaurants in February 2020 (the on–off closures and restrictions applicable to restaurants across the country during the COVID-19 pandemic halted ratings and rankings of restaurants over that time; these are just getting back up again as I write). Bombay Canteen's executive chef, Thomas Zacharias, draws inspiration from regional food styles and his grandmother's domestic cookery to devise the applauded and awarded food served here. In my conversations with food people in Mumbai, when I asked what they thought might be influencing the strong trend towards regional food in restaurants, several of them pointed to Bombay Canteen and Zacharias as a key influence. Restaurant impresario A. D. Singh described the place as a 'game changer' in respect to regional food, and food retailer Avni Biyani said it had been 'very influential in changing the view of Indian [regional] food'.

When I met Sameer Seth, co-owner of The Bombay Canteen, we had a wide-ranging conversation about India's changing foodscape, during which he said that 'nostalgia is having a lot of influence on food in India right now'. While nostalgia has long been a stalwart device of food advertising and marketing, others also mentioned it as a potent contemporary influence. So, I was curious to explore this further with Seth. If nostalgia was a food trend, then was it possible that the uber successful Bombay Canteen might have influenced this, or had they just picked up early on underlying currents? To explore this further, I am first going to share Seth's story about the ideas behind Bombay Canteen, then I am going to explore what nostalgia is, and finally suggest how this all links to the rise of regionalism in food.

Seth and his partners have lived across the years when restaurants in India were places to escape the everyday to experience luxury and sophistication on special occasions to them becoming a commonplace experience for many urban Indians rather than an exception; and they wanted to create a restaurant that people would feel comfortable coming to every day (no white tablecloths here). What better to inspire a sense of comfort than the domestic home? Particularly because it pertains to one's earlier years and offers the assuredness of family—or at least the gilded imagining that passing time crafts of it. Bombay Canteen is often described as having an 'old world' feeling or charm, albeit one reminiscent of the past three or four decades or so when Seth and his partners, and many of their customers, would have been living and eating in the family home. When it came to the food offered at the restaurant, Seth said that they were as aiming to offer menus of 'comfort and difference'. The comfort coming from drawing on dishes or food concepts that arouse memories, stir emotions, and inspire a sense of fun associated with family and food. Comfort equates with familiarity. Conversely, 'difference' is something at variance with what one is accustomed to, something that can be critical to the success of a restaurant because newness or novelty is a primary driver of choice for dining out. The 'difference' in the food at Bombay Canteen is created by breaking down familiar dishes, drawn from a region or home food, into elements of flavour and form and putting these back together in unexpected forms or combinations, such as millet haleem, lamb pao, puffed millets, crispy lotus root, malai kofta stuffed with Stracciatella cheese in a pumpkin curry, or a coffee rasgulla sundae. A regional dish would be familiar to a person who comes from that region (making it comfortable), and the same dish would be different for someone who comes from another community or region. In a place like Mumbai, home to Indians from across the country, people come together through professional and social connections to eat in places like Bombay Canteen, where the context of comfort (food I am familiar with) and difference (food that is unusual to me) sparks conversations between diners. Memories are shared and discussed, and people get to know each other a little better, all through sharing a meal. Building understanding of others helps us feel more at ease, more comfortable with each other. The excitement and anticipation of new food experiences can also cause feelings of anxiety: Will I like the food? Will I know how to eat it the right way? What if I do not like the taste? This can prevent some people from trying new things. Stimulating nostalgia can inspire people to explore cuisines that they may never have otherwise discovered.

This Thing Called Nostalgia

Nostalgia is hardwired into us. It is a complex emotion and a potent attractor because it makes us feel good about ourselves and others. Nostalgia can build feelings of belonging and affiliation with others to create stronger social connectedness. Entertaining nostalgic thoughts or telling nostalgic stories can reduce anxiety, increase feelings of being loved and protected, inspire generosity towards others, and help us deal with transitions. Feeling nostalgic generates positive memories and recollections of past times when we felt loved, comforted, protected, or connected with others, and the feeling is easily triggered by smells, sights, sounds, and tastes. As adults, we commonly look back to our childhoods with longing as a time when we were relatively carefree because adults looked after us, including preparing food for us, making food a particularly powerful stimulator of nostalgia. Nostalgia is strongly intertwined with whatever/wherever we consider as 'home'.

> [The coming year] will see nostalgic diners . . . ordering food [ghar-ka khana] that reminds them of their own [home food] more often than ever before.[12]

Nostalgia for food can be individual and related to food that is specific to a home or more widely shared around the food of a community or region. It can also be more pan-Indian, generated by nationally available commercial food products refashioned into contemporary dishes. During my research, I ate Parle-G cheesecake, a play on the common childhood experience of eating these biscuits with milk; deep-fried 5 Star chocolate bars; and Bourbon biscuits in cake, ice-cream, and milkshakes. In the very contemporary Comorin restaurant in Gurugram, cheeni malai toast, an upgraded version of cream on toast sprinkled with sugar, a beloved childhood snack of many grown-up Indians, is one of the most-ordered items.

Urban Tension

If nostalgia is a significant factor influencing the trend towards regional food in restaurants and other commercial food products, then what is creating the impulse towards nostalgia? The answer is multifaceted, but urbanization plays a significant role.

The disinterest in food that I had felt during my childhood years was transformed into a new kind of need for that food as an essential connection to home. I longed for my native food as I dealt with my dislocation from the throbbing Bombay metropolis.[13]

People migrating into or between India's metros face being distanced or even dislocated from their origins, moving away from extended families into more individualistic living situations: batching with friends, residing alone, or in smaller nuclear families. The opportunities of urban living are varied and exciting—work, money, and better educational and professional opportunities are usually the driving forces behind a move to a big city. Once there, one might also enjoy greater social freedom, meeting and mixing with people from a wider range of backgrounds. A big city affords more anonymity, and one can try new food without their grandmother knowing of it and reading eternal doom into the act or enjoy an alcoholic drink in a bar and not have to hide the fact: It can be an exciting and liberating process. On the other hand, moving to a metro can evoke uncertainties: 'Where will I live?' 'Will I be safe?' 'What will I eat?' 'What sort of people will be around me?' The process can be destabilizing, at least for a time. It is an irony of human psychology that feeling stable helps us make changes. Nostalgia can help people feel connected to the roots of their identity; the sense of security engendered by feeling this connection can provide a stable foundation to be more able to cope with change.

> Food stands in as a potent signifier of connection with a place 'back there'.[14]

We go to a restaurant; we find a dish that reminds us of home or a happy past situation; we eat it; it lifts our spirits; we are reminded of love or connection, or we feel self-assured; it soothes us in our urban disorientation. If we share this food with others, it can help build connectedness and cement social bonds, enhancing our sense of belonging. Life in the city begins to look good: We have satiated our appetite for physical and emotional nourishment.

According to writer Anoothi Vishal, the protracted pandemic lockdowns of 2020–21 spurred a 'surge in interest in traditional foods and long-forgotten recipes that perhaps give us a sense of rootedness at a time when all certainties are crumbling away'.[15] During this time, people around the world re-familiarized themselves with their kitchens, taking the time to cook from scratch—to which the international craze for baking sourdough bread attests—and favouring so-called 'comfort food'. Indians were no different: Digging out old family recipes, 'deriving pleasure in the simple things . . . going back to their roots, recalling their childhood favourites, re-creating these in their kitchens . . . And, most importantly, eating meals together as a family',[16] i.e., seeking out the experience of connectedness and safety. If, as predicted, COVID-19 permanently changes our working lives with fewer people working from central-city-based offices, then India's urbanization might slow down, and the turn towards nostalgia might dissipate, although it is unlikely to go away. In fact, nostalgia around food could heighten because in adjusting to the post-COVID world many of us will need to come to terms with a sense of loss of life as we knew it, and perhaps it might also ease the disfranchisement of a future with far less human contact in it.

As we willingly participate in the elimination of a broader range of interpersonal interactions from our lives in favour of virtual transactions, such as online meal delivery and food shopping (see Chapters 2 and 3), many of us will start to miss the seemingly trifling human interactions with restaurant staff, retail assistants, or the man who used to bring his fruit cart to our door each morning. Some people can engage with food in a purely transactional way, they eat because it is necessary and take little pleasure in it (I can't imagine how that is possible!), but for many of us, food is intertwined with our feelings, which is why nostalgia is so powerful.

'Authentic' Nostalgia

Shilpa Sharma is a successful entrepreneur and co-founder of the popular Mustard restaurant in Mumbai and Goa. She and I met by chance at a Delhi food event, where regional food was in focus, and we decided to meet again a few days later to continue our conversation on this trend. Shilpa suggested the turn towards regional food was being influenced by people seeking out 'authentic' food, describing this as food that was 'safe and comfortable', trusting that it had been cooked for you with love and care, and enjoying it in surroundings that were relaxing and did not require too much formality and social performance. Authentic might also be experienced as something belonging to the place you come from. All of which could be seen to replicate the feeling of eating in a family home. The desire for 'authentic' food is also related to health and trusting what you eat to be good for you. As India's regional cuisines have developed in symbiosis with the environmental conditions of a locality and its particular seasons and are often built on enduring ideas about supporting well-being through food, traditional foodways are increasingly being understood as offering a 'healthier' way of eating. As the desire for convenience becomes an increasingly powerful driver of Indians' food choices, leading them to purchase more processed, pre-prepared, and take-out foods, there is considerable concern about the detrimental health implications of this. Traditional foods and cookery are, thus, being looked to as superior dietary choices for maintaining good health.

> We [want] to eat what the west is eating but [are] starting to realise that what our grandmothers were eating was healthy.[17]

Like Mustard, Bengaluru Oota Company (Oota), focuses on two cuisines, both belonging to Karnataka: One representing the sub-region of Mangaluru and the other the Gowda community, traditional Karnataka farmers. Oota is the creation of Vishal Shetty and Divya Prabhakar.

The pair were inspired by a mutual ambition to create an eatery that was not a typical restaurant. Instead, the eating space at Oota is the 'tasting room'; accessible only by advance booking and limited to thirty-five people at a time; the menu changes daily, based on what is local, seasonal, and available in the market. The food is prepared by a team of local women, none of whom are formally trained cooks, who built their skills and knowledge by learning from their mothers and grandmothers and by cooking for their own families. Oota feels personal; the style and ambience are like being in a tasteful residence, with either Vishal or Divya there to explain the menu and talk with guests as if you were at their home. There is a human connection here, and with the food being rooted in domestic cookery, it is trustworthy: This place feels authentic. As online social interactions become increasingly dominant in our daily lives, real-life interpersonal experience might become more highly valued, even aspirational. Then we will want to go out to eat in places where we feel cared for and human, a place like Oota, where we are welcome to open the kitchen door to say hello to the people preparing our meal and see them smile back at us. More recently, Chef Mehrotra has decided to serve 'at least one course on [their] tasting menu [at Indian Accent] in the kitchen [in order to reduce the] distance between the server and the served'[18]—another sign of the heightened need for human connection when it comes to the food we eat, be it psychological (nostalgia) or physical proximity to those who are cooking for us, in the post-pandemic world.

Oota has been winning awards and accolades since it opened in 2018, and it exemplifies the currents of change in contemporary food as discussed in this chapter. It focuses on regional cuisine, bringing it out of its concealment in domestic privacy into a public place that still feels like a home. Depending on the backgrounds of the diners, Oota offers them experiences of familiarity, novelty, comfort, nostalgia, and authenticity, as well as satisfying material appetites with superb food, and it illustrates the growing influence of women as change makers in Indian food in the public arena. Oota also points to India's food future in offering diners an in-depth experience of regional cuisine(s).

People like to eat familiar food because it tastes good to them. If something is too different or confronting, we just won't like it. Indians also have palates attuned to strong flavours—spices, chillies, aromatic cooking oils—such that other cuisines can taste bland or too strange and ultimately unsatisfying.[19] While Indians enjoy discovering and experimenting with new foods, these still need to 'fit' their gustatory preferences. Talking with A. D. Singh about regional food in a restaurant setting, he commented, 'Customers are happy to try new things as long as the flavours are approachable.' India's regional cuisines can offer both new food experiences and satisfy Indian taste preferences.

The focus on India's regional cuisines is only intensifying as chefs, researchers, food producers, and writers delve deeper into exploring the food of regions *within* regions, community food traditions and histories, forgotten or neglected indigenous ingredients, and family food practices. In a recent article titled '40 Under 40: India's Most Exciting Young Chefs', each chef featured spoke about their inspiration and aspirations for their cookery. There was much in what they said that resonates with the themes in this chapter:[20]

Sheik Mohideen once believed South Indian food was [merely] 'home food' and preferred cooking 'Western' meals. 'I appreciate Indian food better now.'

Aketoli Zhimomi is reviving lost recipes because she wants to 'show travellers that Naga food is more than just Naga chillies and dog meat'.

[Pankaj] Sharma's tasting menu celebrates local ingredients like sea buckthorn and Ladakhi capers. 'We start by looking at hyperlocal ingredients and how they're consumed locally, and then add our personality to the dish.'

'With her sustainable approach to cooking, Radhika Khandelwal [Delhi's Fig & Maple and Ivy-n-Beans] aims to make homely food hot.'

Prateek Sadhu has brought little-known Kashmiri ingredients to the fore, foraging and collaborating actively to bring revelatory dishes to diners. 'My mother always says we need to preserve two things—food and language,' he says. 'We may be gone one day, but these are our identity and legacy . . . I want to delve into familiar dishes and elevate them to restaurant-quality fare.'

The French built their international reputation for 'great' cuisine by bringing everyday food out of homes and into restaurants. The way these young chefs are talking, they are well on the way to doing the same. Before he headed off to the kitchen to oversee that evening's service at Indian Accent, Chef Mehrotra wound up our conversation saying, 'There is no need [for Indian chefs] to look outwards [to other countries] for new ideas and ingredients, all I have to do is explore my own country.' In other words, looking 'inside' is the answer.

2

Software Eats India

What's Cricket Got to Do with It?

It was the third day of my first visit to India. I had made the obligatory tourist pilgrimage to the Taj Mahal, where I was standing on the forecourt absorbed in its memorial splendour when a male voice intruded on my contemplation.

'Madam, where are you from?'

'Australia,' I replied.

'Oh Madam, very good cricket team . . . David Boone, Shane Warne, Alan Border.'

I smiled and nodded bemusedly. Watching men hurl a hard ball faster than the eye can see towards another attempting to hit it with a piece of sculpted willow is something many Australians love to watch. But its appeal had always passed me by, and I was unable to name any cricketer off the bat (pardon the pun) in response to this fellow's exclamation. This same interaction dogged me across India, and it has persisted across the years with a changing mix of contemporary and legendary Australian players' names sung out—I eventually learnt to reciprocate with 'Sachin Tendulkar', delighting my Indian interlocutors. However, it was more than this enduring good-natured exchange that caused me to notice the World Cup series in the summer of 2019. In Farzi Café, a Connaught Place eatery popular with the capital's youth, cricket commentary replaced the usual piped rock music; in the dining room of the Nashik hotel I was staying in, businessmen craned their necks to watch game highlights on a huge television in the lobby area while eating their breakfast; as I walked through the lobby of my Central Delhi accommodation returning from a late dinner elsewhere, cheering erupted from its upmarket restaurant, still full with diners watching a match on a specially erected theatre-sized screen. It is a particular claim of mine that I can make a connection between food and just about any other aspect of our existence, and because I was being confronted by cricket so often in eateries in India while researching for this book, I began to ponder how I might make a connection between food and cricket. It took a few days for the answer to materialize, but there it was: Cricket connects to one of the biggest contemporary food stories in India—online food delivery . . . admittedly it is a tenuous association.

I had been in the Nashik hotel I mentioned, observing other guests watching cricket, because I had gone there to visit Sula Vineyards, India's biggest wine producer, where Disha Thakkar acquainted me with the company's main operations on the outskirts of this regional city. After much talk of wine and food, which was strictly professional, the conversation turned to Disha's domestic life and the expectation of her as a wife and mother to always be responsible for organizing the family meals, regardless of her working full time. Apropos of this, she mentioned how she, and many of her friends and family, had been spending the summer in front of a screen at home watching cricket and ordering meals via online food delivery apps. Bingo! This was it, the connection between food and cricket. My inquiry began: Disha said she enjoyed cooking despite her gender-determined responsibility, so I was curious to understand what influenced her to use online food delivery apps. Her response was multifaceted: 'It makes it effortless to invite family and friends over for a meal, and then you feel like doing it more often.' When she was late home from work, ordering dinner to be delivered meant more time to help her daughter with her homework; the significant discounts offered by online delivery companies were another key attractor, and it made it easier to satisfy everyone's food preferences. She went on, 'Indians like being at home as there is usually a lot going on there', and with the easy availability of lifestyle goods—big-screen televisions, commodious lounge suites, advanced air-conditioning systems—people have been able to create cosy homes where they can enjoy their leisure time; using online food delivery apps means 'restaurant-quality' food can be added into this scenario, 'minus the effort of going out' to eat it.

The Black Box 'Revolution'

Back in November 2014, I was stuck in traffic on Lala Lajpat Rai Road in south Delhi when I spotted a scooter rider whizz by carrying a large black box emblazoned with the word 'Swiggy'. Having noticed this one distinctive rider made me aware of many others like him who had suddenly appeared on the roads. I was certainly curious to know what this battalion of humpbacked riders was doing, but when I discovered they were 'working' for an online food delivery service, I did not give this any further attention, despite my usual interest in anything new in India's foodways.

Ten years prior, I was living in Delhi, working on a book about the distinctive food culture of Nizamuddin Basti. One evening, two Australian friends arrived to spend the night with me before catching a flight home to Melbourne the following day. Their departure was unexpected and hasty due to a serious family situation, and after our dinner, I thought I would briefly distract them from their worries with the pleasure of a Nirula's hot chocolate fudge sundae for dessert. I phoned the nearest branch of this iconic restaurant chain and ordered three 'HCF' to be delivered to the door. Twenty minutes later, these arrived, slightly softened, but holding form. We three marvelled at this service: it was not possible to have an ice-cream dessert delivered to your doorstep in Australia then, the best you could do was a pizza. When I first arrived in India, I was, therefore, intrigued to learn that it was easy to have all manner of prepared food delivered to your door, from meals to ice creams, in the big cities. This was why Swiggy did not seem novel, nor innovative, to me and initially failed to spark my investigative curiosity. It certainly has now.

India's online food delivery sector is forecast to be worth more than $21 billion by 2026.[1] With the actual market size somewhere in the vicinity of $8 billion in 2022, this growth expectation is considered 'staggering'.[2] Nonetheless, investors have faith in the prospect, pouring in the funds that have enabled India's major food delivery companies to expand the market for their services, but we will get to all of that. Besides its financial potential, online food delivery has low barriers to entry—asset-light and low capital costs—making it an extremely competitive and dynamic industry, and new contenders come and go trying to grab a share of this, so far theoretically, lucrative market. As I write, two companies, Swiggy and Zomato, are the dominant players in food delivery in India, having captured 90 per cent of the market between them, and most of the media attention. So, I am going to use them as exemplars in this chapter.

The frenetic pace of change in the food delivery sector in India over the past few years has made it challenging to keep this chapter up to date as the book's publication was impacted due to COVID-related delays. In fact, the impact of the pandemic, while initially slowing online food delivery patronage in India, accelerated development in the sector and necessitated extending this particular story. By the time you read this work, I expect the details will have changed again; it is even possible that either of the current major players might be knocked out of the game. However, the trajectory of development explained here is more or less how it unfolded.

Player No. 1: Zomato 'started up' in 2008 by compiling menus from restaurants in Delhi NCR onto a website that allowed users to discover eating options near to their location, expanding into online food delivery a few years later. Zomato variously describes its business operation as a 'restaurant review, restaurant discovery, food delivery, and dining out transactions platform' or, alternatively, 'dine-in, food delivery, and search aggregator'. Player No. 2: Swiggy entered the fray in 2014, the year I first noticed their 'delivery executives' out on the road, with a less complicated identity as a 'food ordering and delivery platform'. Despite the grab bag of descriptors, these are copycat operations, with little to distinguish the main service—online food delivery—of one from the other (noting that Zomato also functions as a discovery mechanism for consumers looking for brick-and-mortar eateries to try out). Early on, tech-based food delivery start-ups, such as Zomato and Swiggy, were collectively referred to as food-service aggregators, or FSAs, because they 'aggregate' information about food services across India onto a digital platform. Over time, more terms such as 'ordering platform', 'delivery apps', 'delivery platform', 'aggregator apps', and 'food delivery platforms' have come to be used, and the main players are commonly referred to by their respective names as people are familiar enough with them to understand their business.[3] I am going to largely stay with using 'aggregators' or 'FSAs' to refer to all companies in India whose main business is online food ordering and delivery or, in a newer development, exclusively catering to food for delivery only. From here on, I am also going to use the term 'food delivery' to mean food ordered for delivery from an *online* platform unless otherwise specified.

Food Delivery in India: A Short History

When I first began interviewing Indian restaurateurs and chefs for this book in 2018, I found them generally, sometimes cautiously, enthusiastic about the potential of partnering with FSAs. Online food delivery had opened up new consumer spaces—homes and offices—to sell meals into, offering restaurants the potential to grow their market without the need to expand their kitchen or dining room infrastructure or operate their own delivery service; all they needed was to lay in a stock of packaging material to send out the orders. The FSA would take the food order via its platform, relay it through to the respective restaurant, and arrange for the prepared food to be picked up and delivered to the customer by one of its delivery 'partners'. The respective FSA also took payment for the food, forwarding the monies to the restaurant minus their commission. Restaurateurs expected the commission cost would be made up through increased sales. There was some concern that delivered meals might not be experienced to the same standard as dining in the restaurant because the food had to be packed and transported (in a backpack) to get it onto the customers' plates (if it wasn't eaten straight out of the containers). Other than that, this new frontier in food service looked very promising for both parties to the agreement.

> In a two-sided platform like Zomato, there are indirect network effects. The greater the number of customers, the greater the value for restaurants and vice versa. Now customers have more choices, restaurants have a bigger market, and the delivery network can be utilized more efficiently.[4]

Returning to India in March 2019 to resume my conversations with the food industry, I discovered the attitude of some restaurateurs towards FSAs was not as golden: The gloss had worn off and discontent was brewing. Rather than being a useful revenue source, partnering with aggregator services was turning into a significant cost for restaurants. The FSA commission could be as high as 35 per cent, leaving little or no profit on an order. The restaurants could opt to pay a lesser rate, but then the level of service they received would go down commensurately. If a restaurant paid a more substantive commission, they would appear higher on the results list when a user searched an FSA platform. As most consumers don't go beyond the first page of listings when searching for something online, being on the first page is critical; gaining this position on an aggregator site was a matter of who could pay the most for it.

> The home screens of both apps [Swiggy and Zomato] give top billing to whichever restaurants—usually big chains like Burger King or Domino's Pizza—are offering the biggest deals that day.[5]

Commissions could be forgone if a restaurant offered a discount or incentive to users of a particular FSA. Restaurateurs who took up this type of 'partnership' did so in the hope that offering discounts through aggregator platforms would attract new clientele and build brand loyalty once the customer discovered their food. FSA users were very enthusiastic about taking up offers such as 30–50 per cent discounts, two dishes for the price of one, and bonus food items. Most new customers placed online food orders for, or dined out on, meals and drinks that were discounted. Restaurants who signed up for these schemes found their sales going up and their profits going down. Aggregator discounts were incentivizing patrons to take advantage of whatever deal was available before moving on to 'discovering' the next discount on offer, in whatever place it could be availed. The only loyalty that was being built was to the originating source of the discount, the FSA (I will come to this further on). Aggregators also kept all the customer data, denying restaurants any access to this information; but if something went wrong, say an order did not arrive, it was the restaurant that the customer called to complain to. The massive spike in new users of Zomato from 0.19 million in January 2018 to 2.4 million in September 2018 was attributed to their aggressive discounting strategy. Restaurants felt they were paying the bill, but as Pradeep Shetty of The Federation of Hotel & Restaurant Associations of India described it, not offering discounts was a 'kill switch . . . if a restaurant withdraws from discounting, the FSA app immediately downgrades it and favours another restaurant which may still be in a position to discount . . . [t]his is just not fair'; yet partnering with aggregators became necessary 'to stay relevant'.[6] The National Restaurant Association of India (NRAI) called out the business practices of FSAs as 'unethical', but they kept on with the discounting.[7] Zomato CEO Deepinder Goyal countered these claims, saying his operation provided a valuable service that cost them money to run and was 'underappreciated' by restaurant partners.[8]

Addicted to Discounts

When I talked with Mumbai-based food writer Antoine Lewis in early July 2019, he reiterated the difficulties the Indian restaurant industry was experiencing with FSAs and predicted that a 'backlash' against them would not be far away. It came two months later. In August 2019, the NRAI launched the #LogOut campaign, urging restaurateurs to 'log out' of the dine-in incentive schemes run by FSAs, alleging damaging practices of deep discounting, data masking, and high and uneven commissions. In a statement released by the NRAI, it said the move was a 'protest against aggregators who have distorted a vibrant marketplace by aggressive discounting and predatory pricing' and was necessary to 'detox consumers from discount addiction', which in some cases were leaving restaurateurs literally paying for customers to eat their food.[9]

> Five years into the food delivery boom, many restaurants have now come to the conclusion that they are losing more than they gain. The biggest irritant is the steep discounting game, which has started to hurt margins.[10]

Despite their claims to 'partnership', aggregators seemed to be operating entirely to their own benefit. Two thousand restaurants across the country logged out. In November 2019, 8000 members of the Indian Hotel and Restaurant Association (AHAR) announced that they would be 'unanimously boycotting delivery services by aggregator Zomato under Zomato Gold due to allegations of delivery from illegal [unregistered] kitchens, steep discounts, and unavailability of delivery personnel'.[11] Zomato CEO Deepinder Goyal appeared contrite, proclaiming that #LogOut was a 'wake-up call that we need to do 100x more for our restaurant partners than we have done before'.[12] He 'promised to modify Zomato Gold which will result in a win-win situation' and proceeded to launch a new programme called 'Infinity' which offered Gold subscribers the chance to enjoy unlimited food and drinks at their favourite restaurants.[13] Despite what might have been taken as an empty promise on Goyal's part, there were talks and negotiations. In the end, the restaurants resumed their partnerships with Zomato and other boycotted aggregators, even if it was a cautious rapprochement.

Disgruntlement with aggregators is not universal. Abhay Mangaldas runs the heritage hotel The House of MG in Ahmedabad and its renowned restaurant, Agashiye, which serves traditional Gujarati food. When I met him in the Gujarat capital to talk about how food was changing in one of India's fastest-growing cities, I was surprised by his enthusiasm for online food delivery services. Tradition is his enterprise, so I had assumed he would not welcome the industry disruption that FSAs were fomenting. On the contrary, food delivery services had been good for his enterprise, creating the opportunity to expand its capacity to serve a potentially unlimited number of customers using existing resources, as well as opening previously untapped markets, such as older people who found it difficult to get out of their homes. While the food they sent out via aggregators had to be modified to be delivery friendly and the price reduced to suit the medium, Mangaldas believed people were discerning and understood a restaurant experience to be different from what delivery offers. If customers wanted online delivery, he was happy to work with FSAs to provide food to them in this way, saying, 'people evolve and businesses need to evolve with them'.

When the COVID-19 pandemic hit in March 2020 causing countries to order lockdowns and the closure of storefront restaurants, the demand for online food delivery went ballistic across the world, including in Australia, where spending on it increased by 300 per cent. India bucked this trend: demand for food delivery went down, halting the upward ascent of aggregators and causing Zomato and Swiggy to reduce staff and cut salaries. This decline was slated to a mix of factors: fear of contagion due to the delivery process, a return to home cooking when people found themselves having the time to do it, loss of income, a focus on building health to beat the virus, and the strong nexus in India between wellness and domestic food (see Chapter 3). It turned out to be a temporary wane in demand; after a while, it picked up again, perhaps because Indians were watching even more in-home entertainment in their forced confinement. Sitting on the couch with one's eyes glued to a screen has a strong connection to food delivery. Before the pandemic even hit, the *Economic Times* ran a front-page piece headlined 'Binge Watching Is Big Business for Food Delivery Apps', reporting that many of the 300 million Indians who spend an average of seventy minutes a day watching OTT platforms preferred staying indoors and ordering from food delivery apps, making this combination the 'biggest competitors [for restaurants] . . . rapidly redefining changing consumer preferences of dining'.[14] As the longer-term reality of the pandemic became apparent, restaurants and hotels began to re-embrace the food delivery model: this was going to be their way to survive. The 'ordered online and delivered into homes' model kicked off by FSAs went from being the industry villain to its saviour.

Follow the Money

Priyank Sukanand is young, urbane, smartly dressed, and lives in Bengaluru. He could easily pass off as an IT professional, however, he prefers making bread and biscuits and runs the bakery and confectionery enterprise Bangalore Connection 1888. This date refers to the year his grandfather started baking in that city, but his business is unquestionably contemporary—pop-ups at music festivals and that type of zeitgeist stuff. I anticipated he would be an enthusiast for food delivery. I was wrong again. Sukanand was not against the concept as such; he was concerned that the bigger FSAs were being funded by 'people who don't know about food', that 'big business was taking over' the food space through aggregators, and about the potential consequences this might have for India's food industry and the way Indians eat. His concerns are not unfounded: Success, such as it is, in India's food delivery sector seems to be predicated on access to liberal funding more than anything else.

Indians are now ordering millions of meals every day through aggregator apps. The expectation that they will be ordering many millions more into the future catapulted Zomato's estimated worth to $12.2 billion in July 2021 at the closing of its initial IPO. Swiggy is currently valued at a comparatively modest $5 billion. These are valuations that seem to run counter to the fact that both companies have been running at a loss for all the years they have been operating. It is improbable that any other food business could keep going for as long in the same circumstances. How is it that these two FSAs have been able to endure without profit and hold such incredible financial estimations?

Swiggy and Zomato are backed by some of the world's largest investors, attracting more than two billion dollars of funding from China, South Africa, USA, Singapore, Dubai, and the United Kingdom, and the money keeps coming. The raison de'être of these global investors is to make money, big money. If they are pouring funds into Indian FSAs, it is because they anticipate significant returns. As a rule, these investors would not fund restaurants because their operating costs are too high, the concepts typically unscalable, and their small returns hard gained. But Swiggy and Zomato are not truly in the food business (yet). They are technology companies operating logistics software; as such, their costs are relatively low or should be at some point in the future.[15] Technology companies are known for their lean staffing, and as technology workers improve technology to take over the work of people at scale, their employers can make do with fewer staff and run smaller offices, if any at all. Neither Zomato nor Swiggy employs a large direct workforce.

> Recently, an online food aggregator made news in India for laying off around 10% of its staff . . . [When] the company confirmed that it had, indeed, automated processes and hence rationalized staff, it brought into

stark reality the impacts of a fast-changing technology
landscape.[16]

The so-called 'executives' and 'partners' who make the
food deliveries for aggregators are engaged as 'independent
contractors' with few rights or entitlements.[17] Goyal says
Zomato currently loses money on each delivery, but that
won't happen as per the future business plan. Delivery fees
should cover the costs of delivery, at least, but low-fee,
or free, delivery is an attractor for consumers. So rather
than charge the true cost and perhaps scare off customers,
FSAs make delivery workers bear the burden. Though
the low reimbursement and poor working conditions of
FSA delivery partners have been a point of controversy
for some years, headline stories, investigative articles, and
social media posts about the exploitation of food delivery
workers in India exploded after Zomato's multi-billion
valuation in 2021.[18] This nexus is unsurprising: The fact
that FSAs keep their people costs so low is one of the
primary reasons they are so highly valued in the market;
that, and their potential to reduce reliance on human
workers altogether while being eminently scalable: Swiggy
and Zomato are already operating in more than 500 cities
and towns across India.

Changing Consumer Behaviour 101

Some of the billions invested in FSAs have gone into
building material company operations, but much more has

gone into creating a market in the first instance and then buying customer loyalty. Amongst the considered essays by key Indian food writers, restaurateurs, and producers included in the *Times Food & Nightlife Guide* (Hyderabad edition) of 2018, a copy of which I had found in my hotel room in that city, was a glowing piece about Swiggy. According to its enthusiastic author, the company was on a mission to 'change the way India eats . . . identifying and solving many gaps in the food delivery industry, not only pav[ing] the way for food delivery . . . in India but . . . also revolutionis[ing] the industry for restaurants'.[19] The Swiggy logo also appeared as a banner on quite a number of pages throughout the *Guide*, leading me to consider the possibility that the article on their revolutionary service might be an advertorial rather than an independent opinion. The Times Group have been producing guides to the best eating and drinking places in India for many decades, and the featuring of a new product or service in an established and trusted publication such as the *Food Guide* can help shape its acceptance. People who read restaurant guides want to keep up to date on what is happening in food, and the Swiggy article, appealing to this need to stay relevant, positioned their food delivery service as something new altogether ('revolution'). Claiming there were 'gaps' in the industry suggests that people are being subjected to an unnecessary problem they did not even know they had, for which food delivery was the apparent solution. Zomato employed the same tactics, alerting consumers to another problem they apparently had:

> We [Zomato] want to solve the need to 'cook versus eat
> out/order' and see cooking as something people should
> want to do because it's a joyous activity instead of being
> a chore.[20]

Swiggy and Zomato spent investor monies on advertising to influence Indian consumers to believe that they had problems in their food life, yawning 'gaps' and difficult 'choices', for which these aggregators had designed the solution (actually, they copied it; online food delivery started in the US in 2001). Consumers then become curious to try the suggested solution: A market for online food delivery had thus begun to be created.

It was the next step though—building customer loyalty—that required stupendous spending. Arousing interest in online food delivery was one thing; the hard work was in getting people to form the habit of using a new product or service, and that requires getting them to change. Motivating someone to change and take up a new habit, such as using an app to order food whenever they are hungry, rather than cook, go out to eat, or call the local dhaba to place a direct order, requires incentivizing this choice to make it the most rewarding of the available options, including against competitors in the field, and the key motivational tool used by FSAs is discounting. There is nothing innovative about offering a new product or service at a reduced price. It is a standard commercial strategy to encourage consumers to try something different in the hope that they will like it, and people will more easily try something if it is cheap enough. Getting consumers to use your food delivery service a few times as a novelty is not enough though; you need to entice them to keep using it so that it becomes a habit. Aggregators needed to 'train' people to both use their apps whenever they wanted something to eat and build loyalty to their service, and they did this by offering consumers more discounts and incentives. Food delivery platforms are known to be 'sticky', that is, around 80 per cent of people who sign up for one usually 'stick with it' if they find it rewarding enough, and 'sometimes with all the discounts, it's cheaper for the customer to order online than cook at home', and that is a very attractive incentive.[21]

> Zomato is a money-losing, cash burning enterprise now, but it has immense market potential and is on track to delivering on a viable business model.[22]

FSAs also need to keep attracting new users, and discounts and incentives are key in getting new users to sign up as well. FSAs did get restaurants to bear some of the cost of their discounting strategies, but they paid up too, burning their investors' cash to buy customers or market share.[23] ('Who pays for Zomato burning cash in its operations?' is a question in a 2022 accounting textbook.[24]) Investor funding allowed Zomato and Swiggy to expand quickly, attract customers, and build brand recognition.

> '[In] the winner-take-all dynamic [of the FSA space] the reward goes to the player who can sign up the most customers in the shortest amount of time.'[25]

The Winner Takes It All

The relatively low overheads and infrastructure required to run an online food delivery service mean that the barriers to entry into this industry are low, and that, coupled with the prospect of massive future profits, means new entrants are constantly coming and going in this consumer space. Nonetheless, all food delivery service is essentially the same: An app is used to order the food, and it arrives on the customers' doorsteps in a bag or box. The undifferentiated nature of food delivery has meant that the discounts and incentives initially offered to build customer share have remained as the key point of differentiation amongst its players. In the anonymous world of online food delivery, cashed-up aggregators relied on discounts and rewards to build customer share; in the process, they have trained consumers to expect cheap food from the FSA system, leaving them little choice but to 'maintain aggressive discounting through subsidising the cost of food items on their platforms' with an inevitable race to the bottom on prices.[26] Zomato and Swiggy have now created a very real problem for themselves, but the solution might not be in their control.

Winning the food delivery game will require one player to capture the largest share of the market and not only become the dominant player but also wipe out, or buy out, the competition. But the only way they are going to be able to return the profits expected of them is to cut costs.[27] The bigger the network of a tech company, the more valuable they are since scalability reduces costs. Where else can cost savings be made? Cutting staff is one measure; cutting the fee paid to delivery drivers is another. When Zomato announced that it was cutting 520 people from its workforce in May 2021, it claimed this action was necessary due to the impact of the pandemic; however, this seems at odds with the massive valuation the company received just two months later. A cynic might suggest that the real impetus for the job losses might have had more to do with preparing for the IPO offering.

The Restaurant at the End of the App

Restaurants are expensive to run, and profit margins are notoriously slim, even when these are not being encroached on by commissions. There are three major costs: physical infrastructure, including location—a good location will command a high rent—and fit-out, staff, and food. If you did away with the front end of a restaurant by removing the dining room, or any area where customers might come onto the premise, then you would not need any floor staff, nor any tableware or interior design. This would make restaurants far more profitable: Enter the 'cloud' kitchen, aka a ghost, dark, virtual, invisible, or shadow kitchen. By any name, it is a facility where meals are prepared, but there is no street presence and no means for customers to enter or contact the place directly. Anonymous commercial food production facilities are not new; airlines, hospitals, and event caterers operate this way; however, these produce standardized, limited-choice menus of advance ordered food for specific situations where people cannot cook. Cloud kitchens differ because the food is cooked to order (not all of the time though) from a wider range of choices. Cloud kitchens have a presence in a virtual 'shop front' on an app or website, and the food can only be ordered online—hence 'cloud'. Cloud kitchens are purpose-built for food delivery and are integrated with FSAs. There are different types of cloud kitchens: small independent kitchens run by a sole operator (perhaps a woman working from her home) or a restaurant; industrial-scale central kitchens, where bulk meals are prepared, semi-cooked, snap frozen, and shipped out to small satellite kitchens across a city where they are finished to order; and commissary kitchens, which are shared by different restaurants or food brands.

India has the largest number of cloud kitchens in the world, and the development and operation of these is the fastest-growing area of the country's restaurant industry.[28] Rebel Foods is India's most successful 'food-on-demand' delivery-only company, operating 3000 virtual restaurants and food brands from 300 'Multipurpose Invisible Kitchens' across the country. In an article on the Rebel Foods blog, CEO Jaydeep Barman pronounced:

> In the next decade or so . . . F&B behemoths shall be built on the cloud—making delicious food optimized for delivery at your doorstep, operating at a fundamentally altered economic structure . . . We are not dependent on high street costly locations.[29]

The rise of cloud kitchens in India is inextricably linked to app-based food delivery: This service had to exist for cloud kitchens to emerge. All the same, FSAs are currently debarred from setting up their own cloud kitchen brands due to government concern about the high level of foreign direct investment into food aggregators. The restaurant industry has also petitioned India's antitrust regulators to block FSAs from creating in-house food brands for fear that they would monopolize the industry. I expect FSAs will lobby for a change to this law. If they could run their own cloud kitchen brands, they could gain complete control over costs and pricing and potentially pay out the return their investors are anticipating.

For now, though, Swiggy and Zomato have a workaround, expanding from software operations to being good old-fashioned landlords, setting up commissary cloud kitchens that provide licensed professional infrastructure—commercial cooking equipment, refrigeration, storage, packing, and pick-up facilities, maintenance, and technology—to other food brands.[30] The food brand pays a nominal rent and a commission of 5–10 per cent of gross sales to use the facility, providing their own staff, food, and packaging. 'Swiggy Access' is a service leveraged off this model that helps restaurants open delivery-only kitchens, but this is a kind of peonage as the operator can only run its service through the Swiggy platform. Commissary kitchens do allow operators to quickly launch a delivery-only brand without the 'tyranny of location' or the 'monstrosity of committed costs' of a traditional restaurant.[31] The concept is attracting brand operators and investors alike, who are backing delivery-only kitchen brands to constitute as much as 35–40 per cent of the market for 'restaurant food' in India by 2022.[32]

> Cloud kitchen will be the most important part of the growth because that is changing the matrix and whatever profitability we are seeing is coming because of that— low capex, no depreciation. So the whole balance sheet looks completely different.[33]

If You Can't Beat Them . . .

Zomato and Swiggy largely did the work of establishing online food delivery as a habit with Indian consumers. While this was self-serving on their part, perhaps all the discounts and incentives that restaurants paid out for were money well spent after all.

> The online food aggregators are here to stay . . . customers have gotten used to them. Every [restaurant] player must get into cloud kitchens either today or tomorrow.[34]

To survive COVID-19 lockdowns and ongoing restrictions, restaurants had to embrace online food delivery and the cloud kitchen model. Many established restaurant brands have become hybrid operators since March 2020, setting up their own cloud kitchens and developing delivery-only brands, which may or may not involve an FSA as the delivery intermediary. This development was an expedient response to this crisis, but the cloud kitchen delivery-only model is set to endure as a key element of the 'new normal' in the Indian food industry.

> The aggregators need to be more business-friendly; one can't deny the role they have played in creating a robust distribution channel and driving up volumes for the restaurants. We, therefore, will continue to co-exist in the typical love-hate relationship. Tech, after all has to be an enabler, and not a distorter.[35]

Even as people have started returning to dining rooms, operating a cloud kitchen brand/s will allow restaurants to expand their market with much lower risk than opening a new venue, and if they operate their own delivery service, it will allow them more control in the online space, all of which I am going to return to further on.

> Futuristic technologies like drones, robotics, and autonomous vehicles can further reduce delivery costs [for food aggregators].[36]

The long game for FSAs is automated production and delivery. Whether they intended to or not, the dominant aggregators have set a precedent, creating a segment of consumers who expect to pay less for food. If food needs to remain cheap to hold users to aggregator services, then taking humans out of the process and installing robotic cooks will lower costs. Cloud kitchens are key to this. Commercial food production is already highly automated: Much of the packaged foods we buy in a food store are processed and packed by machines. We accept this because we do not see the process. We tend to be a bit more squeamish around the idea of eating fresh meals produced by robots, but the advent and uptake of online food delivery have inured Indians to minimal human interaction in obtaining 'restaurant quality' meals. The work that currently takes place in cloud kitchens to produce delivered meals is completely 'invisible' to the consumer; it would hardly matter then if a robot was doing it: Out of sight, out of mind. Indeed, given the trepidation around food hygiene since COVID-19, knowing that your meal is being prepared by a lifeless, therefore germless, automaton might even be appealing. Delivering the meals prepared in cloud kitchens by drones or driverless vehicles would reduce costs further by eliminating the need to pay delivery workers and allow for potentially unlimited and more efficient delivery capacity, although achieving this is probably further off into the future than robot cooks.

Automation of food production requires standardization. If menu items can be regularized, then production can be standardized and robots could be programmed to get to work—I do not discount the possibility of AI becoming so sophisticated that any type of dish could be produced, perhaps even bespoke meals whereby the customer inputs their recipe, and the robot makes it. Even now, in large cloud kitchen operations, chefs are employed to standardize recipes to reduce the complexity of the preparation and cooking processes such that low-skilled and, therefore, low-paid labour can do the work of producing the food for online delivery; these will be the people swapped out for robots. Standardization of meals can also reduce food costs and food waste.

Exactly What the Customer Wants

I find it ironic that big aggregators claim that they want to give more choices to the consumer when their aim is to minimize, even eliminate, competitors. The valuation of Zomato and Swiggy is predicated on their dominance, and they have already absorbed other operators, including Zomato's buyout of Uber Eats in India for $206 million in 2020. If competitors are reduced, and you have created a market habitually using food delivery, then consumers would actually end up with less choice in suppliers; this, coupled with standardization of menus, would lead towards a smaller selection of food being available from food delivery services as future predictions are pointing to.[37] Every transaction with an FSA provides data on an individual's food preference, aka 'customer intimacy'; 'aggregate' this information from millions of orders each day, and it is 'big data'. An FSA can easily know which dishes are most ordered and, perhaps over time, choose to stop offering less popular eats. Online menus could potentially end up looking very similar, and the FSA-delivery-only model could end up homogenizing and narrowing food choices rather than expanding them for the consumers. Of course, consumers can make informed choices and only use FSAs for certain types of food, possibly at the lower end of the market.

> Using big data, the aggregators have figured out what dishes sell more in what region. Then they have created dark kitchens (cloud kitchens). If a consumer searches for pizza, what is stopping them from diverting the traffic to their kitchen? It is use of a dominant position. It's scary what these guys are trying.[38]

If consumers look to FSAs to provide discounted or low-cost food, then cheap ingredients will inevitably be used to produce it: processed carbohydrates, low-grade oils and fats, and animal products. If consumers prefer low cost and convenience over quality, the health costs down the line might be significant. If people cook less at home, there are potential social and cultural costs as well:

> Dining at a restaurant is an exciting and delicious experience, meant to be shared with family and friends. Consumers lose the restaurant ambience and dining interaction when opting to utilize an online food delivery service. Eating in solitude with only your favourite streaming shows to accompany you . . . fosters an attitude of isolationism, slowly disconnecting you from the outside world.[39]

Who Benefits?

A report in the *Harvard Business Review* in the backdrop of Zomato's successful IPO admired the company's aim to 'transform the way India eats' because 90 per cent of the population does not eat in restaurants due to limited car ownership and cultural taboos about 'outside' food.[40] I would ask though, 'Transform to what and for whom?' I think if FSAs do succeed in transforming the way India eats, it will potentially be by making cheap, low-quality food more easily available to more people, perhaps those who are susceptible to marketing twaddle or for whom convenience is a more powerful influence than health, and potentially disenfranchise people from cooking for themselves and maintaining their well-being through the simplest way possible, i.e., eating fresh home-prepared food. All to the ultimate benefit of their shareholders, many of whom do not live in India, and CEOs.

It is obvious that I am not on the cheer squad for India's FSAs. Still, let me offer a balanced view and consider the ways Indians might be benefitting from their services. As part of the research for this chapter, I read customer reviews, posted on the social sites of Swiggy and Zomato, offering positive feedback about the discounts and incentives, such as free food items, that they had availed of and the convenience of having food delivered. Less positive reviews tended to be about the poor quality of the food and late or non-arrival of an order (not so convenient then).[41] Convenience-seeking with food is one of the major forces driving change in India's food system because it is unquestionably held to benefit people, especially women, by saving them time and effort in food preparation. Many women have also benefitted from the development of India's food delivery industry by setting up their own small 'cloud' kitchens, usually in their homes, and putting their cookery skills to work to generate income (see Chapter 3). The convenience of contemporary food delivery is reliant on food packaging, and the demand for food-packaging products has boomed. India's food packaging industry then is a beneficiary of the FSA system. It might not be as beneficial for the environment though, as one delivered meal creates an average of 100 grams of packaging waste. However, FSAs have begun implementing measures to try and counter this, such as Zomato making 'no cutlery' the default mode on orders.[42]

In 2021, the NRAI started conducting 'bootcamps' to help restaurateurs and food businesses set up their own independent direct online order service, and in 2022, the organization ran a convention dedicated to sharing knowledge and practice about cloud kitchens.[43] Other alternatives to mainstream aggregators are also emerging, such as Thrive, which has a capped commission of just 1–3 per cent and, equally importantly, gives the food businesses working with them the ownership of customer data, making the people they are serving more visible to them.[44] The Kerala Hotel and Restaurant Association has also launched its own food delivery app called Rezoy to ensure 'all stakeholders benefit', not just the aggregator:

'When you factor in the overheads, which include raw material cost and salaries, a restaurant owner is not left with much to run the business. Sometimes the bill amount [on a particular order] may not justify the commission. We needed to do something about it in order to continue in the business,' says Asees Moosa, Ernakulam district president of KHRA.[45]

Another interesting development is restaurant impresario Riyaaz Amlani's tie-up with Mumbai dabbawallas, the city's famed conveyors of home-made lunches, to have them deliver restaurant meals as well. After all the angst, if restaurants and small food businesses can control their own delivery operations, and/or work with less avaricious aggregators, and expand their businesses and serve more customers than otherwise would have been possible, then it might be that the Indian restaurant industry could end up being one of biggest beneficiaries of the work the cashed-up dominant aggregators have done to establish the market for food delivery services throughout the country.

According to a recent Rabobank report, the only way large aggregators such as Zomato and Swiggy can succeed and deliver on their valuations is if one or the other gains hold of the greater share of India's food delivery sector.[46] With the continual emergence of new delivery operators and the developing trend of restaurants moving to direct-order operations, it is going to be a constant battle to quash the competition. The biggest winner then will be the consumer, provided paying less for food turns out to be for the good.

> It appears to be a case of multiple Davids banding against a few Goliaths, in a tussle that promises to be fascinating, and ultimately rewarding for customers.[47]

Outside to Inside

Returning to the theme of the shifting of domestic, or inside, food to outside the home. Online food delivery has done the reverse and brought 'outside' food inside, and with it, a degree of trust that the food is prepared in a manner and under conditions that are suitably hygienic and culturally safe, even without seeing the kitchen it is made in. This got me wondering, in an oblique way, why, as someone with an avid interest in India's food and food systems, I didn't take more notice of the FSA phenomena before I felt compelled to do so for this book. Certainly, I did not think food delivery was innovative in India and therefore not persuasive of my interest, but I realized it was also because it is a system that is largely concealed. I could not see its workings beyond the delivery riders, and as it continues to develop, it is moving towards making kitchen work 'invisible' through cloud kitchens. This seems ironic given the popularity of food and cookery on television and social media platforms, which have made the workings of the kitchen highly visible. Are Indians becoming more interested in *watching* food being made than *doing* the work of making it? Could India's urban food move outside the domestic kitchen altogether?

> We can operate from our designed-for-delivery cloud kitchens with a totally altered cost structure of running an F&B business. Remember mobile leapfrogging expansion of landline telephony in India?[48]

India has a remarked tendency to pass over earlier iterations of technologies, usually on their way to redundancy, directly to the most advanced systems, for example, in solar energy and mobile telephony (an important factor in the take-up on online food delivery and in the predictions for its future growth); I recall my friend Amrita laughing when I mentioned watching 'videos' [video cassettes or VCR] in Australia in 2000 as India had leapt over this 'prehistoric' technology to DVD systems. There have been ongoing predictions in the West about the demise of the kitchen. But with the recent rise of cojoined food delivery and cloud kitchens, these prognostications appear less futuristic and more of a possibility. Perhaps urban India might 'leapfrog' into this future.[49] Concurrently, though, the lack of human interaction in this system might make eating out in restaurants and cafés, where there are real people to see and interact, and 'uniquely human skills', such as having your meal cooked by a skilled chef rather than a robot, 'become more valuable'.[50] On my first trip back to India post COVID-19, in April 2022, the restaurants in the central Delhi neighbourhood where I stay and in the big malls I visited were bustling with patrons once again. Anecdotal reports from friends suggest the same, especially younger Indians returning to social eating out with gusto.[51] Food delivery is not going to go away though, and consumers will 'vote' for how much the sector grows and who owns it by where they choose to spend their money.

> The nice thing is [India] appreciates high quality. This wasn't always the case as it was very price sensitive. But now India is a country where if you provide superior quality, customers are willing to pay for it.[52]

3

Women: Agents of Change

Late January 1998. It was the last week of my first trip to India. I took an early afternoon train to the rural town of Rudrapur, 250 kilometres northeast from Delhi, to stay with Kini and Gogi, the family of my friend Amar, whom I had met at university in Melbourne.[1] This was my first experience of Indian domestic life, and twenty-three years later, I retain two abiding memories of that time. It was late winter and still bitterly cold at night. I had been travelling on a student budget, and until this point, my accommodation had been in low-budget places furnished with beds of immutable firmness and meagre covers. On that first night in Rudrapur, when I climbed into bed, I slid in between smooth fresh sheets, felt the weight of expertly layered quilts, and my toes unexpectedly encountered the warmth of a hot water bottle, placed there earlier when the bed was turned down for me; it felt like being simultaneously enveloped in velvet and a warm bath. This recollection is a fragment of pleasure, a clear singular moment; the other is fuzzier in detail though its impact was more significant. I had climbed into that soft cocoon of bedding, feeling satiated after a delicious dinner, and over the following days, I learnt, in Kini's kitchen and at her dining table, how different the food cooked in Indian homes was from my commercial experience of it. I realized that if I truly wanted to understand India's food, I would have to get into her domestic kitchens.

This understanding was regularly reinforced: So often when I mentioned to an Indian acquaintance that I was interested in learning about India's food, they would respond with something along these lines (aside from the disparaging stereotypes of the food of other communities that were also shared with me as mentioned in Chapter 1):

> India's best food is in her homes . . . unbeatable by any other country in the world.
>
> You must visit people in their homes to know about the food [in India].
>
> My mother/sister/grandmother is an excellent cook. If you are going to visit [insert place name], you must go and learn from her when you are there.'

People regularly offered up their own, or their relations', kitchens for me to visit and learn in, and I keenly took up these offers wherever I could. If I can lay some claim to having a well-informed understanding of India's living food culture and its historical making, it is in large part because of people's generosity in taking me into their private domains, sometimes on the slightest association. It would require quite a feat of memory for me to list each Indian kitchen I have been in over the past twenty years, but I can recall the few occasions when a male, who was a family member and not a paid worker, cooked for me. Most memorably in the mountain town of Chamba in Himachal Pradesh, where Dr Mohammed Hamid, a passionate home cook who regularly prepared the family meals, taught me how to make a local version of pulao from scratch. Another time it was in Kota, Rajasthan, where friends Jaiwardhan and Neelu arranged for me to meet several men they knew to be keen domestic cooks. These fellows enthusiastically shared their knowledge of Rajasthani cuisine with me over several days, culminating in a meal cooked over hot coals under a star-filled sky on a summer night. Male cooks were commonly employed in the elite homes I was invited into. According to the esteemed food scholar Krishnendu Ray, Bengali men actively participate in domestic kitchen work, although he concedes this to be an exception.[2] I acknowledge that my experience of Indian kitchens, while broad, is based on a statistically small sample; nonetheless, other than the experiences mentioned, it was always women doing the domestic cookery work. There is also some statistical support to back up my personal experience: A 2020 study found that just over 6 per cent of Indian men took part in domestic cookery activities.[3] I am going to come back to men in the kitchen, though, because changes in Indian women's lives may affect a change in the number of men cooking at home.

Women's Inner Work

India's cuisine 'springs from its inner world', the private domain of the home and its internal kitchen where women have traditionally carried out the wide range of activities involved in feeding a household.[4] As of 2022, women remain the provisioners of food in most Indian families; it is they who maintain India's everyday food culture and they who will potentially benefit the most, or otherwise, from changes in India's food system. I set out to talk to as many women as I could for this work. I interviewed female journalists, food and travel writers, chefs, restaurateurs, educators, producers, public relations and event professionals, academics, a bartender, and home cooks, and I paid close attention to women in retail food stores, public eateries, and in food production. Several female interviewees described India's domestic food arrangements as persistently patriarchal, saying that they were expected to take responsibility for organizing their family meals despite having to work:

> Men still prefer a woman in the kitchen to serve them.
>   Dinner can be an expression of social patriarchy as rotis need to be cooked on the spot, there is a fetish about them being hot, this keeps women in the kitchen.

Responsibility for organizing family meals does not necessarily mean that a woman has to cook these;

sometimes, it is more about organizing the food. Higher–income households typically employ domestic help, ranging from a maid who might help with food preparation as part of her work to a full-time cook, such that some women might simply provide instructions on the meals to be prepared, or they might take a more active role in the kitchen. The availability, or otherwise, of domestic workers and the nuclearization of families in urban India are factors influencing change in domestic food. If India's 'best food', her regional, traditional, and community cuisines 'spring' from the home, then it is the women who do the labour of maintaining this; and as women's lives are changing, this is also transforming India's foodways.

Agents of Change

Demographic, social, cultural, economic, and technological changes have contributed to the increasing consumption of commercial meals in India over the past two decades, especially in urban areas where there is greater accessibility and choice available. Yet, the majority of Indians, 80–90 per cent of them, eat home-cooked meals most of the time. There are around 250 million households in India, with an average size of 4.8 people, most with a woman in charge of meal provision. It is women, then, who decide what most Indians eat, the ingredients for these meals, and where they are purchased. If a new food or food product is brought into a household and becomes a regular part of a family's food habits, it is more likely that a woman made the decision to buy it; even if it was initially introduced by another family member, it is she who will eventually control whether it appears regularly.[5] Women have a lot of power when it comes to food, and as they start changing what, how, when, or even if they are cooking, this will exert transformational influence on the way India eats. It is what Indians do in their domestic food lives that will affect irrevocable shifts in the food system. As women predominantly remain responsible for household food production, this makes them the major agents of change in the evolution of food in India.

November 2018. This was the first time I travelled in a women's carriage on the Delhi metro during peak hour. It was so tightly packed I imagined that if I fainted, no one would notice because I would be held upright by the pressure exerted by others' bodies. Observing the women surrounding me, many more of them in jeans, and some in body-hugging 'athleisure wear', than saris and salwar kameez, set me to musing how much Indian women's lives have changed over the previous two decades (although the necessity for women-only carriages suggests there is more change needed). Many more women are working (in paid roles), and they have increased financial independence and social freedom, even if gendered social mores around family food provision are lagging. Commercial food producers are more up with the times, and India's urban food environment is altering in women's favour with an ever-increasing range of products coming into the market to make the task of meal provision easier.

The Convenience of Convenience

Seeking 'convenience' in food is a key driver of change in India's food system, and the demand for more expedient food is primarily coming from women. I use the term 'convenience' in its broadest sense to encompass any type of commercial food, or food service, that reduces or removes the labour of creating domestic meals—ranging from breakfast foods and snacks to pre-cooked meal components and complete fresh or frozen meals to domestic help and food delivery services. There is also a broad spectrum of quality in convenience food, ranging from home-delivered meals from high-end restaurants to mass-produced fast food, from freshly cut salads to ultra-processed items. In Indian cities, a woman can call into a store—the neighbourhood kirana, green grocer, supermarket, or confectioner—to pick up pre-cleaned and soaked dal, pre-cut individual and mixed vegetables, sliced and marinated meats, or semi and fully-prepared meals that only require heating and plating up. Or she has the option of using online readymade-food delivery apps for completely effortless meals in the home. The range of convenience food now available in urban India is such that a family might, if they were so inclined, completely outsource the production of their meals to external providers and do away with any domestic cookery activity altogether.

I first met Kavita Chesetty in October 2010. Two months earlier, I had fallen into a conversation with her cousin Sundhya at a mutual friend's party in Melbourne.

We were talking about Indian food, and I mentioned my forthcoming research trip to India for what was to be *The Penguin Food Guide*, and she said, 'You must go to Chennai and meet my cousin Kavita; she is totally into food.' She connected us. Kavita invited me to stay at her home. I took up the invitation. At the time, she had two young daughters, had independently established a local food magazine, and was active in championing and promoting local food producers, chefs, restaurants, cookery writers, and cookbooks. Despite the demands of her professional life, she insisted on preparing most of her family's meals. And in case she was unable to do it herself, she had trained a cook to produce the standard of food she required. Each evening, she prepared south-Indian style coffee that slowly dripped through a filter to be ready for the morning and ground the batter to prepare fresh idli or dosa for breakfast. I was impressed by Kavita's dedication to, and enjoyment of, cooking for her family when she could have easily opted out of it. Nine years later, I return to Chennai, again with another warm welcome into Kavita's household. I have asked her to help me explore contemporary changes in Chennai's food scene—the 2010 visit had been focused on food traditions. She took me to bakeries and pastry cooks, fashionable cafés and restaurants, and fresh- and packaged-food retailers. She was particularly keen to show me the range of convenience foods designed for local tastes that had come into the market in recent years: pre-made idli/dosa batter and filter coffee in packets, pre-cut vegetable mixes specific to local dishes, and readymade millet drinks and fresh spice bases. While Kavita still cooked most days, she said that she used the dosa batter and coffee products regularly because the quality met her expectations while saving her a lot of time and effort. Her keen adoption of pre-made foods gave me pause. Here was someone who loved to cook, who was so painstaking in preparing food for her family, now singing the praises of convenience food products. In the years between my visits with Kavita, she had established a very successful café-bakery and then a boutique cake and confectionery business. Like many other working women, perhaps using convenience foods helped her ease the tensions between working and the prevailing expectations on Indian women to provide family meals.

When I talked with Rahul Singh, restaurant entrepreneur and owner of The Beer Café chain, he described how the 'shrinking size' of contemporary families in India—siblings choosing separate homes, kids going off to live on their own, and older parents leading active and independent lives—meant that there were often fewer people at home to cook meals for, such that the impetus for cooking, even for those who enjoy it, was diminished with no one around to appreciate the effort. Kavita's daughters were now grown up and in and out of home, depending on their college schedules and social lives, so the occasions when they ate at home were fewer and more random. Why not opt for easier meal options then? Kavita, like many Indian women, is relishing the availability of convenience foods, which allows her to provision family meals when needed and yet have time to do things other than cooking. For women who find cooking an unwanted burden, convenience foods offer potential liberation from the kitchen. The easy availability of commercial foods could also help fill the gap if India's domestic workforce shrinks in the future.

Domestic Help

The only experience I had of domestic workers—people employed to do work, such as cooking and cleaning, in an individual household on a daily or live-in basis—before I came to India was reading about them in history books or novels. Australians had been enthusiastic employers of cooks and maids up until the early twentieth century, but as women became more educated and more job opportunities were available to them, they moved away from domestic employment and this industry faded away. This is a common historic pattern, intertwined with the rising economic prosperity of a society, the emergence of a large middle class, and more egalitarian social norms: very similar conditions to those that India has been experiencing since liberalization in the early 1990s. Nonetheless, India is as yet bucking this historical trend—possibly because the achievement of something resembling an egalitarian society is a long way off, if at all.

As India has become more prosperous, more Indian women are prolonging their formal education and entering the workforce, and Indian families are becoming smaller. Precisely due to these conditions, the country's demand for domestic workers has grown, not diminished. There are a greater number of female domestic workers, more than four million of them, employed than ever before, the majority in metropolitan India.[6] Despite the existence of this large sector of paid household 'workers', domestic capabilities are looked at as 'unskilled' and considered innate in Indian women and not valued as 'work'.[7] It is an attitude that results in Indian women doing thirty-five hours of household chores a week on average, while men do just two. Small wonder that women working outside the home persist in employing other women to help them manage their households if they can afford it.

The historical pattern of declining employment of domestic workers in western countries did not occur because households did not want servants or could not afford them; it was largely because they became less available. This is not the case in India. Urban Indians still have a huge labour pool of workers, belonging to lower socio-economic class, to draw from; people who are poorly educated, even illiterate, and/or are from states and rural areas, where work opportunities are limited, poorly paid, and diminishing, and where there are no 'dark satanic mills' to absorb them as had happened in the industrializing West, migrate to the big cities to find employment. For females who are uneducated and lack the skills demanded by a formal job, domestic work is the most viable employment, providing more prosperous urban dwellers with a ready supply of household help; or at least it did—the recent pandemic might have a lasting impact on this, but we will get to that.

The Changing Home

Food is changing in India because women are coming out of the home. It is also changing because the home itself is altering with the broader transformation of Indian family life. The size of Indian families began shrinking after Independence, and economic liberalization accelerated this trend. The tradition of multigenerational family living has also been diminishing, and people are increasingly splitting off into smaller independent, or 'nuclear', households, a happenstance intertwined with urbanization. The high cost of real estate in India's metros means apartments are the most affordable residential option. These are typically designed to accommodate a smaller number of inhabitants. Living in a singular family unit means individuals might loosen the influence of family members who insist on maintaining community, caste, and gender norms, giving them more freedom to make their own choices, including what, where, how, and when they eat. On the other hand, working women living in an apartment in an Indian metro might miss out on the support a communal living situation might have offered her to manage her allotted domestic responsibilities.

The competing demands of having a career and managing their family's nutritional needs, all without the support of family members may have played an important role in steering these women away from cooking healthy traditional Indian meals, and resorting to convenience and fast foods instead . . . the phenomenon of the lack of social support, facilitation and interaction, especially during mealtimes, was identified as a strong theme contributing to changes in their food preparation and consumption habits.[8]

Without relatives to share the work of cooking and other domestic tasks, many urban women are filling this gap with domestic workers. However, the trend towards smaller families living in smaller homes, especially in urban India, is changing how families employ domestic help. When living in a smaller space, the need for a full-time domestic help might not be justified, or affordable, or even practical. Instead, a maid/cook might be employed only for a few hours, and she might work for several households across the course of the day, to do cooking tasks ranging from cutting up vegetables and making roti dough to pre-cooking the entire family meal. From my conversations with women for this book, it seemed this was common practice:

> Every colony or apartment block has women who work in different homes there.
>
> There is plenty of [paid] work for women who do domestic cookery work. Many of them work in several homes each day.

Marryam H. Reshii has been writing about food in India for the past three decades, scribing a regular food column, restaurant reviews, and several food-focused books, including most recently, *The Flavour of Spice*. Her observations on how food is changing in India are amongst the best informed I could have sought out. According to Marryam, the increasing participation of urban women in the workforce is affecting the most significant change on food in India and contributing to a decline in food standards. When I spoke with Marryam, she described the situation as she saw it: 'When a woman is getting home from work at 7 p.m., she will prioritize doing homework with her kids. So, she employs a maid to do the cooking for the family. She could bring a maid from her own region or community who is familiar with the type of food her family prefers. But if she makes this choice, then she faces other problems: Where will the maid sleep? Whom will she talk to? Where will she do the shopping to buy the food we like?' The easier solution is to employ a maid from the pool of women working in her colony; she will have her own accommodation, know where to shop, and have a social network. 'However, this maid will not understand how you like your family food to be, nor the community or the idiosyncratic nuances of flavour and texture preferred.' Now, this maid only comes in for a fixed time, and as her employer's time is circumscribed by her work and other commitments, does the employer choose to try and train her maid in the standards she prefers? 'Or does she dismiss that as too hard and just let the maid do things her own way?' In the end, it might just be too hard to tackle a part-time maid, so she chooses the latter option. It is not ideal, but it is expedient, and the process gets a good enough meal onto the table. This expediency might extend to using convenience products, such as pre-made spice mixes ground by a machine in the anonymity of a factory or even generic flavour enhancers such as Maggi sauce. Over time, the complexity of Indian food is diminished, and although Marryam did not say this, it is through this process that people become accepting of, or resigned to, less sophisticated flavours and quality in their food.

Food writer Antoine Lewis suggested to me that 'not cooking' might be seen as a sign of wealth and that the status gained by having the wherewithal to employ another person to cook for you might be more important than the quality of the food on the table.[9] Many Indian women who have no impetus to work outside the home in formal employment still employ domestic help, and wealthier homes are more likely to have a full-time cook whether a woman works or not. From my observations, it is the food lives of the wealthiest women in India that have changed the least, except that they now have a much greater choice of food products, restaurants and cafés, and other food experiences easily available to them. This situation might be altering though. In my broad-ranging conversation with Manish Mehrotra, we were talking about how the broader socio-economic framework of India is changing, and he commented: 'I do not think my maid will want her daughter to be a maid because there are more work opportunities for women now.' Perhaps India might just be a generation behind on the historical pattern of a disappearing domestic workforce. Mehrotra and I were talking in October 2019. Six months later, when the Indian government announced the country would go into a lockdown to stave off the advancement of COVID-19, millions of migrant workers, including domestic workers, fled India's cities to return to their villages. This left many affluent urban households with reduced help in their homes, or no help at all, forcing them to get their own meals. Some resolved the situation by cooking for themselves, others by accessing convenience foods and food delivery options, or a combination of these choices. It is an experience that might have shown some Indians who had relied on domestic help that the contemporary food system makes it possible to produce meals without domestic help relatively easily, whether they like this or not. Despite predictions that migrant workers would not return to India's cities in the same numbers as those who departed, and government schemes to help people stay in regional and rural areas, there are signs that people who left the cities are returning, or want to return, there to work. I asked some friends in Delhi in 2021, admittedly another small sample (n = 3), about their experience with domestic help with respect to the exodus of migrant workers from this city, and all reported that they had as many workers as they needed. If it does turn out that fewer domestic workers are available to help do the work of household cookery, it is probable that urban women will rely more on convenience foods to replace them.

The Costs of Convenience

Convenience foods undeniably serve to ease the labour of food production for women. The nature of convenience foods is that these are processed and packaged (to varying extents), creating additional benefits, such as ease of handling and storage, consistency of product quality and hygiene standards. Purchasing and using convenience foods might also support an identity of modernity. But what are the potential costs of taking cooking out of the domestic kitchen? The concomitant forces of industrialization, economic prosperity, urbanization, increasing education levels, and social liberalization drawing women out of the domestic kitchens in India have historically caused a decline in eating standards. Marryam's previous comments demonstrate how this might happen for people with the means to afford domestic help, but for people with smaller economic means, the decline can be especially pernicious.[10]

One of the costs of convenience food is its monetary price. Producing convenience food is a commercial undertaking, and companies and individuals who make and provide it do so seeking to make a profit from their enterprise. The fact of this almost always makes convenience food more expensive than home cooking, if you want to eat well, that is—cheap convenience food is inevitably produced from poor-quality ingredients. The ability to be flexible with how you source your food is a characteristic of affluent societies or of the more affluent citizens of a society. India's wealthier women can not only afford to pay for convenience food, they can also buy quality food products and services and are potentially spared having to choose between caring for their family's health and easing the work of meal provision, assuming their time to be more valuable than investing it in domestic work. Indeed, women who can afford the services of full-time domestic help to cook for their households already enjoy the ultimate convenience when it comes to domestic eating. Buying convenience may not impact the quality of the food eaten by high-income Indians, or it might. For those with less disposable income, what they can afford might undermine their health in the long run.

> The food business, like any other business, is about the bottom line and the best way to improve that is to get ingredients and use technology that will make you feel like you are still eating food, but unlike real food these will not have the problems of perishability and loss of taste with time, and who cares about loss of nutrients . . . easy to procure, easy to handle and, most important, cheaper.[11]

It is easy to understand why convenience foods are deemed attractive by India's less well-off working women—women who might be working as maids—who have had no choice but to prepare family meals even after working all day. Access to convenience foods means spending less time on food production, but the choices available to them might force them to choose between health and easing the burden of their work. A panel focused on the health benefits of eating millet at the 2019 Tasting India Symposium included two women from lower socio-economic circumstances who had participated in a programme to learn to use whole grain millets to prepare healthy snacks and meals for their children. They described how they struggled financially to meet their children's demands for packaged ready-to-eat foods, saying they often refused to eat anything other than these items, and as many of their peers were also eating these, it was difficult to deny them. They were also acutely aware of the potential health costs of consuming these foods. Despite the demands on their time, they wanted to provide nutritious meals for their families and were prepared to do the labour for this. There is no doubt that Indian women, no matter their background, still prioritize their family's health when planning and preparing family food. However, maintaining this habit in practice will increasingly be challenged by 'market forces'.

If convenience foods are used more regularly in everyday meals to replace fresh foods, whole grains, and cereals, which require more preparation, this might undermine family nutrition. Indian nutritionist and author Rujuta Diwekar advocates an intelligent approach to eating (and is a voice of reason on food trends). She is concerned that as Indians spend less time cooking for themselves and come to rely on convenience in the food they will be 'eating more like each other than unlike each other: More packaged cereals, more juices, more soda, more cupcakes, everything more than ever'.[12] When Marryam H. Reshii suggested to me that Indian food was on 'the decline', she wasn't just referring to the immediate replacement of home-cooked food with purchased food, or the merely serviceable output of a maid, but also the culminating loss of culinary skills and knowledge. If more convenience foods are used in domestic meal production, cookery skills will fall away, and culturally distinct food practices and knowledge might potentially disappear. Most people learn to cook at home, in both a technical and cultural sense—an Indian work colleague recently told me that while he did not learn to cook in his parents' home, he was very aware of what went on in the kitchen there, such that when he came to live in Australia, he found that he was able to cook by remembering what he observed while growing up. Even if Indian men are not actually learning to cook at home, their domestic food experiences can help them develop an expectation of wholesome eating if nothing else. If there is not much domestic cooking taking place, this not only inhibits learning to cook, and/or eat well, it also sends a message that preparing food is not something worth taking too much trouble over. If people lose, or do not gain, cookery skills, their capacity to feed themselves well dissipates, and enhances their vulnerability to the marketing claims of food producers more interested in selling their products than in the physical and cultural well-being of their consumers (see Chapter 5).

Cast Out

It seems as if food is being cast out of the home in India into a new space, a consumer space—public dining rooms, disposable packets, boxes, and plastic containers—rather than a place associated with familial nurturing and care.

For commercial food providers, there is huge potential in the Indian market if food production can be lured out of the domestic kitchen into the consumer sphere. In the early decades of the twentieth century, middle-class Indian housewives were encouraged through cookbooks, health guides, and food advertising to imagine food as the key to a 'successful transition to modernity'.[13] I think a similar process is taking place in India now, except that twenty-first-century Indian women are being 'encouraged' to use commercial food offerings to contribute to shaping India into a 'modern' economy—a fully fledged consumer-capitalist society in which food becomes a commodity bought outside the home, ideally freeing up more women to enter into formal work or just freeing themselves from the domestic realm even when they do not have to go out and earn a living. In my conversation with restaurateur Rahul Singh, he also told me that groups of women socializing over food and drink make up a third of the business of his Beer Café chain, many of them of a generation who would have previously met at home for a lunch or dinner event or a kitty party, who now prefer to enjoy their social lives in commercial spaces, their ability to pay allowing them to eliminate the effort and expectations of domestic entertaining.

Making the Invisible Visible

As women are stepping out of India's home kitchens, out of the 'inside', they have made what they were doing in there more visible precisely because they are not there anymore. The COVID-19 lockdowns, ongoing restrictions, and avoidance of commercial eating places and services caused many Indians to return to the domestic kitchen with enthusiasm, in large part because the situation allowed them the time to cook. This led to a prediction that Indians will keep up with home cooking over the longer term. I am doubtful of this—the same prediction was made in Australia, most notably because people started making their own sourdough bread during the lockdown, leading to a huge increase in the demand for flour, but even before we were released from confinement most people had returned to buying readymade bread, having been affirmed through this experience that it was much easier to buy it. I think the idea that cooking takes up time better spent on other activities, such as watching cookery shows, has taken hold, and there are too many commercial food producers and services in the market now to let India's food make a return to the inside, at least not without creating pathways to putting meals into that space.

Writing of the pandemic trend of replicating restaurant-style food at home, food writer Anoothi Vishal describes this as an irony, given the popular trend of putting 'home food' on the menu in restaurants.

> We don't know yet for how long this kind of entertainment will keep us in thrall. Yet, even when we begin to escape our isolation, this inspiration towards restaurant-ness at home, whether at the level of a

chowmein stall or World's 50 best, means that a new cooking culture is emerging.[14]

While home food is entering restaurants, there is also home food at home, except it is cooked in somebody else's home. There is a rapidly growing industry in India created by women, for the most part, who have not given up cooking; in fact, it is the opposite. They are using their domestic culinary skills to become food entrepreneurs, turning their home kitchens into places of commercial enterprise, using online platforms to advertise their offerings and have these delivered to customers. Some of these home cooks specialize in a particular regional cuisine and/or cater to the dietary preferences of a particular community or ethnic group. Opportunities to earn income from their home cooking are being created by women all over India. The absence of their cook during the lockdown prompted my friend Vishu, who lives in a town in eastern Madhya Pradesh, to go online and see what food was available for delivery there. He was surprised by what he found: Instead of the restaurant and fast-food options he had expected, there were local women offering home-cooked meals, ordered online and home delivered, to suit the dietary preferences of each different community in the township, including Anglo-Indian, Jain, Marwari, Brahmin, and Muslim. Jonty Rajagopalan runs bespoke tours of Hyderabad, which typically include immersion into some aspect of this Deccan city's venerable food culture. When we met there, she described a distinct trend of women preparing *swagruha*, or 'our house', foods in their home kitchens to sell to others, including products such as pickles, papads, and snacks, as well as labour-intensive Telugu-style curries and jowar roti, which were once made in every home, but which have migrated to commercial production because of the time involved in making them.

When I first drafted this chapter in March 2020, just before the pandemic took hold in India, I had described the home cooking phenomenon as a 'micro-industry', but I think it could move beyond that. The circumstances of COVID-19 inspired the opening of thousands more home kitchens and home-made food delivery services across India. Professional cooks and hospitality workers put out of work by the pandemic also started some of these, but the majority were being operated by home cooks. Demand boomed for meals prepared by these home-cookery enterprises, possibly because people had less, or no, domestic help. Paradoxically, several established home cooks reported in August 2020 of having to reduce their output because they did not have any domestic help to assist them.[15] In 2021, a survey found that a significant number of Indian restaurateurs and food service experts expected meals delivered from home-chef kitchens to be the fastest-growing sector of the commercial food industry.[16] While I could not find any further numbers around this trend (at the time of writing) in 2022, home chefs are being described as 'changing the food game' in India.[17] Popular food writer and blogger Kalyan Karmakar has also started a 'Home Cheffies' award to celebrate India's home cooks. The fact that this event is sponsored by several multinational food brands is a clear signal of the expectation of growth of the commercial home cook industry.

Several specialized food aggregator services have emerged that are focused on working with home cooks. One of these services, Curryful, describes its customers as people who want home-cooked meals delivered as they trust this food to be reliably healthy because a home cook can be trusted to use fresh ingredients, no preservatives, and less oil.

> Home food. The words invoke a sense of nostalgia. It's never only about the food; it's the story of each dish, the love, the creativity and the purity of recipes nurtured in family kitchens.[18]

There has been a prevailing attitude in India that food prepared in the home, 'inside' food, is the 'most natural and nutritive' because the people who prepare it, female family members, would unquestionably cook in the best interests of their families, producing unadulterated food to nourish and sustain the body and suit the family's taste and cultural needs.[19] When Indians order home-made meals online, they seemingly make the assumption that these will also be prepared in their best interests. Yet, it is actually food prepared 'outside' their homes, so they cannot know whether the ingredients are pure or if it is made with love. While I am not suggesting that this is not the case, I comment on this, as I have mentioned previously, because of the trajectory of India's food from inside the home to outside it and the increasing acceptance of this.

> So much great food is emerging from hitherto undiscovered sources. Unpretentious, original and straight from home kitchens. May Delhi's cuisine undergo a metamorphosis led by home cooks![20]

India's home cooks have also been stepping out of their home kitchens into commercial kitchens—in hotels, restaurants, resorts, and event spaces—where they are invited to create menus for food festivals, pop-ups, special events ; some of their dishes may even end up included as everyday items. They collaborate with the cookery staff to reproduce home dishes such that these retain their distinctive qualities but are suitable for production in a commercial kitchen. In the process, professional and domestic cookery is becoming more closely interdependent. I learnt from my conversations with India's cookery professionals that they understand that Indian cooking will advance from its domestic hearths, from the 'inside', and bringing home cooks into commercial kitchens gives them access to the vast culinary wealth of the country; for a professional cook, it is like reaching into a living encyclopaedia of food to learn from. For the women involved, it gives them recognition as well as income; and utilizing home cooks in restaurant and hotel kitchens offers patrons opportunities to discover more and more of India's regional cuisines.

Women in a Man's Kitchen

> When a man cooks, he should be a 'chef' but in the case
> of women, it is always said it is her responsibility.[21]

Just as there has been a cultural demarcation of inside and
outside food in India, the domestic kitchen, the inside, has
been designated as a place for women. Perhaps Indian men
have not been active in domestic cookery because they have
not, generally, been welcomed in home kitchens.

> My mother always attended to, and still does to this
> day—every little thing in the kitchen. She doesn't think
> it is a man's job to contribute or even take part in any of
> these chores. I grew up that way, and amongst that kind
> of attitude.[22]

The one kitchen that has never been a female space in
India is the commercial kitchen—this one has been
male-dominated—and women have not been necessarily
encouraged or welcomed in it.

> Despite being a cuisine chef, Urvika Kanoi was often
> told to manage baking at the beginning of her career.
> 'I was not allowed to butcher or grill meat because
> "women were not cut out for the job"'.[23]

The professional kitchen was not considered a suitable place
for women to work. It was an 'unsafe' environment because

it required close physical proximity to men—jostling and reaching around other team members during service is a necessary part of the job—it is physically demanding work, and women were not thought to have the strength and stamina to cope with it, and such labour was considered unseemly for a female (at least publicly). The long hours stretching into the evening were also incompatible with a woman's family role, and it could be both dangerous and socially unacceptable for her to travel home by herself late at night. Consequently, enrolment in India's professional cookery schools have been male-dominated, but India has not been without female chefs and professional cooks. Women have been working in hotel food service for decades, but they have been few in number, and it has been tough for some of them beyond the challenges of the work itself: I have heard stories of sexual harassment, unequal pay, subordination and lack of promotion, and women being overlooked in favour of less skilled male colleagues. More positively, I have also heard experiences of support, encouragement, mentorship, and advancement for female chefs if they found the right employer. And with more 'right' employers emerging, more women are becoming chefs and cookery professionals in India. A 2019 listing of India's '40 most exciting young chefs' included eleven women—decent odds considering there were only two women in the prestigious San Pellegrino ranking of the world's top 100 chefs in that same year.[24]

Ritu Dalmia is one of India's most respected and enduring 'celebrity chefs': a self-made restaurateur for twenty-five years, running restaurants in Italy and Delhi, as well as a catering business, authoring several cookbooks, and hosting television food programmes. When I interviewed leading food importer Jehangir Lawyer, he described Ritu as a major influence on India's contemporary food culture, declaring that she had 'chang[ed] the way we [Indians] eat'. Ritu comes from a background that allowed her the social leeway and resources to do anything she wanted with her life. Yet, as she shared when I spoke with her, the people around her were perplexed when she decided to pursue cookery and open a restaurant as they could not believe it was something she would seriously pursue. Her success has been an example for other women interested in professional cookery in India, although, as she said of herself in our interview, she has always 'been her own boss' and done her own thing, training her staff from scratch because she wants them to be able to 'think outside the box and not be caught up in the orthodoxies taught in catering colleges and hotel training schools'. When she started out in the early 1990s, she said that there were few women available to work in her restaurants because it was hard for them to meet the dual demands of home and work. Nonetheless, she has focused on mentoring and developing women chefs in her kitchens, building them up as a key part of her staff. She believes that as more women come into professional kitchens and stake their claim to equity there, it will, in turn, attract more women into them.

Megha Kohli has been consistently rated as one of India's best young chefs for several years now.[25] She began her chef training and cookery career with Oberoi Hotels when she was seventeen but found that the hotel kitchen model—the menu designed by an executive chef and execution focused on homogenous impersonal consistency of product—did not offer her the scope to be creative. She left to join the Olive Group, where she flourished and was able to discover her own style. A consultancy in Kolkata inspired her to take more of an interest in regional food, particularly the cookery legacy of the Armenian community in that city, leading her to develop the recipes for the Kolkata-Armenian-inspired food at the Lavaash by Saby restaurant in Delhi and head its kitchen. Having experienced difficult conditions in male-dominated hotel kitchens early on, she actively works to create a kitchen environment that is safe and supportive for women. When two young women approached me at an event in Delhi to ask me to sign their copies of *The Penguin Food Guide*, I asked them about their interest in food, and they said that they were both chefs happily working with Megha at Lavaash (she has moved on since she and I spoke and has turned her talent to another restaurant in Goa).

> Megha Kohli is considered one of the few and finest women in professional kitchens in India. But it has also been one of her biggest challenges. A new supplier, for instance, would much rather speak to a man, even if he were a junior, than address her. Kohli, though, has been creating waves outside the 'woman chef' box.[26]

Anahita Dhondy, former chef-partner at the popular SodaBottleOpenerWala restaurant brand, is inspired by Mumbai's iconic Parsi-run Irani cafés and her own Parsi heritage. I met her in my favourite Delhi branch of this chain in late 2019, where we talked about her career experiences up until then. While her own family were supportive of her choice to pursue a career in professional cookery, she said this was unusual ten years ago when she did her training, as 'middle-class parents looked down on cookery as a career', especially for women, preferring their educated kids to take up 'safe' professional occupations as doctors, accountants, and engineers, and there were only four other women in her batch when she did her training. Nowadays, the same course can have anywhere between twenty to forty women enrolled in it. According to Dhondy, a culinary career has become more acceptable for women because of the high profile that chefs, professional cookery, and the food business have gained over the past decade as subjects of television programmes and social media. Initially, Anahita found it intimidating to work in a kitchen in which she was the only woman, saying that she had to work harder than anyone else to be 'taken seriously' by her male colleagues. Having endured this to take her place as a professional, it is important to her to be seen as a 'chef', not as a 'woman or female chef', and to not be treated differently from the men she works with.

I always look forward to a meal at Bengaluru's Mavalli Tiffin Rooms (MTR) whenever I am in that city, so I was excited when Hemamalini Maiya, owner of this iconic restaurant, agreed to talk with me there. She told me that running the restaurant was not something she had ever expected to do, but when its previous proprietor, her father, Harishchandra Maiya, died suddenly, she had to take over its operation. While MTR had been the family business for several generations, she had no preparation at all for running the place because the entire operation was run and staffed by men—who, she said, had to 'resign [themselves] to the fact' of her becoming their boss even though they did not like it. Dedicated male customers who came to the restaurant for coffee every day were discombobulated, asking if she was a daughter-in-law married into the family—they had never seen her before despite their enduring patronage—as they could not conceive of a direct female member of the Maiya family doing such work. Nobody thought she would last, and people kept asking her when she was going to get married and leave. That was not her intention. Despite the unsought challenge of the task, she took over the restaurant, determined that it would continue, and resolved to do whatever was needed to make that happen.

MTR serves Karnataka Brahmin food, and the kitchen adheres to orthodox Brahminical hierarchies and practices. Nobody wears shoes inside the kitchen, and in the past, customers even entered via the kitchen so they could be assured of appropriate levels of cleanliness being maintained. Many of the cooks had been working at MTR for decades when Hemamalini took over and were rusted on to its traditional operational environment. Accepting a woman as their boss was a huge challenge, unleashing the egos of senior kitchen staff for whom working under female leadership was a personal and social affront. After their initial resignation to her leadership, they began actively resisting it (the shock of it must have set in late). Hemamalini was not going to be done in by them. She focused on earning their trust while making it clear that she was the boss and they had to do things the way she wanted them done. She also had to deal with male food vendors who, despite having provided quality food while her father was alive, decided that they could take advantage of a woman being in charge and started supplying watered-down milk, amongst other things. As Hemamalini describes it: 'I had to be like a man, but do more than a man would do to be seen as the boss. I became extremely aggressive in those early days. I was always fighting.' This approach eventually took a toll on her health. But she says it is a much better environment now. Most of the older staff have retired, and the newer ones have a different perspective; 'there is a different attitude to women in business now, and the younger staff have no issue with a female as their boss.' Hemamalini said she would love to employ more women to cook but would have to bring them from rural settings, as she does not think contemporary urban women would know how to, nor want to, work with the enduring orthodox processes of the MTR kitchen.

Women have always been in charge of food in India, just not in the public domain, which historically has been the least of it. As food is shifting out of the inside/the domestic sphere into outside/commercial food production, women too are shifting their influence on food into the public domain through social media, journalism, and writing. Food journalism, researching and writing about food, teaching cookery, product development, business consultancy are all areas in which women have created work for themselves, without having to be in the kitchen of a hotel or restaurant, but contributing to the evolution of food in India in independent, thoughtful, and creative ways. It has been the work of women that has arguably had the greatest impact on bringing India's food from inside to outside and generated popular interest in her multiplicity of foodways overall. When I look at my collection of Indian regional cookery books, almost all of them have been written by women about their familiar domestic cuisine; it was Indian women who ardently took to blogging about their cookery in the early days of the internet; and now, it is women bringing home food outside through the home chef phenomenon and who are acting as consultants to the commercial food industry, and, as just mentioned, in the wider media sphere. Perhaps though, as women become more involved in food-related enterprise, this might contribute to them cooking less at home (see below). When I am in the process of writing a book, I still cook for myself, but I get into a repeat pattern of meals, i.e., eating the same thing for breakfast, lunch, and dinner for weeks at a time, as this saves me having to use up my thinking energy (writing is essentially relentless problem solving, and it is tiring on the brain), and I use a bit more 'convenience' food, pre-made stock for example, than I would otherwise.

As promised at the start of this chapter, I am going to discuss men's position in all of this. I have noticed amongst younger urban Indians I have met an expectation of more equitable sharing of domestic responsibilities with their partner, such that more males are taking a role in preparing, or at least organizing, family meals.

> I have previously argued that Indian men must learn to cook for many reasons: social, economic and moral. The Indian woman can no longer be allowed to bear the burden of household work because it is not just holding her back but holding India back. Indian men do far less housework than men of almost all nationalities.[27]

And it is not only the younger generation of males doing more kitchen work, it seems that as food and cookery have grown as a popular subject in the Indian media, men of all ages have become more interested, or at least convinced that they need to, in taking a role in producing domestic meals. There are also some male cooks amongst the home cooks selling their fare.

> The great Indian kitchen . . . is changing. One little recipe and baby step at a time. From a father who makes a hot *roti* for his daughter, a husband who learns how to wash dishes and cut onions after a decade of being spoilt and pampered by his mother, a brother who brushes up

his *batata poha* skills during the pandemic. To a mother who insists that the kitchen and its many duties belongs to, and should be claimed by everyone, and not just by the women in the household. A mother who vows to raise her children differently, ensuring that cooking is not a skill dictated by one's gender.[28]

It seems that as urban women are moving out of the domestic kitchen, they are making space for men to come into it. We can only wait and see how men get on with it.

4

New Influences on Indian Food

Thumbs Up for Cake

19 January 2018. A day before flying home to Australia, I collected an artwork I'd had framed from a framing store in Delhi's Khan Market. It was a business I had been a customer of for some time. In October of that same year, I returned to this upmarket consumer precinct intending to drop off a small painting purchased in Puducherry to the same framer to have it mounted, except the business wasn't there. Instead, I found myself looking into the window of an upmarket patisserie. I was more interested, at this point, in finding the framer and set off to investigate if they had relocated elsewhere in the complex. I noticed another patisserie and then two more cake shops, all just doors apart. These stores had not been there eleven months ago. I forgot about the framing and turned my attention to exploring these recently materialized purveyors of sweet confections.[1]

A Sweet History

India was one of the earliest producers of the crystalline substance created by boiling the extracted juice of *Saccharum officinarum*, or sugar cane, known as sugar. Mention of its use in a range of foods, including milk puddings and fermented drinks, first appeared in Indian texts circa 400 BC—a time when sugar was hardly known to the rest of the world. When the army of Alexander the Great came into north India in 327 BC, one of his generals noted a local phenomenon, a 'reed which brings forth honey without the help of bees from which an intoxicating drink is made, though the plant bears no fruit'. What he is describing is sugar cane, making it clear that the Mediterranean invaders had no experience of cane-derived sugar.[2] Two millennia later, India is one of the world's largest producers of sugar, and Indians are amongst the highest consumers of sucrose. The collective Indian 'sweet tooth' has a venerable as well as an ancient lineage. Sugar cane was being offered to the gods at least as early as 600 BC, and sweet dishes and drinks are considered the favourite foods of the Hindu deities.

India has a vast, possibly countless, repertoire of indigenous sweetmeats and sweet dishes: a short list of some of my favourites includes sooji ka halwa, mishti doi, shrikhand, jalebi, milk cake, sohan halwa, phirni, suterfeni, chenna poda, bal mithai, sondesh, malpua, rasmalai, unnakkaya, and lagan nu custard. Many Indian sweets are confected from milk in various forms—lightly reduced for payasam or kheer, curdled such as yoghurt or chenna, or condensed to a thick pliable paste (khoya); some are also fried in ghee. Besides milk, all kinds of ingredients are used to fashion sweet items: wheat, rice and chickpea flour, nuts, seeds, semolina, coconut (fresh, dried, and milk), fresh and dried fruit of all kinds as well as vegetables such as carrot (gajar ka halwa) and ash gourd (petha). The use of cream, butter, and eggs is uncommon in Indian confectionery, nor is there a customary domestic practice of baking cakes, pastries, or bread, with notable exceptions of places such as Goa and Mangaluru and in Parsi and Anglo-Indian communities with strong European influences (Portuguese and British respectively). I have several Indian friends who, whenever I stay with them, graciously ask if they might prevail upon me to prepare a few western-style dishes for them: My consent is always greeted with great delight. They typically request baked items: cheese pie, lasagne, apple crumble, lemon delicious pudding, chocolate self-saucing pudding, and lemon meringue pie are all favourites—they also enjoy the salads I make up, perhaps to balance the nutritive ledger. For me, these dishes are commonplace, simple to make and less complex in production and flavour profile than most Indian dishes. For my friends, anything out of the oven is novel and exotic as it is not the food of their everyday lives.

India does have a more recent 'tradition' of commercial production of European-style baked goods, which began in the late nineteenth century with the local manufacturing of sweet biscuits. By the time I arrived on the subcontinent a century or so later, cake, bread (colloquially known as 'double roti' in north India), and biscuits were commonly available in food stores, although the variety was limited, and most were relatively plain and less sweet than Indian mithai. For something fancier, there was the cake for special occasions, a sponge filled with jam and cream (of a type) decorated with exuberantly coloured imitation butter frosting, perhaps best exemplified by a Monginis classic. I have always found these whimsical cakes charming, igniting nostalgia for childhood birthday parties, and noticed that these have been evolving into even more elaborate versions. Visiting the former French colony of Yanam near Andhra Pradesh on 31 December 2018, I revelled in juvenile pleasure in walking the lanes of the town's commercial centre, inspecting the cakes decorated in high style with grass, flowers, swans, hearts, tear drops, and scalloped and swirled edges fashioned from soft icings, variously coloured dayglo pink, luminous green, bright cornflower blue, ivory white, and golden yellow, displayed by local confectioners to celebrate the new year. This experience also set me to wonder if this heightened use of vivid colours and elaborate decorations might be in response to new competition in India's sweets market.

Given the Indian penchant for sugary confections and fondness for baked goods, it seemed to me that there was an obvious gap in the market for good European-style desserts, cakes, pastries (patisserie), and leavened breads. You could get these items in hotel bakeries and breakfast buffets, but they just weren't quite up to the mark. Breads, cakes, and muffins did not rise into soft crumbly volume, tending to be dry and heavy, and pastries that should have been light and flaky were dense, due in part to the stone-ground wheat flour commonly used in India, a process which denatures the starch and protein in the wheat, adding more flavour to the flatbreads it is commonly used for, but handicapping its rising potential. The lower fat content of local milk[3] meant fresh cream could not be whipped up easily to hold soft peaks, and a heavier mock 'cream', prepared from butter and commercial vegetable shortening, was usually substituted; this product also has more capacity to hold its texture, i.e., not melt or curdle, in a hot climate. Egg-based custard dishes were often prepared with cornflower-based custard powder, accommodating the strong demand in India for egg-free dishes but diminishing their flavour and texture. Even as I preferred to indulge in Indian sweet treats and desserts, I noticed a steady evolution in the range and quality of European-style baked and patisserie items available in India, as well as the proliferation of cafés serving espresso coffee and western-style cakes and sandwiches. Still, this sudden appearance of four stores, just metres apart, dedicated to fine patisserie and cakes—I could have been looking at a display of sweet comestibles in Sydney, London, or Paris—in a matter of ten months, what had led to this? I started to ask around.

The *MasterChef* Effect: Part II

Apparently, the answer to my question as to why all these cake stores had opened in Khan Market was 'Australian

MasterChef'. It is possible that I received this response because the show and I share a nationality—at a cooking competition in rural Jharkhand, when the judges, of whom I was one, were invited on the stage to announce the winners, I was introduced as 'Dr O'Brien, from the land of *MasterChef*'. Though not everyone I asked pointed directly to this Antipodean culinary game show, all cited television as a key influence on this trend.

Cooking shows have been a television stalwart for decades, aired during the day for an audience of women responsible for cooking food at home. That cooking has now become primetime viewing, attracting huge audiences of both genders and across all ages, is a more recent happenstance, propelled by shows that have turned meal production into a competition. Others have made food the focus of visually seductive travel narratives or given audiences an inside view into the dramatic machinations of esteemed chefs in restaurant kitchens.

> Food, earlier a domestic unalterable, has fled the confines of the kitchen and become a national adventure. Foodies, once a select band . . . have blended in. Food writers, both rude and polite, have become celebrities by discussing the intricacies of a creme brulee. Food shows, now even on news channels, have transformed restaurateurs from humble khansamas to courted celebrities.[4]

The impact of contemporary media in all its forms on how Indians are currently cooking and eating, or aspiring to, is inarguable, but television programmes are perhaps the most influential, and by 'television', I mean to include cooking- and food-focused programmes on OTT and digital platforms. At any time of the day, there are around twenty different food programmes being aired on Indian television. India has many of her own influential television celebrity chefs, food personalities, and food shows: Sanjeev Kapoor—one of the most watched and best-known chefs in the world with an annual television audience of 500 million viewers, Vikas Khanna, *Urban Tadka*, *Mummy Ka Magic*, *Vicky Goes Veg*, and *MasterChef India* are amongst the most highly rated. I am going to use *MasterChef Australia* as my example though, not from any instinctive bias for my countrymen, rather as it was my Indian interviewees who nominated it as having a direct influence on the cake phenomenon, and it is also representative of global media influence on contemporary food trends in India.

Creating fine European patisserie, desserts, and baked goods takes skilled and painstaking work requiring specific conditions, ingredients, and equipment to execute to a professional standard—as is true for the professional confectioner of Indian sweetmeats. Producing elaborate and novel high-end restaurant-style desserts and sweet treats was a feature of *MasterChef Australia*—pastry chefs Adriano Zumbo and Anna Polyviou both became celebrity confectioners after their appearance on the show. The three million Indians watching the programme had a whole new world of exciting desserts and sweetmeats laid out, visually, before them, which would have left many hankering to consume these in real life. Some viewers might have tried making these elaborate items at home, but given the skill and equipment required to do so, how many people would really want to put in the effort? It is much easier to buy these treats. With media-stimulated appetites for European-style confections and the economic wherewithal to spend regularly on such discretionary indulgences, the demand for these items burgeoned. Indian chefs, cooks, and aspiring food business owners had, in the meantime, having discerned the potential of the cakes and bakes market in India, been training as pastry cooks and bakers at places such as Le Cordon Bleu in London and Paris, or cookery schools in Australia—the popular north Indian European-style bakery chain, Nik Baker's, has as its tagline 'Run by a Professional Baker from Australia'—and/or at India's culinary schools to skill themselves up as bakers and confectionery makers. Their skills and ambition connected with a growing consumer demand, hence the flourishing of cake stores in Khan Market and elsewhere in urban India—as an aside I counted 100 plus varieties of cakes, biscuits, tarts, and slices at The Big Chill Cakery in Delhi.

October 2019. I purposefully arrived early for a lunch meeting with my editor Richa at Cyber Hub, the restaurant/café and pub precinct of the futuristic tech-business park Cyber City in Gurugram, so I could do some field research. I wandered around inspecting the food offerings and counted eight eateries devoted solely to cakes, desserts, chocolates, and ice-creams, including 'on trend' Nutella-filled doughnuts, banana bread, and gluten-free brownies. I am going to evolve the style of cakes and bakes from here on into 'Euro–American' as social media has embedded its parent (USA) food preferences into this category of eats. These venues cater to people working in the shimmering corporate office towers encircling the Hub and a younger crowd of leisure seekers—or at least it did so before COVID-19 depopulated the offices. You could be in a technology-business park in any big city around the globe here, although the collective smorgasboard of sweet items was a distinctive feature. Every day I was in Mumbai that same year, I took a walk in a different direction around the streets of Colaba and the surrounding residential neighbourhoods, noting on these meanderings that just in this section of the city alone, stores selling cupcakes, elaborately decorated birthday cakes, iced-doughnuts, muffins, macaroons, fancy breads, dessert cakes, filled pastries, and a lot of chocolates and chocolate-based confections had proliferated since my last visit nine years previously. Even the Monginis store had updated and expanded its range to include contemporary 'designer' cakes. Fifteen years ago, my Chennai-based friend Kavita Chesetty travelled to Australia to train with one of the country's best pastry chefs with the intention of opening a store in Chennai selling fine pastry and cakes as there was nothing like this available in the Tamil Nadu capital. She duly opened a bakery and café called Amore, and this venture was a great success. In December 2019, Kavita is taking me around Chennai, visiting contemporary food businesses for my research for this book, including a raft of bakeries and patisseries, selling cakes, croissants and pastries, leavened breads, cookies, and richly iced small cakes, that have all opened in the past five years.

Media-fuelled hunger for sugary confections has not been exclusive to Indians. In Sydney, long queues formed outside Adriano Zumbo's cake store every day for several years, with people eager to buy the sort of items they saw him create on television. Other popular cooking programmes such as *The Great British Bake Off* and *Chef's Table* too have contributed to an increasing global appetite for Euro–American cakes, desserts, and sweet pastries. As a curious side note, this has happened concurrently with the emergence of the anti-sugar movement, perhaps an example of the disparity that often exists between our espoused values (sugar is 'bad'; I will eat less of it) and lived values (enthusiastic consumption of sweets). *MasterChef* is additionally credited with changing the Indian understanding of the potentialities of the visual appeal of food. Focusing on the appearance of food is essential on television because you cannot taste or smell it; visuality is the only way for consumers to connect with it. The same is true for social media. Desserts and cakes can be made visually spectacular—an effect you can't quite achieve with a bowl of pasta. India's cakes and bakes trend is not solely born out of television. It is also interconnected with economic prosperity, travel, and social media. Nor it is just about the material elements of food. Having a slice of cake and a coffee is an affordable indulgence, especially for young people wanting to socialize in a fashionable venue, who might find the cost of a full meal prohibitive.

Modern Mithai

Back in 1993, when Vineet Bhatia, the first Indian chef to get a Michelin star for his restaurant, invented the chocolate samosa on a whim in London, it did not cause even a ripple back home because mithai was then seen in restaurants and hotels as the domain of the un-inventive halwai.[5]

If the Indian halwai was the purveyor of predictable confections in 1993, his customers were perhaps as unimaginative as to what they would accept as his 'art'. This is no longer the case—and India's professional confectioners are also no longer exclusively male. Indian pastry cooks and confectioners are working with traditional sweetmeats to fashion these in a more contemporary style, a movement said to have been spearheaded by the invention of the doda barfi treacle tart by Chef Mehrotra at Indian Accent. The Bombay Sweet Shop in Mumbai is 'bringing back the magic of mithai' by refashioning traditional Indian confectionery, such as laddoos, barfi, chikki, pak, pedha, and milk cake, infusing some with modern flavours such as caramel, coffee, and pepper, and presenting them in highly designed contemporary packaging that plays on nostalgia but repositions these sweetmeats to look more like a box of chocolates or some other novel treat. Khoya Mithai in

Delhi is another business finessing classic Indian sweets with visually seductive packaging, albeit designed to appeal to consumers with more traditional Indian sensibilities. This brand also has a tie-in with a popular television talk show, such is the 'celebrity' of food.

The Social Media Effect

Shahdol is a regional city in eastern Madhya Pradesh. It is the administrative headquarters of a district with a population of one million, and the town centre bustles with commercial and agricultural activity. I have been coming to Shahdol almost annually since 2009 to visit my friends Bharti and Vishu. There are some small temples here of the same era and style as the famed shrines of Khajuraho, but this is no tourist territory—Vishu jokes I am the only foreigner to have come here besides a man named Robert O'Brien in 1879 and says it must be in the bloodline. This is everyday regional India, an ordinary place like that of R. K. Narayan's fictional Malgudi, vibrantly alive with the intricacy of human relations played out in the complexity of Indian society. Each time I visit, we make a trip to Mahadev Fruits, the fanciest grocery store in town, to stock up on ingredients so that I can prepare western-style cakes and bakes for them, although the limited availability of suitable food items meant I often had to settle for substitutes.

Around 2016, the range of 'foreign' ingredients available at Mahadev Fruits suddenly expanded: good quality olive oil (in large bottles rather than small 'medicinal' tins), rolled oats, dried blueberries, multi-grain bread, pecan nuts, real fresh cream (not in a tetra pack), a range of dark chocolate, cacao powder, cream cheese, almond meal, amongst other seemingly random imported food products. There was also a newly installed bank of freezer cabinets packed with convenience foods and a refrigerated cabinet dedicated to those fancy iced cakes I mentioned. Each time I went to the store thereafter, I noticed that new imported food products had appeared on the shelves, also noting that items that had been available the previous year had often disappeared from sale. One evening, I was waiting for our goods to be packed when a stack of square silver-wrapped packets the size and shape of a block of paneer sitting on the countertop caught my eye. I picked one up to discover that it was tofu. I was surprised: 'Tofu! In Shahdol?' This Asian soya bean product has a distinct taste and texture that many people baulk at, and it seemed incongruent here; I would not have imagined it to appeal to the Indian palate, especially not in conservative small-town India. I asked the gentleman who runs the store: 'Who buys this?' His reply: 'People who go to the gym.' Then it all fell into place. Many of the new foods I was seeing in Mahadev Fruits were of the type that goes into the 'power smoothies', 'health shakes', and 'protein breakfast bowls' eaten by people, predominantly young men and women, who 'work out' in gyms across the world to achieve a universal body type popularized through social media. In addition to hefting weights, achieving this look apparently requires adherence to a homogeneous set of dietary precepts, which includes tofu. YouTube and

Instagram were connecting the citizens of Shahdol to international trends and influencing what they were eating, although the faddishness of social media means many of the food concepts popularized via this medium don't stick in people's everyday lives.

The tofu sold in Mahadev Fruits was made locally, and I asked Vishu if he could find out where it was being manufactured. When I returned the following year, we drove to a facility outside the town where a tofu production unit had been set up as part of a local government economic development programme. The sprawling complex of buildings we arrived at seemed deserted except for some boys playing cricket in a far corner of the desiccated grounds. We walked around trying to peer through windows to see if we could find any evidence of tofu production. The caretaker eventually appeared and said that there was no one around because it was a holiday. We asked him about the tofu: 'Bundh hai'. The operation had closed down. Apparently, the demand for the 'vegetarian paneer' (as the caretaker described it) had been short-lived. I was impressed though that someone had thought that there might be a potential market for tofu in this part of rural India and had gone so far as to set up a unit to produce it.

The Medium Is the Message

Manu Chandra is one of India's most influential chefs and an astute food industry operator. During our conversation together in Bengaluru in 2018, he declared that having a social media presence was 'not optional' for chefs and food professionals—whether they liked it or not. Every TV chef or cooking programme inevitably has a strong social media engagement as intertwining the two mediums bolsters the impact of the other. Social media is unquestionably influencing what Indians choose to cook and eat, where they eat or would like to, what foods and food services they buy, the type of diets they might choose to follow, even aspirations they might have about a career in food—but how much it might influence a longer-term change in food systems is debatable.[6] It certainly stimulates food trends and fashions that come and go as its predominant nature is to provide instant gratification, a way of experiencing pleasure and fulfilment without delay or patience and getting a spike in dopamine without effort or discipline. Dopamine is produced in our brain in response to pleasure, and it makes us feel good; understandably, we like it. Seeking dopamine release is the beating neurobiological heart of addictive behaviour. Social media is designed to facilitate instantaneous access to information; anything we want to know about is just a finger movement or voice command away. If we want to look at fancy cakes, we can do that instantaneously and get a dopamine kick, and our desire has been fulfilled for now. We continue to search to get more of the dopamine hit. Receiving notifications also stimulates a momentary mood uplift. What is actually happening is that people are engaging with the tool—social media apps on a device—which is what is providing the pleasure, not necessarily the products they are looking at. Continued use of social media has been shown to 'kill . . . desires, motivation, and goal-directed behaviour' in many users; young people are particularly vulnerable to this effect.[7] Social media could be all talk and no action: Users look and 'like' before moving on to the next thing. The swift pace of social media brings fads in quickly, but real shifts are a bit slower, and social media might be generating potential change so quickly that nothing much sticks. For food businesses, it can be hard to keep up with consumer whims driven by social media feeds. One restaurateur explained that his approach is to hold social-media-inspired fashions lightly, because what the customer is willing to come back for regularly is more stable and enduring. This is possibly more so since COVID-19, which has set off a pattern of seeking comfort in food, and comfort foods tend to be those associated with domestic meals and sweet treats.

Indians of all ages are enthusiastic consumers of social media, and their collective usage of it is amongst the highest in the world. India is also a young nation, with more than half the population aged below thirty-eight. This cohort, typically collectivized as 'millennials' and 'Gen Z', constitutes the most prolific users of social media in the country and the biggest potential consumer market in India. It is their tastes and preferences that will exert significant influence over changes in India's food system, including the hospitality industry, into the future.[8] Younger people are also the most vulnerable to marketing, although not exclusively so, which for their generation comes in the form of social media influencers and other covert, as well as overt, methods of online consumer persuasion. Any one of us engaging with social media, no matter our age, is being influenced by it to some degree, but older generations tend to have more affirmed habits, tastes, and lifestyle patterns and can be less malleable to change than their youthful offspring. Young people are not yet set in their ways and are more open to taking on new things, including migrating to big cities to work and live. They are known to seek novelty, and being up-to-date with the 'latest' consumer products can confer status amongst peers.

> The huge amount of food blogging on Instagram has turned the conversation around food into a cacophony and you have to sift hard to remove the phony from it.[9]

The vicarious pleasure we experience from looking at a photograph of a cake on a social media platform might, in fact, create a desire for that food such that we seek it out and purchase it—as the proliferation of cake stores and confectionery items in India demonstrates. It is this consumer behaviour, i.e., taking action with their money, that social media marketers and many influencers (not all of them) are aiming to inspire, not just 'likes', although that helps attract advertisers and freebies. If enough people start purchasing products or services and keep doing so for long enough, then a trend can evolve into a transformational change. Young people are more likely to be change agents because they have not settled into the status quo, and creating a unique identity is one of the key developmental tasks of adolescence and young adulthood. The irony is that young people also copy each other a lot since the need for peer acceptance is as strong in them as the drive to be different—although this is more about differentiating themselves from their parents' generation. Social media fosters copycatting on a global scale, such that what Indian millennials are eating in cafés in urban India has become much like what is being eaten by their age peers in Melbourne, San Francisco, and London— the tacos in India might have more spice in the filling though. This age group holds strong universal concerns around the production of food related to climate change, environmental degradation, and animal welfare, as well as a strong focus on individual health. These concerns have led to the inclusion of 'plant-based'/vegan items on contemporary menus and the development of food products that address these concerns. Speaking on a panel at the 2019 Tasting India Symposium on India's food future, Varun Deshpande, Managing Director of The Good Food Institute in India, spoke about the buoyant work happening on developing processed/ready-to-eat plant-based foods (another form of convenience food) and lab-grown meats to meet expected future market demands. I find the emergence of the global concept of 'plant-based' foods in contemporary India another irony: After all, isn't that what the traditional Indian diet largely is?[10]

India's young, better-off urbanites are curious, value immediate experience, and are in the habit of socializing in commercial eating places rather than at home, with many of them going out four or five times a week, if not daily, to eat and drink—COVID-19 curtailed this for a while, but from what I saw in Delhi in April 2022, they have enthusiastically returned to it. Younger Indians don't always have a lot of money, so they tend to patronize more casual cafés and coffee shops rather than fine dining restaurants. The Olive Group, a leader in innovation in Indian dining, opened The Grammar Room in Delhi specifically aimed at a millennial clientele, an indication of the growing clout of young people on shaping food in India, and because they are so swayed by social media, what they will want to eat and where they will want to eat, will continue to be heavily influenced by this medium. On the other hand, it is entirely possible that they will get fed up with it and move on to something else . . . perhaps taking up a lifestyle devoid of social media.

Waves of Change

Sourish Bhattacharyya is an established journalist and food writer, a co-convenor of the Tasting India Symposium, and a dedicated observer and ardent champion of India's hospitality industry. I whiled away a hot July afternoon in the cool of his Delhi home, enjoying cups of sweet tea as we talked about changes in Indian food. Sourish believes social media has impacted a sea change for young people in India, including those living in India's villages and small towns, affording them a way to be part of a bigger conversation about what is going on in the world, be it in food or anything else, especially as the visual nature of social media enables young Indians who do not speak English very well to relate more easily to what is happening nationally and globally. The egalitarian nature of social media also mirrors the increasing social mobility of Indians, allowing young people to see that greater possibilities might be available to them. In his book, *The Game Changers*, Vir Sanghvi elaborates the impact of social media further as a powerful social leveller:

> [It] has no sense of the complex and insidious divides within the Indian middle class, and in [a] country where hopes and dreams have been constrained by the circumstances of our birth it allows people more opportunity to push past those constraints.[11]

Two days before 2019 rolled over into 2020, and COVID-19 was just a news item in India, R and I were driving from Delhi to Kapurthala in Punjab. We pulled off the NH-44 at Khanna, a prospering regional city, into a shopping mall precinct to take a break at a branch of a popular coffee shop chain. This compact café space had an upbeat vibe as it was tightly packed with young guys and girls drinking coffee and milkshakes and eating generic mass-produced pizza, sandwiches, cake, brownies, and cookies. We were hungry too and ordered a sandwich each along with our drinks from the small menu of western-style food. The hot beverages were good, but the cellophane-packaged sandwiches were very average, particularly in comparison to the freshly made stuffed parathas with curd and pickle we had eaten some hours earlier at a highway mega-dhaba in Haryana. 'Why', I thought, 'would these kids want to eat this bland lifeless food when they could enjoy much tastier Indian snacks?' Then I reminded myself that their patronage of this café had little to do with the quality of the food. They were here to hang out with their friends in a place that felt contemporary and offered a similar experience as being in a bigger city, Delhi or Mumbai, or Singapore or Palo Alto.

Food has always defined social groups—rich or poor, old or young, rural or urban, Gujarati or Punjabi. Social media has allowed young people to see what others their age around the world are doing in a way that has never existed before. Social media models the global aspirations of their generation for young Indians and directs them to the products they need to consume and the habits they need to adopt to achieve this 'lifestyle'. If Nutella waffles or tofu cocoa Buddha bowls are in fashion in San Francisco, then young people all over India, be they in Khanna or Shahdol, can know about it directly. But younger Indians are not all slavishly taking on western food fads. They are also creating local trends and enthusiastically engaging with their own food heritage (discussed in Chapter 1).

Food trends have always come and gone. Most die out, but some take root and anchor into everyday food; social media might stimulate a faster rate of food fads than ever before, but the lasting impact of social media influencers is under question by Indian restaurateurs and public relations professionals specializing in food. The commercial relationship between influencers and food businesses, i.e., the provision of free meals and paid reviews, has tarnished the value of social media opinion for some consumers. Social media might be concurrently generating 'disorientation' with respect to food, as well as an orientation to what may emerge as more enduring change.

> With the top tier of eateries working to introduce regional cuisines and sometimes, new dishes, restaurateurs are seeking bloggers who have the knowledge to educate their audience with posts or long captions, rather than just dish names and a great photograph.[12]

Food and Luggage

The Rajiv Chowk metro station is a subterranean world of railway lines, platforms, and walkways located beneath the Connaught Place commercial area in Central Delhi. One of the busiest stops on this system, its location has made it easy for people from across the sprawling NCR to travel to the capital's mercantile centre to eat and drink and promenade along its colonnaded walkways and seemingly to buy luggage. It had been some years since I had spent any time wandering about perusing the precinct's retail stores and eateries, but when I returned to do exactly that in 2019, one of things that was most noticeable was the numerous travel goods stores had opened here—a testament to Indians' recent metamorphosis into avid travellers. This boom in travel is the result of a confluence of factors: increased incomes, low-cost airlines, vastly expanded air travel infrastructure, and easy access to information and booking procedures online. Travel has influenced a strong interest amongst Indians in their own food cultures, and travel experiences can make people more open to trying new foods at home.[13]

When I met Mumbai-based travel writer Prachi Joshi, she said Indians have become more adventurous with their travel, no longer sightseeing in the 'safety' of large groups and seeking out more 'offbeat' or less circumscribed tourist experiences. Discovering local food, be it from street stalls, in markets, food stores, and restaurants or attending cooking classes has also become an important part of the travel agenda for many Indians; for some, culinary discovery is the sole purpose of their travels. Even when food is not a focus, travel exposes people to different ideas and varieties of food if they are open to it. Television and social media have also played a role in inspiring Indian travel aspirations, including food-focused adventures. Seeing a food destination, say northern Kerala, featured on a travel programme is known to spark visitor interest: Plans for the next long weekend break become focused on travelling to Kozhikode to try the fish biryani at Paragon and the chicken biryani with freshly grated coconut, onion raita, lime pickle, and pathiri at Zain's. Travel writing in print media is another source of inspiration for Indians to explore new places, and describing local food has become an essential element of general travel writing.

Travelling has become an expected, if not normative, experience for young people around the world, and younger Indians are no exception in this. They are travelling earlier and more often than their parents; many of them have studied or lived abroad and have enjoyed a different type of lifestyle, including socializing in informal cafés drinking coffee and eating cakes or in bars eating and drinking with friends, likely of significant diversity. When they return to India, they want to continue to enjoy this type of lifestyle, creating a demand for similar services and patronizing such places, potentially igniting transformative change because these venues are not necessarily about food and drink, even if this is the obvious focus. Casual cafés and bars represent generational change and increasing social freedom for young Indians (and not exclusively so). Having learnt this model from the West, be it through experience and/or digital and social media, when it's replicated in India, it looks and feels just like eating cheesecake-filled cronuts and sipping a latte made with quadruple cold-filtered single-estate almond milk anywhere in the westernized world.

Inside–Outside

Social media, television, and travel are connecting Indians more closely to the rest of the world and have influenced their adoption of homogenous global food trends at the same time as increasing the enthusiasm amongst Indians for their own foodways and regional cuisines.

> The Indian foodie is now learning to love his roots, especially now that it has been validated by the West.[14]

If the 'West' has inspired Indians to feel more passionate about their food 'roots', this influence has chiefly emanated from digital and social media. As Indians have engaged with a plethora of images and programmes celebrating the food of other countries and/or the food cultures of the diverse peoples living in places such as Australia, the United States, and the United Kingdom, I think they have been compelled to turn their gaze inwards. Indian chefs, cooks, restaurateurs, food writers and journalists, nutritionists, and food producers have also been instrumental in inspiring popular interest in India's own foodways. The work they are doing is bringing India's traditional and regional foods out of the domestic sphere (inside) to the outside, onto menus and into food products, articles, images, recipes, videos, food tours, and food events such that Indians are no longer 'locked out' by physical and cultural barriers from experiencing the fullness of their nation's cuisines.

If westerners have been ignorant of India's food beyond a menu of curries and tandoori, it is because that is all they have been offered in Indian restaurants in the West. Contemporary media platforms are also allowing Indians to escort the wider world into their kitchens, and these outsiders are getting very interested in learning more about India's 'real' food. On the 2021 season of *MasterChef Australia*, contestant Kishwar Chowdhury prepared the everyday Bengali dish macher jhol, which wowed the judges and audience alike and inspired growing media interest in India's 'real' food.[15] As I am writing an Australian documentary series, *India Unplated*—telling the 'untold' story of India's food is being aired by a national broadcaster—looking at my own social media feed, there seems to be a growing international awareness of the vast diversity of India's food.

> Indian cuisine, diverse and varied, has long struggled to establish itself beyond the standard butter chicken-naan fare and $ 9.99 all-you-can eat buffets in an America of increasingly sophisticated palates. In recent years though there has been an explosion of Indian restaurants beyond Punjabi fare, showcasing both India's culinary diversity and refinement.[16]

Once people feel safe to travel again, they are going to want to experience what they have been seeing of Indian food in the media and trying out in local food venues at the source. I believe India's cuisine and her talented chefs and cooks are on the verge of taking their long overdue place on the world stage.

5

Supermarkets and Superfoods

In a Place in the World

When I was a young teen, my mother purchased a 'yoghurt maker', a cylindrical metal container similar to a thermos, that came with a packet of a powdered curdling agent. A spoonful of this substance was mixed with a measured amount of warm milk and decanted into the container, which was then wrapped in a towel and placed in a cabinet to keep it warm overnight. The thin, loosely set yoghurt this process produced the next morning was unimpressive. After a few more attempts with identical results, this contraption was banished to the recesses of a kitchen cupboard. We resumed buying yoghurt in plastic containers from the local supermarket, and I was left with the impression that it was something difficult to make. Even through my professional cookery training, any yoghurt we used came out of a pre-packaged tub. When I took up residence in a south Delhi suburb in 2000, I was lamenting the difficulty of buying yoghurt to my friend Kini. She said it was because it was something Indians generally made at home and explained to me how to go about this. Following her instructions, I got a small portion of curd from a local confectioner—discovering in the process that one could buy yoghurt, it just didn't come in labelled tubs, but never mind, I was keen to make it now—and filled my own small stainless pail with milk from the 'electronic cow' at the Mother Dairy booth across from my apartment. That evening, I warmed the milk, added the curd, covered the container, and left it sitting on the bench. In the morning, I had yoghurt. It was that easy, and there was no packaging. I made yoghurt most days from then on. I loved the whole process; it felt self-sufficient and wholesome. I was equally enamoured with the food system in my immediate neighbourhood.

Each morning, a vegetable vendor pushed a handcart loaded with fresh produce along the street, stopping at each residence to call out his presence. I would go downstairs with a basket and choose the vegetables I wanted for that day, then cross the road to the fruit seller stationed under a tree and buy seasonal fruit. No plastic bags or plastic wrap, no packaging at all. Next to the Mother Dairy booth was a kirana store where I could buy dry goods, spices, dals, and sugar, all of which was packaged up in newspaper twists or recycled paper bags. There was also a *chakkiwallah*, where I bought freshly ground wheat and corn flour and fresh-pressed sesame oil poured into my own jar—this service was unheard of in Australia. In the summer, mango vendors set up along the colony's main thoroughfare, and I gained an education on this fruit as different varieties came into season over those hot months. In June, bunches of pink-shelled lychees appeared, then disappeared again soon after, but what pleasure it was eating this superlative fruit every day while it lasted. A nearby market serviced the local Bengali community, and from there I could buy excellent seafood, watching with awe as the fishmonger took a whole fish and processed it into delicate fingers of flesh with a few strokes across a sharp *boti* positioned between his feet. All the foods available locally were intended for producing fresh home-cooked Indian meals. There was very little convenience food apart from biscuits and snacks. If I wanted any western foodstuff, I had to go further afield to the INA Market or one of the grocery stores in Khan Market that serviced Delhi's expatriate community and locals with cosmopolitan tastes. Part of the appeal of shopping like this was in its novelty. I come from a country with a food system dominated by two supermarket chains, a circumstance contributing to the development of a homogenized diet across the entire continent, and which usually necessitates travelling by vehicle to access a store. But having all this food on my doorstep was to my mind the ultimate convenience.

Exploring food retail in any country offers deep insight into the real food habits of a population and is arguably the truest indication of what people eat in their day-to-day lives. The changes that have taken place as to where Indians are purchasing their domestic food, and what they are buying, in the years since I had to make yoghurt in my

Delhi apartment, demonstrate how 'worldwide diffusion of notions of Western modernity' are influencing the development of India's contemporary foodways.[1] This chapter explores how the changing food-shopping habits of urban Indians are becoming more uniform with the rest of the affluent middle-class world and the aligned adoption of global food trends that purport to support health and well-being.

Anywhere in the World

December 2019. It has been nearly twenty years since I lived in that south Delhi suburb, and I am in the basement of the city's glamorous glossy Chanakya shopping mall wandering the aisles of Foodhall, a 'premium lifestyle food superstore' [that] offers its customers 'flavours from around the world [in] a space that every food lover would enjoy. A place that allows you to not only buy unique, rare ingredients but also taste fresh food as you explore the store – indulging all five senses.'[2]

It is indeed a beautiful store, a pleasure to be in. The fresh produce sparkles, the expansive delicatessen section offers a cornucopia of cheese, charcuterie, and tracklements, and the shelves bulge with on-trend packaged food products and hard to resist international confections. Here I could buy crisp lettuce, robust olive oil, aged balsamic vinegar, and real French mustard to make the salads I craved but could not get the ingredients for in 2000. The only distinctive Indian elements in the place were an artisan mithai counter and a pharmacopeia-like display of spices and spice mixes in sleek glass jars; in this retail environment, I could have been shopping in an upmarket food store anywhere in the world.

There are nine Foodhall stores across Delhi, Mumbai, and Bengaluru. The chain is the creation of Avni Biyani, whom I met in a very zeitgeist, shared office space in a corporate complex in Mumbai, where we talked about the inception of this retail concept, its place in the family business, and the changing foodscape of India. Foodhall is part of the Future Group, one of India's largest retail companies.[3] Speaking of the wider company, Avni said its success came from an acute, and deeply researched, sensitivity to the Indian market; its Big Bazaar food retail chain is attuned to middle-class Indians and Foodhall to a sector of the Indian market 'tuned into global food trends who want to replicate these with high-quality foods'. She pointed to avocados as an example. When avocado on toast become an international fashion in the early 2010s—a fad that began in a beachside café in Sydney—cosmopolitan Indian consumers also wanted to spread the waxy green flesh of this fruit on their toast, but avocados are not commercially grown in India, with the exception of some small production out of Kerala and Karnataka.[4] To meet the emerging demand for this Central American native, Avni built a supply chain procuring avocados from different places—California, Mexico and Australia—at different times of the year depending on the season, to ensure her customers a year-round supply; Foodhall also stocks sourdough bread for the accompanying toast. By her own admission, she told me that she has been criticized for flying in food from around the world, but Avni believes what happens at Foodhall can influence change in India's food preferences. The 'foodie generation' who buy their groceries at Foodhall comprises India's wealthier citizens, and what they choose to buy and eat can shape the choices and food habits of the wider population. For example, social media posts of celebrities/influencers gushing over something they are eating, say avocado on toast, can send foods on a trajectory from exclusivity into the mainstream. This 'approval' of a certain food from a high-status group inspires others to try it, and as demand grows, supply comes up to meet this, which in this case could result in the development of a local avocado industry mitigating the need to fly in as much fruit: The price drops, and perhaps in a decade avocado has become commonplace in the middle-class Indian diet. Or this trend might be nothing but a memory by then. A couple of recent salient avocado examples to consider about the impact of food trends:

1. In 2021, avocados were being called out as unstainable food in the same privileged spheres of food influence, although not necessarily by the same individuals, where, earlier, the praises of this fruit had been vigorously proclaimed.[5]

2. The 'avo on toast' trend began in Australia and in 2017 became the subject of a national polemic when a property millionaire said that it was a wonder that

the nation's millennials could not afford to buy homes when they were spending AUS $20 to eat a serve of this simple dish in the fashionable cafés they frequented.[6] This in no way quelled demand for avocados, and Australian farmers enthusiastically planted hectares and hectares of trees with the result that there is a glut of fruit in 2022, and prices have fallen significantly—from anywhere between AUS $3–5 a piece to AUS $1.00. But India is being eyed as the potential saviour in this situation.

Avocados Australia chairman Jim Kochi suggested that the simplest solution was to increase the volume of avocados to the export market:

> 'We have markets in South-East Asia and, hopefully, India that will take avocados,' he said. 'It's complementary to what we do here in Australia because some of the sizes, particularly the smaller sizes and the really big sizes, aren't all that favoured on the Australian market but are favoured by the export markets.'[7]

It is probably all to the good if Indian farmers are not putting their resources into growing this 'unsustainable' fruit if cheap ones from the Antipodes flood the market.

When the automated glass doors slid apart to usher me into the recently opened SPAR Hyper market store in Bengaluru's Koramangala neighbourhood, it felt surreal: I could have been in a supermarket in suburban Sydney. All the hallmarks of the western shopping experience, purposefully designed to manipulate shoppers to buy more, were in place: wide aisles, large trolleys, bright lighting, shelves stacked high with an apparently endless variety of goods— the differentiation largely achieved through branding—all made convenient to take off the shelf and stack in the trolley through packaging. At first glance, the most distinctively Indian aspect was the section of pooja supplies, but as I inspected the stock more closely, I discovered that the food was more to Indian tastes than otherwise; although a large range of international-style foods was available, it was the setting that was entirely westernized.

Contrary to the western idea of wide aisles making shopping more appealing, the layout of the Krishna Supermarché 37 in Delhi's Safdarjung Enclave is aligned with a distinctly Indian retail mentality, the 'butt and brush' theory that posits Indian shoppers prefer an overcrowded environment.[8] However, while its aisles were narrow, its trolleys more compact than the SUV version of SPAR Hyper market, and the shelves groaning with goods all the way to the ceiling, the food itself was more indicative of a global urban food style: cold cabinets filled with cheeses, dips, butter and yoghurt products, and ready-to-eat snacks and meals; gourmet ice-cream and other dessert products; there was a bakery section, a range of pre-prepared Asian sauces, and an impressive range of chocolates. Amma Naana is a stalwart food retailer in Chennai operating from the same corner location for close to forty years; once described as a 'departmental store', it is now designated a 'supermarket'.

I first shopped here in 2000, and ten years later, it looks no different from the outside and little has changed inside, except what was the lobby space is now occupied by a bank of refrigerated cabinets, and several rows of display cases filled with local and imported confectionery. It was truly impressive to see how many more products had been fitted into the same shelving arrangements, all 6500 of them, including a 'plethora of foreign-made brands' and Indian-made western-style foods such as cheeses, processed meats, sausages, fresh pasta, ready-to-eat pasta meals, soups, dips, dairy desserts, cakes, and bread, along with any food item you would need to make any international-style meal, cake, or dessert, few of which were stocked here a decade ago. Another interesting development was the range of south Indian convenience foods that had become available. All three of these supermarkets, and the Foodhall stores, cater to more affluent urban Indians; local tastes and needs are serviced, yet all these are examples of the globalization of food retail in India, be it of design or content.

> Globally flowing, industrially produced commodities [that] grease the skids of capitalism as it extends market reach . . . easing people worldwide along a path of capitalist acquisition and consumption . . . globalize and homogenize tastes around the world while teaching new populations to desire and seek more of the same.[9]

India is one of the biggest retail food markets in the world with huge growth predicted in the formal sector such as supermarkets. Major international food retailers have been attempting to set up operations in India since the 1990s. Every so often, I would see a headline such as 'Supermarkets in India—Will they work?' or 'India opens doors to foreign supermarket chains' or 'India prepares for the supermarket revolution' in relation to the imminent arrival of a major international food retailer, leading me to think, 'here it comes, the supermarket take-over', but it didn't happen. Most of these ventures failed, perhaps because their operating model of standardized inventory across all stores that works to flatten the foodscape, in order to scale and be profitable, could not serve the diversity of socio-economic segments and regional food preferences of Indian consumers, or perhaps Indians were resistant to the supermarket model because they were satisfied with small neighbourhood stores and doorstep fruit and vegetable vendors, or maybe it was that they had not yet been primed as a market for this style of shopping. Prosperity, technology and media, malls, and Big Bazaar have since done this work, and after spending time in these and other food retail stores in Indian cities and towns (Mumbai, Hyderabad, Ahmedabad, Shahdol, Rudrapur, Karpurthala) in 2019 I thought, 'ok, so this it, the Indian market is ready for big supermarket retail'. This might still prove true, but then a pandemic happened.

Shopping in the Cloud

Prior to March 2020, online shopping was reported to have huge potential to become a significant force in Indian food retailing, although its uptake was relatively small: COVID-19 was a gift to its development. Having been pushed to use online shopping by the circumstances of the lockdown, many urban Indians are keeping up the habit, in part because the only human interaction involved is when the goods are delivered, and even that can be contactless, and being able to choose your groceries from home at any time, day or night, and have these delivered to your doorstep is ultra-convenient. Before the pandemic, it was thought that a lack of trust might hinder the uptake of online grocery shopping as Indian consumers largely preferred the familiarity of purchasing from a local kirana store where they knew the owner.[10] Having been forced out of that habit of shopping in-store, they may not return to it, something the Indian government is directly facilitating:

> The Central government of India has designed and developed smart cities with a state-of-the-art infrastructure for setting up different models of e-commerce and online transactions. Owing to these reasons, the online grocery retail market is witnessing a growth rate of 25–30% in the Indian metropolitans, and other emerging smart cities.[11]

This national investment in technology has enhanced the vast potential of online food retailing in India, offering further incentives to private investors to pour significant monies into this sector. As with online food delivery, online food shopping removes all the experiential elements of in-store shopping—ambience, 'butt and brush', personal service, touch, feel, and smell—leaving retailers little to compete on.[12] A visually appealing website with informative blogs and videos, an easy-to-navigate app, and 'free shipping' are potential attractors, but online stores allow consumers to easily compare prices, and the most competitive advantage for online retailers is cost. In the precarious economic conditions post-COVID-19, Indian consumers are expected to be cautious with their spending, with value and price remaining the primary drivers of purchase decisions into the future.[13]

> Most of the customers in India often show a tendency of switching between different online grocers, with special inclination towards those who provide more discounts, charge less for delivery, and generate a higher value of coupon offers.[14]

Amazon Pantry has become one of India's biggest online food retailers. The modus operandi of this global giant is undercutting prices to gain market dominance.[15] A visit to their website offers a clear demonstration that their appeal to Indian consumers is all about paying less, and the company's well-documented competitiveness will force a race to the bottom on prices. Other major Indian online retailers such as Grofers and Big Basket also focus on cost saving. Consumers are the apparent beneficiaries of this, yet what might be the potential consequences?

Is [Jeff] Bezos laughing at people's manipulated
susceptibility for convenience . . . Amazon's customers
are robbed of the experience of actively going to local
businesses where they can actively engage with others,
get offered on the spot bargains and build relationships
for all kinds of social, civic and charitable activities.[16]

A common theme in the work of the well-known Indian
environmental activist Vandana Shiva is the 'true cost' of cheap
food.[17] Building consumer expectation of paying less for food
will lead to increasing industrialization and homogenization
of India's mainstream food supply. Major online retailers
in India have co-opted the 'farm to fork' concept, building
their own direct supply chains to agriculturists, purporting
to cut out the middleman when they are, in fact, simply
taking his place. For consumers, imagining that their food
is coming directly from a farm—perhaps unaware that the
logistics of a big chain directs all fresh food into warehouses
where it is stored and packed before being distributed into
stores—is attractive, but low prices are more so, and retailers
will be looking to cut costs with supply, something that does
not bode well for farmers.[18] When Indian farmers went on
strike in 2020, one of their main concerns was that the direct
intervention of major retailers in agriculture would lead to
them being screwed down on prices. Cheaper imports might
even be bought into the market to keep the prices low.

Although [big corporations] will bring much-needed
investment, they could also skew the playing field, with

small farmers unlikely to match them in bargaining power.[19]

The opposite view is that consumers should pay more for food to ensure the growth of better-quality primary produce, through practices that are less environmentally damaging, and not all online food retailers in India use a discount strategy to attract customers. The online service of the Nature's Basket chain differentiates its brand through selling 'healthier' food to wealthier urbanites for whom buying products that they believe will better support their well-being is of greater value than price (I will come back to this later). The development of online food retail in India hasn't all been about big players. It has been a boon for many small food suppliers, allowing them to retail their produce and products directly to customers, creating the potential for more equitable trade for both the producer and consumer.

I think that India might now leapfrog the large supermarket model that dominates food retailing in the West to food retailing largely taking place online, at least in urban India. As a retailer, why would you bear the costs of brick-and-mortar stores when you could cut that out? Women predominantly do the grocery shopping in India, and as they are more inclined to shop online in general, they are likely to continue shopping for their groceries in this way as well.[20] Others are confident that Indian consumers will return to favouring in-store food shopping.[21]

Plain Organic

If I wanted to buy produce and whole foods specifically labelled as organic in Delhi twenty years ago, it meant travelling outside of my neighbourhood food bubble to the nearest Navdanya store, a place with an austere look and atmosphere that suggested that one should eat only as a duty to life and no more. There was no attempt to beguile the customer with any artful displays or seductive packaging; the fresh produce was stacked in plain metal containers and dry goods were packed as simply as possible, with no claims made for these as aids to weight loss or anti-ageing. The products were affordable. The people I saw shopping at Navdanya looked as if they subscribed to Gandhian principles—ascetic over aesthetics. Nothing much has changed at the Navdanya store in south Delhi that I patronized two decades ago, although I expect its customer base to have broadened because there have been big changes with retailing organic food in India. Demand for organic produce and products is a major trend in urban India; organic food stores have become very attractive places to shop, and 'organics' a 'lucrative market to venture into' as affluent consumers are 'willing to pay more for organic food because they are prioritising their health over cost'.[22]

What Exactly Is 'Organic' Food?

Technically, all plant and animal food is organic because it is derived from living matter. Nonetheless, when a consumer buys fresh produce, animal products, dry goods, or processed edibles specifically labelled organic, what they should be getting is food grown without the employment of chemicals, fertilizers, GMOs, or artificial additives. An organic farmer relies on crop rotation, animal and plant manure, and biological pest controls to grow crops. Animals raised for organic meat or milk production should be fed 100 per cent organic feed, be freely able to roam around outdoors with access to natural pasture, and have no antibiotics or synthetic growth hormones used on them. Writing this reminds me of travelling through the Pathankot hills in Punjab in the autumn and seeing groups of Gujjars bringing their flocks down from the high mountains; the meat from these animals would be 100 per cent organic as a matter of course. Producing and eating organic food is widely considered to be good for people, animals, and the planet. Organic foods are popularly proclaimed to be a better choice than conventional food because they contain more nutrients and many health claims are made for it. Consumers say they buy organic food because it tastes better and is 'healthier for them'. Yet, there is no conclusive scientific evidence to support the claim that organic food is more nutritious or that it has enhanced flavour.[23] It is often those retailing organic food making the most definitive claims for it.[24] Evidence-based research is not infallible and the results reported can depend on who is funding this work, but the claims of the organic food industry also need to be considered for bias and cherry-picking from favourable research. Another reason consumers increasingly say that they prefer organic food is because it is better for the environment; perhaps any additional health benefits are due more to the absence of chemical inputs than any nutritional superiority. However, organic food production requires more land and there are concerns as to whether organic agriculture would be capable of producing enough food to meet the ongoing increase in global food demand.[25]

Better for Whom?

I am not trying to argue one way or another on organic food, I just wanted to show how, like many aspects of contemporary life, it is complicated due to the prevalence of complex and competing evidence and views. The one thing I can say definitively from my experience is that in a retail setting, in India and around the world, specifically labelled organic food is always more expensive than so-called conventional food, recalling that consumer willingness to pay extra for organic food is what makes it a 'lucrative' business in India.

> 'When we make a paradigm shift toward organic farming and food systems, there is no reason to repeat the past mistake of keeping food cheap.'[26]

Information about the cost of producing organic food is also complex and confusing. There are claims that 'price, in fact, shouldn't be a factor and that there is no real reason for organic food to be more expensive than non-organic, and experts agree that there is hardly any difference in the cost of normal and organic farming'.[27] Others argue that the higher price is necessary and justified because of the additional costs of producing and processing organic foods, or that most of the high incremental pricing is made up of taxes as it is considered a rich man's purchase and, therefore, taxed heavily.[28] Again, my intention is not to argue the case either way; what interests me is that because labelled organic food is more expensive, I have found it commonly referred to as the prerogative of the 'wealthy elite', 'the well-heeled', and the 'affluent', and this gels with my field research in India's retail food environment. Market demand for labelled organic food is most vigorous amongst high-income Indians increasingly focused on their health—a focus intensified by COVID-19—and organic food certainly looks more elite these days than it did twenty years ago: beautifully displayed, packaged, and presented on store shelves, or sold at charming urban 'farmers' markets' patronized by the 'upper crust'. Perhaps the cost is part of the appeal: The very fact of organic food being expensive confers prestige because the high-cost limits wider access to it, and limited access confers a distinction on consumer items and the people who can afford to buy them. The rhetoric around 'organic' food might also be seen to be making a moral judgement around food: Because of its price, wealthier Indians get to eat 'good/superior/super' organic, and the less well-off get to eat 'inadequate' conventional food.

Given that they can afford the choice, anyone would want to eat food free of potentially toxic additives and produced sustainably, but unless there is a genuine commitment to an equitable food system, it is likely that 'cheap' organic food will flood into the market as demand for organic products is becoming mainstream in India. Talking with chefs and farmers about organic food, I heard strong concern that the 'fashionable' nature of it was resulting in produce being labelled organic when they were not actually being produced under the specified conditions to qualify as such, especially when bigger producers and companies were involved.

> Given that the term 'organic' attracts premium pricing, there are huge incentives to game the system and sell pretty much anything under the umbrella term.[29]

Meeting the growing demand for organic food from a wider sector of the Indian population and making it affordable could result in even more 'gaming' of consumers. Labelled organic food has thus far been a totally unregulated area in India. According to Pawan Kumar Agarwal, chief executive officer of the Food Safety and Standards Authority of India (FSSAI):

> There is no guarantee that what is being claimed as organic is actually organic, but with new regulations [coming into] force, the organic market will be streamlined and properly regulated. Proper enforcement may take some time.[30]

In the meantime, there is little to prevent companies from cashing in on the organic label rather than doing what it takes to produce the genuine product. The willingness of Indian consumers to pay more for organic products has also seen Indian food companies producing a huge range of organic products including snack foods, ready-to-eat cereals, juices and other packaged drinks, biscuits, sauces, and confectionery. The fact that these products are all processed foods and might well be regarded as detrimental to health when made with 'conventional' ingredients seems to be willingly overlooked because of the organic label: a potent example of what has become known as 'health washing'.

In the Field

Chef Manish Mehrotra believes that the way a lot of food is grown in India, particularly by small and dryland farmers, is 'more or less organic' and that many rural Indians eat organic food as a matter of course. While their produce might be grown sustainably, rural agriculturists may not have the education, connections, or resources to benefit from the higher prices paid for organic food in the same way as their fellows who can access urban farmers' markets, wield social media influence, or run retail food enterprises. Having a farm or particular foods certified as organic by reputable bodies is also an expensive process. While this book is predominantly concerned with the changing foodscape of urban India, this is inextricably connected to rural farms and fields, culturally, economically, and materially, and I want to include some exploration around change, or otherwise, in food outside the city.

Rural Organic

In the Kumaon hills of Uttarakhand in the village of Chatola, I visited the small family farm of Mr Sibata T.T. Pardi, a marvellously sprightly nonagenarian with some 70 years of experience cultivating this land. As he and I, and his son Ganesh, who has taken over the running of the farm, along with my translator Akash, sat in the sunny stone-flagged courtyard of the Pardi farmhouse sipping tea, the senior man shared his experience of growing apples, pears, apricots, peaches, plums, and almonds as commercial crops, along with vegetables and dals for family use, selling any excess in the market (along the way, he also demonstrated how he carried the stone used for the house and yards on his back from the local quarry). Chemicals have never been used on the farm; fertilizers and pesticides are made from natural ingredients as is common practice in the region. Pardi describes the food produced on his farm as 'organic', but it is not distinguished as such. Harvested crops are carried up to the roadside to be picked up by a truck and taken to the regional mandi in Haldwani and sold alongside all the other produce brought in on the day for the same market price. Some of this produce stays in the local area, with the greater part shipped to the wholesale markets in Delhi to eventually be sold by vendors across the city, where Delhiites of all classes buy it at a reasonable price because it is not labelled organic.

From the Pardi farm, we walked further on to meet farmer Ved Prakash. I guess Prakash must be a good half-century younger than Pardi, but like the elder man, he has been farming here all his adult life, taking over the family's commercial apple, pear, and stone fruit orchards from his father, adding peas, tomato, eggplant, green capsicum, potatoes, and cabbage to send to the market as cash crops. Prakash said he briefly experimented with chemical fertilizers and pesticides but found his plants were badly affected by these, so he returned to a completely organic system: raking the pine and oak leaf bedding he lays down for his cows out of their pens after they have slept and manured on it to use in the fertilizer he makes; producing insecticide from ash, walnut leaves, and red chilli; and saving seeds to produce subsequent crops. He is well aware that the food he produces is 'organic', saying 'other people get the benefit of that', but he does not have the connections or the capacity to promote his food as organic and potentially make a better financial return on it.

I have heard it expressed and read it in print that rural Indians are unaware of the harmful effects of conventionally grown food.[31] Prakash and Pardi are both keenly alert to the impact of chemical pesticides and fertilizers on crops, and they are experiencing the impact of climate change first-hand. Both men said the winter was becoming warmer and that this change has affected the apricot crops. The cold weather usually kills the insects that damage this fruit tree, and because it was not as cold, the insects were thriving. The higher temperatures also meant that there was less snow and consequently not as much water available for agriculture. They were also concerned about the broader change in the local food environment. According to their individual reports, local youngsters were more interested in eating the packaged snacks and 'junk'—pizza, noodles, soft drinks—sold in restaurants in the nearby hamlet of Sitla, a popular tourist destination. As Pardi explained, as more wealthy urbanites build holiday homes in the area, they employ more local people as domestic workers, taking them away from farm work and exposing them to urbanized foodways. People who come from cities like Delhi and Mumbai to their hill retreats stick to their food habits even when they are in the region; it is their demand for their food preferences to be met that is changing local supply and, thereby, local habits. People are buying more food from stores because more has become available due to the demand and the financial capacity of urban migrants and tourists. I see this as an example of class differentiation between who eats what; in this case, it translates into the impression that rural people are not as savvy about what they eat as urbanites, whereas it might be the other way round.[32]

31 July 2019. I headed out early on this Sunday morning to Delhi's Earth Collective Market to avoid the mid-summer heat, but it had settled in by the time I arrived at this artisanal food market held weekly at Sunder Nursery heritage park in Delhi. I wandered amongst the fresh

produce: crates of seasonal mangoes, just-picked summer
corn, pink lychees, bunches of leafy green vegetables and
herbs, pumpkin, bhindi, lauki, green onions, and one very
large jackfruit grown on a nearby urban farm. There was
artisanal bread and muffins, exotic mushrooms, grains,
and cereals grown in neighbouring Haryana and cheese
produced in the Kumaon hills. There were also stalls selling
cooked food, and as I had forgone breakfast in my haste
to get here, I picked up a rustic spinach chaat, millet idli,
and a jaggery-sweetened ginger tea and sat down at one of
the tables on the adjacent lawn to enjoy it. The table was
also occupied by a young couple, Dave and Saee, and we
easily fell into a conversation: Dave told me about his work
with the Australian cricket team and I told them about
my interest in Indian food and the subject of the book
I was then researching. Saee then said, 'My family runs
an agricultural development trust in rural Maharashtra'
and proceeded to tell me of all the different projects it
operated. 'You should go there,' she said. 'Where exactly is
it?' I asked. 'Baramati'. A fortuitous happenchance: I was
heading to Nashik the following day, and Baramati was
only a few hundred kilometres down the road from there.
We exchanged contact details, and by the time I reached
Nashik the following evening, my visit to Baramati had
been organized.

   After finishing my work in Nashik, I took a taxi
290 kilometres south across inland Maharashtra and the
rocky outcrops of the Deccan Plateau to Baramati and
the Agricultural Development Trust, Baramati (KVK

Baramati). I was welcomed at the Trust guesthouse by Dr Hemangi Raul, a senior staff member of the impressive education facility for rural children operated under the auspices of the KVK. For the next few days, Hemangi took me on an assiduous exploration of the Trust's projects and local food enterprises. We visited every grade level of the school, inspected various departments of the college, including its contemporary commercial bakery training unit, and I gave a talk to the hospitality students to share my experiences and impressions of India's food culture. I was treated with such reverence and curiosity that I felt like Princess Diana. We spent a morning at the Trust's science centre and instructional farm, where agriculturists from across the region come to learn how to apply the latest technology to their farms; we walked over its acres inspecting experimental vegetable and floriculture greenhouses, aquaculture ponds, beehives, and groves of fruit-bearing trees. Another morning was spent looking over the extensive water conservation projects underway on the dry side of the region. We ate at a popular local fish restaurant, where all the food is cooked over wood fire, and I was sweetly felicitated with flowers just for eating there. After this, we visited various food enterprises operating in the town, including a slick contemporary chai shop selling nothing but excellent spiced tea, some thousands of cups a day of it. At Triveni Oils, I watched the process of making small batch, aka artisan, cold pressed peanut oil using a traditional conical wooden press. I was invited to two different homes for dinner, where there was much apology on both occasions that the food was all vegetarian because it was the annual Pandharpur Wari pilgrimage festival—this was no matter for me as all the food was excellent, but my hosts were concerned that by missing out on non-veg dishes, I was being short-changed on experiencing the best local cuisine.

Our Baramati itinerary also included a visit to a small organic farm run by Mrs Sangita Deokate and her family. I was welcomed here with a vegetarian lunch prepared from their own produce, after which I was taken to see all the workings of their enterprise. Beginning with an introduction to jeevamrut, the traditional Indian organic fertilizer prepared from the dung and urine of the desi (native) cow—a critical component as the waste products of imported cows are not considered efficacious—jaggery, ground lentils, water, moringa/drumstick leaves, and a handful of farm soil, the lot mixed together in a large holding vat and left to ferment for several days and turned six times daily. A traditional bio-pesticide prepared from fermented cow urine, custard apple, and neem leaves is also made by the Deokates—I can well imagine that this is a very effective repellent as its smell was so overpowering it caused me to immediately step away from the vat it was brewing in.[33] Hemangi brought me to the Deokate farm because she buys her vegetables from them using the instant messaging platform WhatsApp. Each afternoon, the Deokates inspect the farm to determine what will be ready for harvest the following morning and send a group message out to their customers letting them know what is available. They subsequently place orders, and the vegetables are picked and delivered the following day. The produce is a little more expensive than the vegetables sold in the market, but Hemangi assures me that it is affordable for 'every day' families, and the Deokates make a decent living from their small farm enterprise.

The three farmers I met in Baramati and Uttarakhand all use similar organic farming methods to grow produce suited to local conditions. Still, only the Deokates describe their food as organic, and from what I saw, it seems that they reap greater monetary benefit from their farm than Pardi or Prakash, even though they have a smaller land holding. A range of factors would account for their relative prosperities, including that Baramati is a more populated and prosperous region overall than the Kumaon Himalaya region. But putting this aside, what I noticed is that the Deokates have a better understanding of how to use technology to directly connect with a market willing to pay for organic produce—there is no middleman involved in their transaction. On the other hand, Prakash understands that what he is growing is valuable to certain consumers, but he does not know how to directly connect with this market.

> Getting people to eat higher quality food is a type of bigotry because it feeds into pernicious social divides. Equitable does not have to mean the way food is defined by higher status people, or people seeking status and distinction through food . . . [there is a need

to] create structures for people to make real choices in context.[34]

My visit to the KVK Agricultural College included conversations with its director of education, Prof. Nilesh Nalawade, and board chairman, Mr Rajendra Pawar, who both said the biggest challenge for Indian farmers was market linkage and that it was the agents who knew how to connect into consumer markets who were making the most profit on agricultural produce, including organic food. They believed this to be a problem of education as many farmers were not literate and lacked the confidence to take on new technology. A key focus of the work of the KVK is to educate farmers on the technologies available to them and help them understand how they might use these to improve crop production and link more directly into markets to enjoy more return for their work. KVK have fostered a linkage between organic produce farmers in Baramati and several housing cooperatives in Pune, whereby their produce is sold to cooperative residents directly, a process that raises the return for the farmer and gives consumers affordable access to organic food. An example of how community involvement can create a more equitable food system for the producer and consumer by keeping the exchange relatively local: Digital literacy and online retailing are potentially key enablers in creating this system.

* * *

From Five Star to International Stardom

When I began perusing the shelves of India's supermarkets and retail food stores to research for this book, I discovered that there had been a significant increase in the variety of chocolates available in India: imported international brands spilling from the counters of food stores alongside a growing selection of Indian-made chocolates, from commercial to boutique brands; dedicated chocolate shops selling hand-made chocolates and hot chocolate drinks, and chocolate cakes and desserts were prominent in bakeries and on restaurant menus. What I was seeing was the evidence that India is now one of the world's fastest growing markets for chocolate confectionery products. The growing consumption of chocolate in India straddles the intertwined stories of food retail and how health claims around foods are shaping the buying and eating habits of Indians.

The first Indian chocolate bar I ate was a 5 Star Fruit & Nut. It had a waxy texture and turned into a clay-like paste in the mouth instead of gently melting, was sharply sweet and only vaguely tasted of cocoa. I tried other locally manufactured chocolate confections and found them similar; the best of the lot was Nutties, although these are more substantively nuts and caramel enrobed with a thin coating of chocolate. Some imported chocolates were available in upmarket grocery stores, but they were expensive, and exposure to the hot, humid Indian climate tended to decline the quality of these. The fact of this was an irrelevance for me anyway: with so many indigenous Indian confections to enjoy, there was no point in eating inferior chocolate, and it was hardly a nutritional emergency to go without it. In fact, the situation made it easy for me to bring novel gifts for friends in India: I brought them good chocolate.

Chocolate is made from cocoa derived from the seeds of the *Theobroma cacao* tree, a tropical plant that grows in hot and humid conditions, such as those in Andhra Pradesh, Kerala, Karnataka, and Tamil Nadu, yet when it is processed into chocolate products, these same conditions are anathema to it.[35] The cocoa butter in chocolate melts at 37°C, just below body temperature, causing it to soften quickly when you put it in your mouth and release the flavour components we recognize as chocolate. The difficulty in the predominantly hot Indian climate is that chocolate with a high percentage of cocoa butter had a tendency to melt, or 'bloom' such that its components separated, sitting on a store shelf. The waxy texture of Indian chocolate I found unpleasant was due to the replacement of much of the cocoa butter with vegetable fats such as coconut or palm kernel oil, which remain solid in warm temperatures. Commercial chocolate confectionery produced for the Indian market also had to appeal to and be accessible to local consumers, meeting their preference for saccharine-saturated confections, and as sugar is cheaper than cocoa butter, making it the predominant ingredient made it sit well with the Indian purse as well.

Chocolate, Chocolate Everywhere

November 2018. I am in The Oriental Fruits Mart in Delhi's Connaught Place, a landmark family-run grocery store operating here since 1935. Author and Delhi chronicler Mayank Austen Soofi notes the place has 'changed little in its fit-out since [it opened], the refrigerator is a 1941 model', a fragment of heritage in this 'furiously evolving colonial-era district'.[36] Despite these antique qualities, The Oriental Fruits Mart has always been a harbinger of change when it comes to its stock. When I was living in Delhi in 2000, it was one of the few places where you could get good ground coffee before this beverage became the raison d'etre of a café 'lifestyle', and Soofi credits Oriental as having introduced avocados into Delhi. It had been some years since I had been in the store, and it was a little different—proprietor Mohinder Bal was older, and while there was barely any fresh fruit on offer anymore, there was a very large selection of good chocolate: a portent that this confection was on its way to being more widely consumed in India, subsequently proven true by some unanticipated encounters with this product.

Chocolate Scene No. 1: Araku

December 2019. R and I travelled to the Araku Valley in Andhra Pradesh as I wanted to explore the coffee industry there, and to that end, we visited the local coffee museum. We followed the path set along a series of dioramas and educative panels telling the story of the development of the coffee industry in the region, which at its end channelled us into a large merchandise shop, filled not with coffee products and paraphernalia as one might expect, but with chocolates, a huge array of these, all produced from local cocoa. I was taken by surprise as I had no idea that Araku had a chocolate industry and that the quality of the chocolate was good. We bought up a large selection of these confections for our own consumption and for gifts—the large packet of Araku coffee chocolates I gave my household in Australia were eaten up immediately as they were found to be delicious. There was a small corner of the store selling local coffee, but it was chocolate our fellow visitors were buying as eagerly as we were. Making some inquiries into the matter, we learned that cultivating cocoa has become an additional source of income for local farmers who grow it beneath the tall forest trees alongside their coffee crop.

Chocolate Scene No 2: Anand

If I have anything resembling a travel 'bucket list', it is focused on places related to food. One of these had been the Amul dairy complex in Anand, Gujarat. I had been wanting to visit the headquarters of this iconic Indian brand for many years, finally making it in December 2019. Prior to this, I had tried contacting the company several times to see if I could organize a visit. No one at Amul responded to my inquiries so I decided to just show up there. After a little wrangling at the security gate, I was welcomed in and shown around the huge dairy production complex by public relations officer Richard Christian. As part of my tour, we took in a display of the extensive range of food products the company currently manufactures, including many different varieties of chocolate. Amul has been making chocolate for decades: In a nostalgic piece about childhood and Indian confectionery, Anurag Varma writes, 'If you had one of these [an Amul chocolate bar] . . . you were considered the cool kid with a rich dad', a comment indicating that it was not a common treat, the range of bars was also small.[37] When I remarked on the considerable expansion of the Amul chocolate selection. Christian nodded, 'Yes, the demand for chocolate in India has grown dramatically, we [Amul] have recently opened a dedicated chocolate factory nearby', which he said I was welcome to visit. When we wound up our dairy tour, I headed off down the highway to do exactly that, arriving at a building set in manicured grounds, with a 'Gone with the Wind'-style columned portico leading into a spacious, shining marble-lined lobby, where two smiling staff sat behind a long reception desk to welcome visitors. It seemed more like the entrance to a fancy hotel than a chocolate production unit. Within minutes of arriving, I was taken, along with a family group, on a guided tour of the complex. The factory had been specifically designed to accommodate visitors. We circumnavigated a corridor set around its perimeter, peering through thick glass windows at various stages of the chocolate-production process. In truth, most of this happens inside vast industrial machinery, so you can't see much of it, but I still found it fascinating. Before completing the tour, the guide directed our attention to a display of Amul chocolates, ranging from sweet mass-market confections to high cocoa content single-origin bars made from beans sourced from Africa, South America, and India—representing the world's chocolate-producing regions—including a 90 per cent cocoa bitter chocolate. The fact that Amul had built this industrial complex to produce this range of affordable chocolates was a clear indication of more widespread consumption of it amongst Indians now than just wealthy kids having access to it. As our guide waved his hand across the product display, he confidently pronounced that Indians had 'learnt from television' that 'Indian mithai [sweets] are bad' and that 'chocolate is much better', further claiming that its consumption would 'fix knee problems'. The family group vigorously nodded their heads in agreement. I did not say anything then, but I will say something here about chocolate myths a bit further on. As we departed, a large tour group filed in to take their turn through the factory.

Chocolate Scene No. 3: Chennai

The day after I visited Amul, I returned to Delhi to attend the 2019 Tasting India Symposium. It was obvious from my mix of experiences over the previous weeks that the consumption of chocolate in India had changed considerably. My attention had wandered away from the business of the symposium to wondering who I could talk to about why chocolate had become so popular, when host Sourish Bhattacharyya announced chocolate maker L. Nitin Chordia as a participant on the final panel for the day. The matter under discussion was supporting local farmers and the importance of eating seasonal and local foods, and there was such eagerness amongst the large panel to comment on this subject that Chordia barely got a few words in. As soon as the session ended, I hastened after him, caught him in the foyer, introduced myself, and explained the project I was working on. He was on his way to catch a flight, but he unpacked his bag and gave me an impromptu chocolate tasting. It turned out that he was based in Chennai, and by another fortuitous happenstance, I was going to be in Chennai later that week, and we arranged to meet there.

Nitin was the perfect person for me to talk with about chocolate in India. His background is in retail consulting, and he has a thorough understanding of the Indian retail food market formed from experiences including setting up the gourmet food chain Nature's Basket for the Godrej Group. Travelling around the world to search out food products and retail concepts for this chain, he discovered good chocolate, decided to train as a chocolate taster, and founded an initiative called Kocoatrait through which he produces a range of chocolate bars, offers chocolate-making and chocolate-tasting training, develops chocolate products for other companies, and works to promote Indian chocolate and enhance appreciation of good chocolate in India. He was someone who knew chocolate from all angles.

I joined Nitin on a visit to the plantation on the semi-rural outskirts of Chennai where he works with a farmer to grow the organic cocoa he uses. There was little activity at the plantation as the beans were some time away from harvesting, so we peacefully meandered around the groves of low-growing evergreen cocoa trees shaded by tall coconut palms. Cocoa is an understory crop, like coffee and pepper, thriving in the dappled light created by a canopy of taller trees. Nitin pointed out the delicate pink and white flowers along the limbs of the cacao tree that eventually turn into cocoa fruit, which grow directly from the tree's trunk in the same way as a jackfruit. Most of the cocoa pods were still adolescents, but Nitin searched the trees until he found a couple of more adult specimens, splitting these open to show the cocoa beans encased in a sticky white pulp inside it. Come harvest time proper, the beans are removed from the pulp, put into shallow trays, covered with thick hessian and left to ferment for a week, periodically stirred, and finally dried in the sun, after which they are sent up to the city to be made into chocolate at Chordia's processing unit.

Returning to Chennai and the Kocoatrait headquarters, I'm greeted by the warm aroma of chocolate as soon as I step across the building threshold. This delicious smell is emanating from a batch of cocoa beans being conched—the long, slow process during which roughly ground beans are milled between stones to smooth the particles into finer grains. A conching machine is not unlike the stone grinder used for making idli/dosa batter, and south India is becoming a destination for craft chocolate makers from around the world to source equipment because of local expertise in making food grinding machinery—a contemporary repurposing of a traditional Indian technique. Nitin had invited my friend Kavita and me to a tasting session of the range of chocolates he produces. He makes almost all his products without milk and said that this can make his chocolate challenging for people accustomed to eating mass-produced brands, such as Cadbury—the biggest-selling chocolate brand in India—because these are milk-based, which gives the chocolate a much smoother texture.[38] The sugar content in big-name chocolates is also much higher, up to 56 per cent in some products: Using milk and sugar as the main ingredients in chocolate keeps the price of the product low. Nitin keeps the sugar content in his chocolate products to 36 per cent, the minimum the Indian palate will tolerate. He said that there had been quick adaptation to chocolate in India and that the market was shifting from seeing it as just something sweet to eat to having a more educated understanding of it; subsequently, Indians were becoming more willing to pay for better-quality chocolate. He attributed the interest in it to exposure through media; the novelty appeal of it as a 'western-style' sweet with its lingering luxury aura and its purported health advantages. I told him of the confident claims the guide at Amul had made about the benefits of eating chocolate. He said that as a producer, this idea that chocolate is healthy is good for his business, but he has a far less sensational, and more educated, approach to this, describing chocolate as a 'healthier' option rather than a healthy product per se. He explained that the high milk and sugar content of most commercial chocolate reduces the availability of any antioxidants in chocolate and, therefore, any potential benefits of these.

Indians are not unique in their enhanced predilection for chocolate. It is a worldwide trend, largely inspired by claims that consuming chocolate, especially high cocoa content varieties, is good for us because it reduces the risk of heart disease, helps lower blood pressure and cholesterol, improves memory and athletic and sexual performance, and aids in weight management (oh, glory of glories), even though there is no good evidence to substantiate these claims. Professor Marion Nestle, an eminent nutritional scientist at New York University, says a 'magic trick' has been played on us with chocolate, describing assertions of its benefits as 'nutrifluff', 'sensational claims' made for a single food or nutrient based on marginal research findings, 'usually highly preliminary', from one or a small number of studies.[39] Most 'scientific' research into chocolate tends to be funded by large chocolate manufacturers, such as the Mars company, and they 'set up [research] questions that will give them desirable results, [that] tend to be interpreted in ways that are beneficial to their interests', but the journalists who report on these studies, which is what the layperson reads, rarely mention this, 'exaggerat[ing] findings, and omit [ting] key details and caveats'.[40]

Chai packaging: no chai glass, more waste

Home-delivered millet meal inclusive of sixteen pieces of waste

The Amul chocolate production complex in Anand, Gujarat

Charmaine O'Brien

Two visual slices of cakes

Charmaine O'Brien

Cleaning out an aquaculture tank

Charmaine O'Brien

Selection of locally produced chocolates in Araku, Andhra Pradesh

Making artisan peanut oil in Baramati, Maharashtra

Charmaine O'Brien

Charmaine O'Brien

'Butt and brush' shopping style—Delhi

Charmaine O'Brien

Cheese rondels at Darima Farms,
Uttarakhand

Charmaine O'Brien

The electronic cow:
An endangered species?

Charmaine O'Brien

Convenience for the taking. The frozen food section of a departmental store in Delhi

A newly introduced species. A pile of plastic packets dumped by the roadside in Sitla, Uttarakhand

Charmaine O'Brien

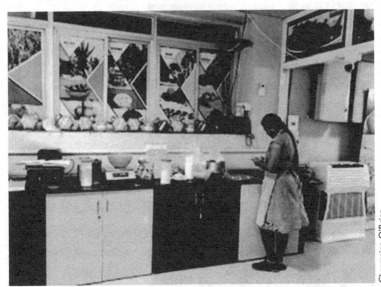

Charmaine O'Brien

A test kitchen at the Indian Council of Agricultural Research (ICAR)-Indian Institute of Millets Research (IIMR), Hyderabad

An urban farmers' market for urbanites in Delhi

A farmers' market
in rural Odhisa

Urban agriculture being carried out in Delhi

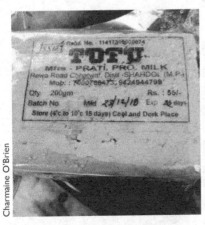

Artisan tofu in Shahdol, Madhya Pradesh

An array of organic food in
Kumaon, Uttarakhand

Fruits and vegetables in plastic wrap at a departmental store

Neatly stacked rows of plastic-wrapped vegetables

Winemaker Karan Vasani of Sula Vineyards, Nashik

Crucially, most recent research has used much higher levels of flavanols than are available in commercial snack products. For example, [a] blood pressure study involved participants getting an average of 670mg of flavanols. Someone would need to consume about 12 standard 100g bars of dark chocolate or about 50 of milk chocolate per day to get that much.[41]

While chocolate is not harmful when eaten in moderation, it is not that healthy either, as Nestle says: 'Chocolate is candy'. Even knowing this, it is unlikely that the rate of chocolate consumption in India will slow.[42] Global confectioners such as Mars are undertaking research and development to make their chocolate confectionery more heat tolerant in order to minimize deterioration during shipping, handling, and storage in countries such as India.[43] Nestec, the technology arm of Nestlé (the company, not the scientist), has developed chocolate products with a 'tropicalized' shell to withstand the tropical conditions of India. Mondelez, the international company that distributes Cadbury products in India, provides coolers to small retailers to help maintain product quality. The chocolate confections produced by these companies are of the sweet, smooth milk type that the Indian palate still largely prefers and are relatively inexpensive.

From unappetizing beginnings, I have become a keen consumer of Indian-made chocolate, especially artisan brands that produce products using local beans that give the chocolate the taste and texture of its terroir, the specific environment the cocoa is grown in, a lauded quality in wine. Indian-grown cocoa has more acidity and spice on the palate and a little more 'grit' in the texture: For some, this does not match up to the model of fine Swiss chocolate, but India's artisan chocolate makers are not aiming to copy. They want their product to speak of where it is from and make a feature of these differences. To this end, they are also creating distinctive local flavours: Kocoatrait's range includes bars flavoured with Tamil coffee, panakkum (lemon juice, jaggery, ginger powder, cardamom powder, and black pepper), and modakam (the coconut-filled rice dumplings beloved of the god Ganesh). And the world is taking notice of India's chocolate: Kocoatrait was recently nominated as one of twenty-five 'world-class Indian food brands' and was featured in a 2020 *New York Times* article on Indian-made chocolate.[44] Other brands have also won international awards for their distinctly Indian chocolates: Paul and Mike for their dark chocolate with jamun; Chitram Craft Chocolates for their moringa and lemon white chocolate; Naviluna for their Tokai Coffee and Pineapple single-origin chocolate. Meanwhile, in Telangana, it is illegal for confectioners to make liquor chocolates, yet the demand for these is such that chocolate producers are willing to risk jail time to supply these 'illicit' sweets to their customers.

Caveat Emptor: Health Halos

Cookbooks these days are obsessed with health . . . the problem with such 'healthy' cooking is that it looks at just one, quasi-scientific, aspect of food, and not all the other reasons we eat it. Food is fuel, but it's also the joy of eating it, the pleasure of the different ingredients that go into it, the connection made through it to the seasons that we eat it in, the people we share it with, the memories it evokes of past meals . . . [t]o consider all these seems to me to be the really healthy, holistic way to eat.[45]

Noticing that global concepts intertwining food, eating styles, and 'health', such as gluten-free, vegan, superfoods, keto, and clean eating, were being eagerly adopted by affluent urban India was one of the things that inspired this book. When I talked with food writer Phorum Dalal, she nominated health concepts as having a significant influence on shaping current food trends in India. Because these trends are global, emanating from the same privileged sectors of affluent countries such as the USA and Australia, I am going to draw on wider sources for this section as well as Indian examples.

Labelling foods as organic, natural, healthy, nutri, ancient, or super, to suggest these confer superior health benefits because they either contain more nutrition than other foods or are 'free' of apparently pernicious elements such as gluten and sugar, eases consumers into paying higher prices for these believing these to be healthier (whatever that might mean). Some of these labels are genuinely indicative and others are marketing nonsense, but all have been commercially co-opted to sell food products to a sector of

Indian consumers increasingly focused on 'healthism', the idea that health should be actively pursued because it's the right thing to do and that food has more to offer than basic nutrition and can cure many ailments. It is a belief that all health problems can be solved at an individual level and manifest when we divide food into 'healthy' and 'unhealthy' categories or say 'I am bad' when we eat supposedly 'unhealthy' food. It has been suggested that healthism has taken over from spiritual devotion. Believing ourselves to be entirely responsible for our health—ignoring the genetic, environmental, and systemic (access to healthcare, class, and education) aspects that impact health—and that we should pursue 'health at all costs', has allowed the idea of well-being to be privatized, such that there is now a 'global wellness industry' worth $4.5 trillion.[46] The 'health food' component of this industry—encompassing all the labelled foods listed above—is estimated to be worth $702 billion. India is currently contributing INR 490 billion to this sector, and Indians' spending on 'health food' is expected to maintain a steep upward ascent.

The connection between food and health is hardly a new concept in India. The key principle of Ayurveda, the thousands-year-old Hindu health system, is that a 'proper natural diet' is essential for attaining and maintaining physical and mental health, ascribing the cause of many ailments to wrong eating habits—essentially, it holds that what and how we eat is the foundation of well-being. Ayurveda concepts of what constitutes a healthful diet are deeply inscribed into everyday Indian cuisine. I have so often been in an Indian home where a woman sharing her cooking with me has picked up an ingredient and said it was 'good for' some element of health—prevention or cure—before adding it to a dish: This was done as a matter of course; there was no fuss, no trumpeting the superior nature of any food. But this idea of achieving health through food has migrated from the practices of the domestic kitchen into the commercial realm and the notion that you can buy health through eating certain foods. In food retailing, 'health' claims for a food item equals a higher return on it. There is concern that less educated Indians might be more susceptible to dubious health and lifestyle claims around food, yet well-educated, high-income urbanites are the biggest market for so-called health foods and just as predisposed to believing spurious claims about food.

Health Washing

The website of an Indian food manufacturer producing a range of Tex Mex-style ready-to-eat foods claims these: 'Are focused on health—our products are vegan and gluten-free . . . so very healthy as well!'[47] Their products may well enhance the health of the people who consume them, but if that is true, it is not because they are gluten-free or vegan. Gluten is a protein found in wheat, barley, and rye that has elastic qualities and can stretch when moistened and not break when heated; it is what allows bread and cakes to rise, pancakes to stick together, and sauces to thicken. There is nothing inherently 'healthy' or good or bad about gluten. People who have coeliac disease are highly allergic to gluten and eating it makes them very sick; this verifiable condition is a genetic one and occurs in a small percentage of any population. The more populist claim is to 'gluten intolerance', whether such a condition exists remains questionable. Regardless, the notion that gluten-free food is healthier has been pervasive in the West for more than a decade and has come into India largely through social media channels.

> It scares me, because there is nothing wrong with being healthy, but the way that culture has developed these days, being healthy is more about performing as healthy for other people. And that performance becomes an identity: 'Like me because I am a healthy role model.' More and more people get their entire identities caught up in whether or not they have put out a blog post or a podcast about their latest health discovery or Instagrammed their #glutenfree meal for others to gaze upon.[48]

Ironically, the growth in demand for gluten-free food is for processed foods: cookies, biscuits, cakes, pizza, pasta, noodles, ready-to-eat packaged soups and sauces, desserts, and snack foods, exactly the same type of items often considered 'unhealthy' in their gluten-containing form. To claim any of these, or any other foods, as healthier because of the absence of gluten is an example of a 'health halo'. Many traditional Indian foods have also been repositioned in retail as gluten-free, such as khakhra, idli and dosa pre-mixes, and papad, none of which have ever contained gluten—another example of a health halo. The marketing misinformation about gluten in India is such that I found a prominent upmarket Indian food retailer selling sooji and dalia as gluten-free when both are 100 per cent wheat, but labelling food as gluten-free means consumers will pay more for them. The increasing demand for gluten-free food by Indian consumers is influenced by a global trend, not by rising numbers of properly diagnosed coeliacs.[49]

Putting a health halo around food can blind people to the reality of what they are eating and paying for. One of the key reasons people give for buying gluten-free food is that they believe it is healthier and, therefore, has less calories and will help them lose weight, which then leads them to believe they can eat more of it. A food that is gluten-free does not contain less calories simply through this omission, and processed gluten-free products are often higher in sugars and fat, therefore, containing more calories: eating a gluten-free diet could even lead to weight gain.

> [L]ately it's become hip to go gluten free. Based on little or no evidence other than testimonials in the media, people have been switching to gluten-free diets to lose weight, boost energy, treat autism, or generally feel healthier . . . but a larger portion will derive no significant benefit from the practice. They'll simply waste their money, because these products are expensive.[50]

Gluten-free is linked to another bogus health trend that proclaims carbohydrates are bad because these make you fat:

> People want to believe that they are gluten intolerant because it's a way for them to avoid carbs, because they also think carbs make them fat.[51]

A key driver of the demand for gluten-free food might then be sublimated angst about weight and appearance that is a universal preoccupation of educated women around the world. Contemporary educated, well-off, urban Indian consumers might be alert to the marketing devices employed by corporate producers of 'fast' or 'junk food', but they are vulnerable to the nonsense health claims made by food companies, industry bodies, and incentivized social media influencers; over-focusing on the health qualities of food can actually lead to poor health outcomes, such as nutritional deficiencies and eating disorders. I do not exclude myself from vulnerability to health claims around food; I too wish I could eat foods that would magically confer glowing svelte youthfulness, but my experience of holding food and health too tightly together actually led to some less-than-healthy outcomes. When I was younger, and naturally glowing, I did not believe myself to be as slim as what popular culture considered attractive. My quest for thinness led me to 'food and health' and an idea that if I ate a vegan diet made up of expensive organic foods, 'free' from gluten, dairy, sugar, and yeast, I would achieve my desired body size and, thereby, become appealing. What I achieved instead was an obsession with the 'health' qualities of food, a condition that has now become so common that it has a name—orthorexia—and is recognized as an eating disorder, and it is happening in India:

> Nutritionist Samridhi Sharma . . . diagnoses at least three to four patients with orthorexia [each month]. 'Very few patients easily accept they have a problem . . . [they do not] believe their [health focus] is a problem and do not believe it can actually be harmful'.[52]

However, having a concern for food and health does not mean someone will develop orthorexia, as it is a condition of extremes. There is no clear figure around its prevalence, although it predominantly shows up in affluent women, who can afford to make such deeply exclusionary choices about what they eat.

> Although being aware of and concerned with the nutritional quality of the food you eat isn't a problem in and of itself, people with orthorexia become so fixated on so-called 'healthy eating' that they actually damage their own well-being.[53]

My experience with this condition left me sceptical about any claims to the superior health benefits of any particular food, and I am not alone on this.

Among the affluent classes who already ate a healthier-than-average diet, the Instagram goddesses created a new model of dietary perfection to aim for. For the rest of the population, however, it simply placed the ideal of healthy food ever further out of reach. Behind the shiny covers of the clean-eating books, there is a harsh form of economic exclusion that says that someone who can't afford wheatgrass or spirulina can never be truly 'well'.[54]

Believing that consuming any one food can lead to specific benefits ignores the complexity of human metabolism. Just because a food has a high level of calcium or zinc does not mean it is made available to us via our metabolic processes, or that we even need a high dose of that nutrient. The moral stance of what constitutes healthy or unhealthy food has changed dramatically over my lifetime. When I was growing up, carbohydrates were apparently 'bad'; then when I was a young adult, suddenly fat was bad and carbohydrates were good (Pritikin); then fat became good and carbohydrates bad again (Atkins); then fat was bad again, and we started consuming low-fat foods full of sugar; then sugar became the dietary bogey-man because it had been put into many foods to make them taste good without any fat; then protein was good and carbohydrates bad again (Paleo/Keto). No wonder people are confused about what to eat, and confusion does not help anyone to eat well. Making oversimplified statements about what food is, or is not, healthy does not originate exclusively from marketers or self-appointed experts on social media, but also from qualified nutritionists and dietitians. This can be confusing, particularly when these claims are contested later on, and there is a lot of ambiguity about what constitutes good or bad food, and this can change. Take eggs, for example; the advice on the healthy consumption of this nutritious protein-rich food keeps changing.[55]

> US scientists have practically absolved fat and cholesterol of their supposed sins. This February, experts advising the committee responsible for developing dietary guidelines admitted there was 'no appreciable relationship' between dietary cholesterol and blood cholesterol.[56]

Nutrition does not rely on a few foods but on our overall pattern of eating. The healthiest diets include a wide variety of foods and varying our food intake takes care of nutrient needs. Labelling a certain food as healthy can lead people to significantly overeat even when 'good' items contain as many or more calories as 'bad' items. The millet chips I found in a Delhi convenience store labelled as 'healthier' have the same calories as conventional potato chips: Conceiving of a food as healthy or 'super' can lead us to ignore what else is in a product, the portion size, or the fact that it might be very calorie-dense. Eating a food item because it has been deemed 'healthy' might be taken as a licence to eat whatever else we want—'I just had a healthy salad, so now I can have dessert and another glass of wine' (I am guilty, guilty, guilty of this!). When consumers eat at restaurants claiming to serve 'healthy' food, they often end up eating more total daily calories than at restaurants that do not make such claims.[57]

When we eat, we eat food, not ingredients or nutrients. If asked to describe what you enjoy about a certain food item, you would most likely refer to its gastronomical qualities: flavour, texture, smell, the way it looks on the plate, and/or it might be psychological, in that it arouses nostalgic feelings, memories of childhood or special events. Research on cultural eating patterns suggests that untangling food from moral notions of 'superfoods', healthy/unhealthy, good/bad, and pure/impure might actually allow us to take more pleasure from food and, therefore, not eat as much—well-being is not determined only by what we put in our bodies. What happens when you focus on the nutrient aspect is that you leave out the enjoyment of food.[58] I am reminded of a comment made by restaurant impresario A. D. Singh during a 2019 event on future food trends in India; the conversation had turned to how consumers were looking for 'healthier' choices on restaurant menus. Singh has been a leader in the Indian hospitality industry for nearly three decades, and he knows what people want when they eat out. His comment in relation to this was: 'No matter what people say about healthy choices, [we] still sell more fried food than anything: People like it.'

If we are truly interested in supporting our well-being through the way we eat, then we need to understand more about why we eat the way we do. Psychological research on eating suggests that allowing ourselves to enjoy food, in moderate portions relative to our calorific needs, to take pleasure in it, and get over food related-guilt might facilitate our well-being more than eating certain foods just because we believe them to be good.[59] This would require us to trust our tastes, trust ourselves, stop labelling our eating behaviours as good or bad, explore new foods to discover what we really like, and question labels suggesting a particular food is healthier than another. We also need to untangle eating from our physical appearance. There is an increased focus on the body in contemporary healthism, and well-being is often a euphemism for weight loss.

> This was before I could recognize wellness culture for what it was—a dangerous con that seduces smart women with pseudoscientific claims of increasing energy, reducing inflammation, lowering the risk of cancer and healing skin, gut and fertility problems. But at its core, 'wellness' is about weight loss . . . preserving a vicious fallacy: Thin is healthy and healthy is thin.[60]

The 'cons' of the contemporary wellness industry are a global, or westernized, phenomenon, and these have clearly taken root in urban India—although Indian foods and health concepts have been purloined by this industry. To mention just a few examples: Rs 4000 haldi vitamin tablets; 'turmeric lattes', aka haldi doodh; and 'fat busting' *Garcinia cambogia*, aka kokum, a key ingredient of Konkani cuisine. How many Indian women, or men, might be buying and eating certain foods or following dietary regimes under the guise of 'wellness' when what they really hope for is to lose weight has not been quantified in any scientific way. However, many Indians are interested in reducing their weight. The nation has a defined weight loss industry currently worth more than $500 million and is estimated to grow significantly in the next decade. Social media is one of the key factors supporting this growth and it is the primary channel for wellness influencers.[61] Wealthier Indian women can be especially concerned about their weight because of social pressure on them to 'be in perfect shape [i.e., thin] all the time'.[62]

When I met with Ahmedabad hotelier and restaurateur Abhay Mangaldas, he said Indians are 'much more informed about food than ever before, making well-educated choices about what they are eating and drinking'. Urban India's food vocabulary has certainly developed. It is undisputable that there is increased interest, knowledge, and experience of international foods and cookery amongst a greater number of Indians as well as much exploration of India's own cuisines. But does this equal being well informed about food from a health perspective? Abhay's view stands in direct contrast to that of nutritionist Kavita Devgan who says knowledge about eating well has gone down amongst Indians, with people spending more on junk food, especially middle-income Indians, and becoming overweight on the outside and nutrition deficient on the inside. The global 'health and food' fashions are often coming to Indians via popular social media influencers. Is the advice of these people sound or does it have any credibility at all? An online Indian journal that identified and directed readers to India's most influential health influencers and blogs claimed that a vegan lifestyle, is unmatchable for a healthy lifestyle'.[63] In my experience, it is a commonly held idea in India, and elsewhere, that being vegan is a 'healthier' way to eat and live but veganism is defined as 'the voluntary abstention from animal derived food-products and a lifestyle governed by non-violent philosophy'.[64] A vegan diet means the exclusion of all animal products; it is an ethical or moral choice, which does not necessarily make it a healthy, let alone healthier, way to eat. I was a vegan once, many years ago when it was considered freaky, not fashionable, and I can assure you, it is possible to eat plenty of 'unhealthy' food that is vegan, i.e., free of any animal products, including fried snack foods, confectionery, highly processed baked and convenience foods and also alcohol. Indians might have a lot more contemporary information about health and well-being, but the sources of this material can be dubious: unsubstantiated hype spouted by the world's better-off citizens.

Superfoods or Super Hype?

December 2013. I was poking around the shelves in Sharda Stores, an upmarket grocery in Delhi, looking for interesting food ingredients with which to prepare 'exotic' western dishes for friends in Madhya Pradesh, where I was travelling to the following day, when I spotted some packets of quinoa on a shelf there. At this time, the hip and the health conscious around the western, and westernized, world were frenziedly consuming this small-grained cereal native to the Andes, cultivated and eaten by rural communities there for hundreds of years, from where it had recently emerged from mountain obscurity to international food stardom through its re-invention as a 'superfood'. I usually disdained buying this grain because it was over-hyped and over-priced, but on this occasion, I included a 500-gram packet of it in my purchases—outrageously priced at Rs 800—because I had seen a recipe for a salad based on it, which sounded delicious despite my misgivings. I decided I would make it for my friends as I figured they would not have eaten quinoa before. Several days later, I am in these friends' kitchen preparing our dinner. I have cooked the quinoa in water, and it is draining in a sieve on the bench. Archana comes in to see what I am doing. She notices the quinoa, peers more closely at it, picks up a spoon, pokes at it and then asks me what it is. I show her the raw product in the packet, give her a spiel about its provenance, tell her how it is in vogue and that people are paying exorbitant prices for it because it has been labelled a 'superfood'. She listens to all of this and then says: 'We have this in our village [in eastern Uttar Pradesh], but only poor people eat it.' I was intrigued. I asked her more about this, because as best as I knew, quinoa was not cultivated in Indian villages. We worked out that what she was referring to was actually pearl millet (bajra), which looks like quinoa. Millet had been a commonly cultivated and eaten staple in her home state until agricultural modernization had made bio-engineered rice and wheat the predominant

crops several decades previously. Lacking the prestige of
modernity, millet became a food eaten only by those who
could not afford 'better' rice and wheat.

December 1998. Exploring western Gujarat with two
other companions, we landed up at the Than monastery in
the Dhinodhar Hills outlying the Great Rann of Kutch,
where we stayed for a couple of days. The resident yogis
were generous, affable hosts, and my time there remains
a vivid memory, no less for the morning we spent walking
through the rugged desert landscape to visit a sadhu living
in a remote cave, followed by ascending a steep hill to meet
another holy man who showed us photographs of himself
pulling a land rover with his penis while we drank tea,
than the food we were served. There was nothing elaborate
about what these yogis cooked and ate. Our evening meal
consisted of bajri rotla, thick millet flatbread smeared with
ghee, a dish of starchy vegetables cooked to just the right
degree of firm-softness, a lump of fresh gur, and a glass
of chilled buttermilk. The ghee and buttermilk had been
made with milk from their own cows, the other ingredients
were all locally produced. Millet is grown as a fodder crop
in Australia, and I had never eaten it before, nor had I
tasted buttermilk. The idea of eating vegetables with
something sweet was also quite extraordinary to me, and I
gingerly tried this combination, only to find it unexpectedly
delicious, as was the nutty substantive bajra rotla and the
light and tangy buttermilk. Laid out, this meal looked
simple, almost austere, and it was in its context, but this
combination of foods, tastes, and textures remain one of

the most remarkable meals I have eaten; it was also a meal that inspired my interest in millets.

A Short History of Indian Millets

Five thousand or so years ago, the urbanites of the Indus Valley ate a variety of millets as part of their everyday fare. Millets, the seeds of a species of grasses, are one of the oldest foods known to mankind and one of the most important cereal crops in the world, of which India has a number of indigenous varieties. Over succeeding millennia, Indians continued to cultivate and eat different types of millets, depending on where they lived on the subcontinent.[65] Up until 50 years ago, millets were the most widely cultivated grains in India. In the 1960s, the country's ongoing struggle to adequately feed all her people post-Independence was exacerbated by massive crop failures. The solution to food scarcity was to transition from small-scale, place-based, poly-agriculture to an industrial system of mono-cropping, predominantly of rice and wheat, using newly developed bio-engineered high-yielding seeds: a transformation known as the Green Revolution. Farmers were offered significant incentives—easy credit, technological education, and support—by the Indian government to shift to growing new wheat and rice varieties, increasing production of these, and amplifying their use in Indian kitchens by making these cereals more accessible and affordable through a subsidized public distribution system.[66] Using industrially processed rice and wheat had distinct advantages for domestic cooks.

For a start, it spared women the 'drudgery' of preparing raw cereals for domestic consumption as it could take hours to de-husk a few kilos of millet; rice and wheat are relatively simpler to cook. Millet is a 'gluten-free' grain, and a dough made from its flour cracks and crumbles if rolled out; so millet rotis have to be pressed into shape by hand, resulting in a thicker bread that takes longer to cook. Gluten-rich wheat is much easier to roll out into thin flatbreads, which reduces labour, cooking time, and fuel consumption. Rice and wheat soon became the dominant cereals in India. There were no technological productivity enhancements for millets, nor financial subsidies, and this food was pushed aside as 'primitive' and 'ancient'—before these features were fashionable in food, but we will come to that—only to be eaten by poor rural folk.

The introduction of modern agrochemical-based agriculture did 'revolutionize' India's food production. It increased the productivity of food, saving millions of lives, and eventually led to foodgrain self-sufficiency. More available food reduced its cost. But increasing India's food production in this way was not without consequence. The new crop varieties required significant inputs of fertilizer, pesticide, and water to facilitate their performance—in fact, they were ineffective without these—and modern farm machinery was needed to maximize the harvest of the increased grain yield. The benefits of the new system were unequal. There might have been greater profits in growing high-yielding crops, but it cost a lot to be in the game in the first place, which favoured wealthier farmers. The price of joining the Green Revolution left many small farmers impoverished; poor farmers could not even afford to try modern agriculture. Filling the bellies of India's hungry widened the financial gap between large landowners and small farmers, enhancing social disparity. Farmers who could not afford to convert to more prestigious agricultural modernity continued to cultivate millets and/or local cereal varieties, further besmirching millet as a food of the underprivileged. The use of millets as human food dissipated, particularly in urban places, and production declined.[67] By the time I came to India in the late 1990s, it was widely understood as a land of rice and wheat, with a clear culinary marker of wheat eaters in the north and rice eaters in the south. Millet did not rate a mention.

A Personal History of Millet Consumption

Millet-based dishes might not have shown up on the menus of Indian restaurants, in general cookbooks, or other popular representations of her cuisines, but millets had not disappeared from Indian kitchens.[68] These continued to be grown, cooked, and eaten throughout the subcontinent, but their use tended to be rural and domestic, low-key, almost hidden, and unmentioned. My first taste of millet in Kutch raised my awareness of this grain and travelling to all corners of India to research her regional cuisines, I came to understand the extent of its use and its value as a sustainable food source. I ate bajre ki roti, a mix of millet and maize, in Punjab; in Uttarakhand, I enjoyed jhangora ki kheer, prepared from local millet (jhangora) cooked in sweetened milk and mandua (finger millet) roti; I had millet porridge with curd for breakfast in Jodhpur and millet roti with my lunch; in Kota, friends prepared soyta, meat cooked with millet that is a speciality of the royal kitchens of Rajasthan; in Goa, I had tizann, a local porridge of soaked and ground finger millet, jaggery and coconut milk; in Mangaluru, it was raagi manni, hot finger millet porridge prepared with jaggery and coconut milk. Karnataka is India's leading producer of millets, and these grains have remained quintessential in local cuisine. There I ate dosa and idli prepared with raagi and jowar/ sorghum, raagi mudde (millet balls) served with vegetable sambhar, and raagi roti (tasty flatbread of millet flour, onions, coriander, ginger, and curd). The traditional foodways of Telangana are also based on millet, and in that state, I ate millet breads accompanied by soupy tamarind and red chilli pulusu as well as khichdi, payasam, and ladoos prepared from millet. In Sindhudurg, a coastal district of Maharashtra, I enjoyed millet vaadi/dumplings accompanied by a rich coconut-based chicken stew; in Pune, there was thalipeeth, a multi-grain soft bread incorporating ground millet; in Gujarat, I ate millet breads across the state; in Sikkim, I drank chhaang, a home-made beer brewed from millet, and in Arunachal Pradesh, kodo ko chhaang, beer made from fermented kodo (a local millet). As I drove along the roads of rural India, I learnt to recognize the different types of millets growing in the fields—hand-shaped finger millet; conical bajra, the same shape as a kulfi; the knobby, tapered macramé of foxtail; barnyard like a thick plait of hair; and the tall staffs of jowar heavy with grain nodding with the breeze. Nobody made a fuss about millet, it was just everyday food in these places, and often the more remote or rural the location, the more millet was grown and eaten.

The environmental and socio-economic costs of the Green Revolution have been increasingly questioned over the past two decades.[69] Growing crops reliant on expensive and potentially hazardous chemical inputs and plentiful water has damaged land, drained water tables, and reduced soil fertility and biodiversity and, thereby, resilience.[70] Millets, on the other hand, are hardy plants that can grow in drier, less fertile areas; are drought, pest, and disease resistant, requiring little water or chemical assistance to flourish, making them a low-cost crop and, subsequently, an inexpensive cereal food. Millets also grow quickly and can adapt to changing environmental conditions.[71] What they could not thrive upon was the heavy chemical regime of the Green Revolution. In retrospect, millets may not have been sidelined because of low yield but because they did not require the expensive chemical inputs profitable to agrochemical corporations.[72] By the time I finished my field research for the *Food Guide* in 2012, I was certain that emerging and intertwined concerns about climate change, nutritional qualities of foods, and newfound interest in India's traditional food systems would see millets stage a comeback.

The Modern Millet Revival

Sure enough, while I was discovering millets in rural India, forward-thinking chefs such as Manu Chandra had started putting these on the menus of upmarket urban restaurants, setting this humbled grain on a trajectory of 'upward social mobility'. When I interviewed Chef Anahita Dhondy, a self-described 'millet ambassador', she described millet as 'India's future grain'; however, she had to ask her grandmother to teach her to how to prepare and cook it in the first place because there was so little urban memory of how to use it. Dhondy believes that chefs can act as a 'bridge between producers and consumers': In choosing to put a particular food on a menu, a chef brings it to the notice of their customers, signalling to them 'this is a food worth eating', elevating its appeal, thereby influencing what people choose to eat. Putting millet on restaurant menus has reintroduced it to urban consumers by making it accessible to people unaccustomed to eating it, and challenging people's perceptions of it. Speaking to a forum of hospitality and catering students at the India Culinary Institute about India's forgotten or neglected indigenous and wild foods, Dr Vibha Varshney encouraged them to seek out these foods, including millets, and cook with them because 'once you put these foods on plates [in restaurants and homes], it ensures these will be protected'.[73] At Chef Abhijit Saha's comfortably elegant upmarket restaurant Salt, in Bengaluru, the focus is on refined interpretations of regional dishes from around the country. When I met

Saha there in 2019, he told me that he was working on a project with a focus on millets with the Culinary Institute of America and that he was planning on including more millets on the menu because he had found that his customers now 'loved' dishes made with this grain.

When I spoke with food writers Phorum Dalal in Delhi and Joanna Lobo in Mumbai in 2019, both nominated millet as a trending food, typically eaten by urbanites in contemporary cafés as the base of a salad topped with globally trending ingredients such as broccoli, avocado, roasted pumpkin, halloumi cheese, and olive oil dressing—the humble millet, 'poor man's food' was now mixing with the latest in fashionable ingredients. At the Godrej 2020 Food Trend Report launch event in Delhi, amidst conversations on trends in sustainable food, local food, unexplored Indian foods, and the longing for authentic home food, the topic of millets kept surfacing. At the 2019 Tasting India Symposium, millets were also a significant topic of discussion, with panelist Joanna Kane-Potaka of the International Crops Research Institute for the Semi-Arid Tropics (ICRISAT) telling the audience, 'You are going to have to get used to eating millets [as] these are the food of the future.' Browsing the shelves of organic and gourmet food stores in Delhi, Mumbai, and Chennai over the past several years, I have found millet-based breakfast cereals, crackers, biscuits, brownies, pasta, and snack foods. These upmarket stores, like high-end restaurants, often lead the way in food trends, and what is on the shelves here can influence what ends up on the shelves of food stores catering to the broader market. My perception is that the growing popular interest in millet is not so much for its qualities as an environmentally sustainable food source, rather for its nutritional profile and reported health benefits. Millets are a source of complex carbohydrates, micronutrients, protein, and dietary fibre. The constituent elements of millets are claimed to be efficacious in reducing diabetes, cardiac problems, blood pressure, obesity, and colon cancer, as well as 'halting' the ageing process—a global vanity issue arguably more influential than actual health concerns—and aiding in weight loss (an example as per the earlier discussion).[74] All of which has led millets to be proclaimed as a 'superfood', potentially the 'next quinoa for the westernized markets [of India]'.[75]

December 2019. Before investigating the elevation of millets to 'super' status, we are going to detour to Hyderabad to the ICAR-Indian Institute of Millets Research. Like Amul, this place had been on my food travel wish list for some time. I had hoped to participate in the millet cookery course the institute runs; unfortunately, my visit did not coincide with its scheduling. Anyway, I was happy to be shown around the experimental millet fields, productive on the edge of the city, and the laboratory–workshop–incubator complex where ICAR develops and prototypes new machinery to process millets from harvest into ready-to-eat products, transferring this technology to external companies to commercialize into the wider market. I am always fascinated to see how food is commercially processed, and enjoyed looking over machines that turned millet into different types of pasta and noodles—thin ragi vermicelli, foxtail macaroni elbows, and small delicate jowar shells—another, resembling a stainless steel cannon, that agitates whole millet and shoots it out as cereal puffs; there was a conveyor belt oven specifically designed for baking millet biscuits; cereal-packing machinery and an array of small mills, cleaners and graders, flaking machines, mixers, and roti cutters, all with enhanced capability for processing millets into consumer-ready foods. Incubator manager, Siddharth Agarwal, says ICAR's work developing technology to process millets into 'modern format products' plays an important role in helping the general public 'rediscover' millets by making it 'relevant' to their needs, i.e., easy and convenient to prepare. I was able to visit the test kitchen, where the cookery classes are held and the institute's home economists develop and test millet recipes for commercial products and cookery books designed for domestic cooks, to help them learn to use millets in regional and contemporary formats.[76] The kitchen walls were lined with pictures of millet fashioned into all types of regional staples and popular pan-Indian dishes: puttu, dhokla, patra, khichdi, pulao, ladoo, pakora, pongal, kheer, barfi, samosa, biryani, and upma, along with more contemporary foods, including pizza, chocolate pudding, pancakes, brownies, leavened bread, and even sorghum chocolate.

The scientists, engineers, and technologists working at ICAR are committed to reinstating millets as a major food source for the wider Indian population. ICAR's principal scientist Dr B. Dayakar Rao believes millets will play an important role in creating nutritional equity for all Indians, saying that they were also 'good for farmers because they do not cost much to grow' and 'good for the climate as they are carbon neutral and naturally organic'. However, he described the 're-discovery' of millets by the already well-nourished sections of Indian society as largely due to the focus on the purported health benefits of consuming these.[77] Rao, scientist that he is, pointed out that some of the health claims made for millets have some evidence to support them and that others need more research. Nonetheless, he was happy for the attention being paid to millets by the 'health and wellness industry as it is good for the millet business'. Hopefully, it will also be good for farmers who grow millets in the long run. In 2022, it was reported that farmers are not getting fair prices for their millet grains, despite the high prices urban consumers are willing to pay for it (relative to wheat), due to the labour-intensive process of de-husking it. There is work being done to develop contemporary de-husking machines to solve this problem.[78] Now, you might think me a naysayer, but let us hope that these emerging technologies do not result in the same unintended consequences of the Green Revolution and cause naturally sustainable millets to become something other than that in order to meet the demand for them.

Word Processing

Food is also 'processed' with words to make it more palatable. In agricultural parlance, millets are 'coarse' cereals and wheat is a 'fine' cereal. While farmers use these descriptors to indicate specific textural qualities in grains, these words might be understood in the broader population to indicate other qualities, e.g., coarse—rough, harsh, or vulgar; fine—high quality, exceptional, first-rate. It might then be inferred that people who eat coarse grains are crude and people who eat fine grains are more refined. I might be stretching things with this particular example, but foods have been imbued with moral qualities—good/bad, healthy/unhealthy, clean/unclean, pure/impure—since antiquity. Endowing particular foods, or eating regimes, with immaterial virtues, or otherwise, is more often shaped by the cultural ideas, customs, and preferences of a society, than by bodily reality or nutritional science. What any of us believe about what we should or should not eat— barring foods that are outright poisonous—is largely socially constructed, that is, we make these 'rules' up to suit the circumstances of time and place and to justify certain lifestyles.

> Culture defines what can and what cannot be eaten. But not only that, culture also distinguishes between good and bad, correct and incorrect edibles.[79]

In traditional Hindu dietetics, guidelines for eating and drinking, what any person eats plays an essential part in maintaining sociocultural notions of caste identity, social status, and ranking. According to this system, eating foods decreed as *tamasic*, such as onions and garlic, are said to increase dark moods, laziness, and an excessive desire for sex; *rajasic* foods, all the 'tempting foods', inflame passion and ambition, making the mind restless and uncontrollable; *sattvic* foods are held to cool the senses and those who eat a diet of these are pure, wise, happy, and joyful.[80] 'Upper castes will [often] not eat onions, garlic, or processed food, believing them to violate principles of purity'.[81] These cultural rules about food are enmeshed with a persistent system of social hierarchy, and eating a *sattvic* diet confers the most distinction on those who can afford to be as selective, and/or restrained, in what they eat. In a contrasting example, continental Europeans hold onions and garlic in high regard. In the nineteenth century, the British claimed kodo millet, widely used in southern Tamil Nadu, was toxic and proposed banning it. There was no evidence to support this claim, instead it derived from a British cultural belief that western grains, wheat, oats, barley (all the 'fine' cereals), were 'higher staple foods' than India's indigenous millets and rice.[82] Moral judgements of food are not artefacts of history, though: these are stronger than ever. Take the global 'ideology' of 'clean food'—equally entangled with socio-economic class—of which the acclaimed food writer Bee Wilson says:

> [It] quickly became clear that 'clean eating' was more than a diet; it was a belief system, which propagated the idea that the way most people eat is not simply fattening, but *impure* [my italics].[83]

From Humble to Super[ior]

Millet has recently undergone a moral transformation; it has shifted from being a primitive poor man's food, 'fit only for animals', to being hailed as a superfood, a nutricereal, and an *adbhut anaj*, a miracle or noble grain.[84] What has changed? Millets have not; instead, they have been re-valued for their age-old properties. It is the words used to describe millet that have altered, words that have made this cereal food more palatable (pun intended) to an urban Indian market focused on a relationship between food and health. The term 'superfood' is understood to indicate foods that promote well-being because they purportedly contain more nutrients than others, and the superfood label has transformed foods that were once negatively seen as low-class and used to discriminate against communities that ate these as backward and uneducated into 'healthy, desirable' commodities for a global westernized market.[85] Yet, this term has no scientific basis and is nutritionally meaningless as it originated in the marketing department of an American fruit company to sell more bananas.[86] 'Superfood' is just a buzzword, a selling strategy.[87] The foods labelled as 'super' are typically minimally processed plant foods—vegetables, fruits, grains, nuts, herbs, and spices—inarguably nutritious foods, but not necessarily better than any other food from the 'earth, trees, or animals . . . which in their largely unprocessed forms . . . are healthful by definition'.[88]

The claims for the superiority of designated 'superfoods' is often based on weak science or no evidence at all, and in some cases, the research upon which health claims are made for particular foods is often industry-funded, as in the case of chocolate.[89] Whole wheat, for example, has approximately the same amount of protein, carbohydrate, and fibre as millets: finger millet has more calcium than wheat; wheat has more phosphorus (essential for bone health and moving muscles) than millets; millets have more fat than wheat.[90] The overall nutritional value of whole wheat is comparable to millets; wheat just lacks fashionable buzzwords to elevate it to the 'super' status. I am not arguing against millets, my purpose is to show how we are influenced to think about food to suit commercial imperatives that are not actually about health. I think the environmental benefits of cultivating millets are paramount, which is an example of a moral claim for a food. What I am saying is that I *believe* environmental concerns should be *valued* over other interests. Someone else might believe that growing enough food for everybody in a population outweighs environmental considerations. Why does it matter if any particular food is called a 'superfood' as long as it is nutritious? It matters because it is a marketing manipulation designed to get consumers to buy more of a food and pay more for it, and the more expensive the food, the more value it gains, feeding into inimical social divides. This is another moral judgement on my part; if I were in business, I might think of this as fair play. In urban India now, the cost of a kilo of ground millet is double that of atta, which is in stark contrast to my experience of millet in rural India where it is the staple food of some of the country's poorest communities.

When I visited the tribal district of Gumla in Jharkhand, I ate momos made from finger millet flour, instead of wheat flour, as this grain is the staple food in this low-income region. Aruna Tirkey, an Oraon woman who runs Ajam Emba, a restaurant specializing in local indigenous recipes in Jharkhand's capital city of Ranchi, says that the resurgence of interest in millets in the urban market through its promotion as 'organic and healthy' might be stymied if 'steep prices make it inaccessible'. Tirkey's concern is that highly priced millet might prevent urbanites from eating it, but if a food's price is inflated because it is claimed to offer superior health benefits, it can distort the market the other way: Marketing millet as a superfood might actually make it unaffordable for the people who have relied on it and end up causing negative social and environmental impacts. Remember the expensive quinoa I bought in Delhi? The worldwide demand for this grain stimulated by calling it 'super' caused its price to skyrocket. Initially, this was good for poor Andean farmers as they earned more for their crops; then the global demand for quinoa led to mechanized production of it in other countries, including India, resulting in overproduction and price collapse. The situation has devastated many small Andean farmers; to try and compete, they switched from traditional farming to more intensive chemical-based production, causing soil degradation and the debt of failed investment.[91] Pronouncing the acai fruit as a 'superfood' has had similar consequences for the Amazonian communities who rely on it as a daily food. The ecological costs of transporting these foods across the globe to benefit the individual health of the world's wealthiest citizens, who already have plenty of food available to them, don't even merit a mention. Superior health claims for foods can potentially undermine the physical, and cultural, well-being of communities reliant on these foods.

Despite the health claims made for the so-called superfoods, there is little research to show that communities consuming these foods as a key part of their diet are any healthier, which should be the case if their food is indeed 'super'. And, if the communities that cultivate and grow foods such as millets enjoy improved well-being, perhaps it has more to do with the fact that they expend considerable labour to cultivate, harvest, and prepare their foods. Perhaps it is the fact of this effort that confers 'super' health benefits rather than any particular food. Makhana is another traditional food that has recently been given the 'superfood' makeover. It requires great effort to harvest and process these seeds of the water lily *Euryale ferox*, and the men who dive into ponds to scoop these from the mud often suffer from skin and respiratory problems from doing this work. I was astounded and incensed when I came across this recent claim about the benefits of eating makhana on a leading Indian food website:

[Fox nuts] slows down the aging process. Flavonoids present in the fox nuts are also antioxidants. It fights

> the free radicals and slows down the process of aging.
> It improves your health. Consuming makhana will
> help inhibit the aging signs like wrinkles, fine lines
> and premature greying of hair. So, start eating fox nuts
> now.[92]

This is a nonsense piece of health washing. Nothing can slow the ageing process, it is the price of human existence, and I find the avocation to eat natural foods to fight ageing quite an irony when it is a *natural* process. Most disturbing in this was the suggestion that eating makhana can inhibit ageing signs 'like wrinkles and fine lines'. This is not just rubbish, it is such a western concept, showing how urban India is taking on supposed 'health' concerns that they need not. From my observation, Indian skin ages very well, and Indians do not get the 'fine lines' westerners have become so obsessively worried about (interesting to note the use of 'fox nuts' as well as this is the western term for makhana). Yet again, this example shows why specific health claims for foods need to be questioned, and there is another moral judgment here: that the ageing process should be battled. If you like makhana, then include it in your diet. It is a nutritious food in the way all unprocessed plant foods are. But if it comes coated in artificial flavour and roasted in cheap oil, then it is little better than eating a packet of potato chips—potatoes, by the way, are also a nutritious food, a good source of Vitamin B6 and Vitamin C and have recently been magicked with the superfood wand in

Australia. The increasing consumption of makhana by urban Indians is good for the rural farmers who produce it, on the assumption that it is increasing their incomes, and as it is a food that grows abundantly naturally, it might be a better choice for the environment. But demand for makhana from urbanites willing to pay more for it has the potential to distort the food system of the communities who rely on it. Already there have been problems with the encroachment of ponds and wetlands in Bihar where most of it is grown.[93]

There are many food producers, usually small and artisanal, and retailers who take great care to ensure that their products are wholesome and as environmentally sound as possible. In my experience, they either do what they are doing as a matter of course and/or shy away from making hype-fuelled claims for their products. The increasing press of highly processed foods into India, supported by influential advertising campaigns of the type only huge corporations can afford, might make it necessary to push the health benefits of food to counteract the enticement of these denatured but convenient and attractively packaged and priced foods.

Promoting traditional foods is important to counter the increasing popularity of junk food in the country. We need to ensure that food does not become a sterile package designed for universal size and taste. This is what is happening today as we eat packaged food from plastic boxes.[94]

However, labelling any food as super, healthy, pure, or nutri to emphasize health claims for it is not necessarily useful in helping people to eat in a way that supports their overall health. Decreeing certain foods as superior to others can orient people to focus on these, ignoring other foods that are equally nutritious but unlabelled and un-hyped, potentially causing people to narrow down the variety of food they eat.

There are many contradictions and paradoxes around food in contemporary India, and food choices are taking place in an environment heavily influenced by the marketing of food corporations, food retailers, and incentivized 'influencers', with respect to the alleged health benefits of foods. It is just as important to be literate and critical of food whenever it is labelled in a way that suggests it is superior, healthier, clean, pure, or natural as it is to challenge the marketing and availability of ultra-processed foods. Journalist Michael Pollan is an influential thinker and internationally acclaimed author on food, cooking, and eating, including the widely referred to *Food Rules: An Eater's Manual*. His work acknowledges the challenges of eating well in a contemporary urbanized society. Although his opinions on food, cooking, and eating are not without fair criticism, I think his ultimate message is the simplest approach to a healthy way of eating: 'Cook most of the food you eat at home, from scratch. No corporation is going to look out for your health, no matter the promises.'[95]

6

India's Drinking Style

The Time It Takes to Make Fine Wine

The British author and critic Christopher Hitchens was an exceptional writer, a shrewd social commentator, and an 'unabashed admirer' of India.[1] I latterly discovered an article he had written on his observations of a changing subcontinent. It was insightful and charming, and I was enjoying reading it, until I got to the part where he described an Indian-made wine, a cabernet sauvignon, as tasting like 'shark repellent'. That got my back up. He said the wine had come from a vineyard near Bengaluru without naming it, but I knew the place he meant and I was familiar with the wine he wrote of; it did not deserve his derogatory description.[2] I then realized that while I was reading the article in 2020, it had been written in 1997, more than twenty years ago, when India's wine industry was small and fledgling. A more recent 2019 article in the *New York Times* by a 'seasoned [American] wine drinker' was hardly more complimentary about the Indian wines he and his wife tried when they visited several wineries in the Nashik region in Maharashtra, although he did write favourably of their travel experience there.[3]

I first tried Indian-made wine, a Grover rosé, around the same time Hitchens wrote his snide critique; unlike him, I enjoyed it and thought it was a good example of the style. Before this, I had been unaware that India produced any wine at all and have since followed the development of India's wine industry with interest, noting that year on year, the wine section of the liquor store in Delhi where I most regularly buy alcohol expands its selection of Indian wine. The wine is kept at the rear of the store, and you must squeeze past a perpetual scrum of men buying the hard liquor and beer that is kept on the shelves adjacent to the front counter, a layout clearly demonstrative of the respective sales volume of wine compared to spirits and beer. Often, when I brought up the subject of local wine with Indian wine drinkers, they would disdain it, automatically dismissing the native vintage as vastly inferior to imported products. I do not have a sommelier's palate, but I have had a solid wine education, and I think India is producing some good wine that needs to be considered in context, not in comparison to Château Lafite.

On my way to Sydney's airport in mid-2019 to take the flight that would begin the trip that would take me to Nashik, I was chatting with my taxi driver, David, an older gentleman, urbane and full of life's experience. When I mentioned I was travelling to India, he was delighted. He had been there some years ago and held fond memories of this time. When I told him that I was visiting India's wine region, he was surprised; he had no idea India produced any wine at all. He pressed me for more information; I gave him an overview and told him that people tended to report negatively on Indian wine, particularly that it was overly sweet. David, it turned out, was a bit of a wine connoisseur. He reminded me that Australia's now much-vaunted wine industry used to produce some very ordinary wines forty years ago. Before the 1980s, being a 'wine drinker' in Australia was considered by most as elitist or pretentious, and the most popular alcoholic beverages were beer, sherry, and port. To expand the market, Australian winemakers started to make what could be described as 'bridging products' to help people orientate their palates to wine, and many of those products were quite sweet—I remember my parents drank a sparkling wine at this time called Passion Pop that was as palatable as a sugary soft drink. While Hitchens would have choked on these products, they were approachable for the novice, gently nudging them into the wine market. Over the subsequent decades, Australians have markedly sophisticated their understanding and appreciation of wine, and it has become inextricably linked with our food culture. David and I agreed that India was probably somewhat akin to Australia in the 1980s with respect to the development of its indigenous wine industry.

A Complicated History

When I told Australian friends that I was planning to visit India's main wine region, they unfailingly, like David, expressed surprise, saying 'I did not know India made any wine', but what I found interesting was that this comment was often followed by another that went something along the lines of 'I thought Indians didn't drink [alcohol]'. When I asked them why they thought this, the answers were also similar: 'Because their religion does not allow it' or 'I did not think it was part of their culture'. Underlying this was the idea that India had some ancient prohibition on alcohol. If you were to describe India's relationship with alcohol, a very contemporary 'it's complicated' would be accurate, these complications having evolved over the course of India's long documented history.

India's material history indicates that her experience in producing alcoholic beverages began (at least) 5000 years ago with the citizens of the Indus Valley civilization, who fermented and distilled grains to make various liquors. As we do not know what these people's values were, we do not know what cultural or social role this alcohol played in their lives, but presumably they drank it.[4] In his authoritative work on India's food history K. T. Achaya details the mention of alcoholic beverages across Vedic literature, suggesting that production and consumption of these was part of life during the time these works refer to.[5] In Vedic cosmology, one of the oceans encircling the seven concentric island continents that make up the world is constituted of wine.[6] Given that the other six are made up of elements essential either to human life or the foundations of the Indian diet—salt water, sugar cane juice, ghee, yoghurt, milk, and sweet water—this also suggests that wine held some significance for that culture. By the later Vedic period, the consumption of alcoholic beverages was sanctioned, in the literature, only for use at ceremonies and condemned otherwise. Perhaps because it was indulged in too enthusiastically, and those with the societal authority to do so considered its use should be repressed to discourage habitual alcohol consumption.[7] Regardless, it seems that liquor continued to have been widely consumed.

'It may be stated that, except for gambling, the greatest vice of the Aryan race in India was drinking.'[8]

In the great Hindu epics of the post-Vedic period, the Mahabharata and Ramayana, frequent references to the production and consumption of alcoholic beverages continue with their use being described in both social and ceremonial situations.[9] However, the general Seleucus Nicator, who had accompanied Alexander to India in 326 BCE and returned again some years later to attempt to take over the territory of Chandragupta Maurya, is reported to have written that the Indian population he observed (in the north), 'never drink wine except at sacrifices'.[10] Early Tamil literature also includes many references to the production and consumption of alcoholic beverages, while the precepts of Buddhism and Jainism recommended abstinence from any intoxicants.[11] All in all, what emerges from the historical record is that a complex attitude to the production and consumption of alcoholic beverages was well developed in India by the early medieval period.[12]

It is important to understand that the core beliefs and practices with the Hindu traditions have, over the millennia, interwoven permissive alcohol use patterns in some parts of society with strong anti-alcohol restrictions, particularly for the high-caste Brahmins. The Vedic scriptures set the tone of ambivalence quite clearly—strong drink is part of religious ritual in some situations; is a regular part of important social occasions, yet it is sinful and dangerous. The complex history of India has produced sharply different patterns of relationships to alcohol use in the different ethnic, religious, and caste communities.[13]

While alcohol is technically prohibited in Islam, when India was under Muslim rule, it remained part of court life during the Sultanate and Mughal periods. It was not until Aurangzeb took the throne in the seventeenth century, some two hundred years into his family's dynastic reign, that there was an official proclamation against it.[14] Nonetheless, by the time the British co-opted rule of India in the nineteenth century, the Indian population was producing and drinking a huge variety of alcoholic beverages across the subcontinent fermented and/or distilled from rice, the sap of palms, millet or barley, flowers, and sugar cane. These 'country liquors' were made in small batches in the home or by a local bootlegger. Alcohol was not used as an ingredient in Indian food though. It was the British who introduced mass brewing of beer and distillation of spirits, taking arrack and turning it into rum and creating the commercial alcohol industry in India—a legacy still evident in the naming of liquor stores as 'English wine shops', an amusing misnomer as these rarely stocked any wine until recently, and England is not a wine-producing country.

In the early twentieth century, Indian nationalists actively campaigned for the prohibition of alcohol because the British had created, and subsequently controlled, the commercial production and retailing of alcohol. They believed selling alcohol exploited the poor, and 'commercially distributed alcohol was viewed as an unpopular imposition of English rule and drinking a peculiarly English vice'.[15] Gandhi called alcohol an 'evil' plaguing India and stressed the urgent need for its abolition.[16] This attitude was incorporated into the Constitution of independent India in Article 47, which directs the state to bring about the prohibition of alcohol. However, the Constitution also allows state control of all aspects of the production and sale of liquor, and each state operates its own regulations, duties, and taxes on alcohol; several states prohibit it and most others levy high taxes on it, making it expensive to buy from a retail store and creating a complicated and complex financial, legal, and logistical system around the production, sale, and consumption of liquor across India. Another significant issue is that bootleggers serve less affluent drinkers in India, especially in rural areas. Their illegal brews often poison people, sometimes resulting in significant casualties.[17] Post-Independence, attitudes to drinking alcohol remained 'extremely ambivalent and contradictory'; it was either an 'affectation of the upper classes' or 'an atavistic trait of the poor tribal and other socially and economically marginalized sectors of society', and the middle-class abjured it, at least publicly.[18]

I think this historical legacy, whereby alcohol use has been overtly frowned upon in the middle class and hidden away in the social extremities on either side of this, contributes to outsiders imagining India to be a uniformly abstentious society. For Indian women who are economically powerless and living in more traditional communities, having a husband who habitually drinks can be 'devastating', and a disdain for alcohol and demand for its prohibition seems inarguable in these circumstances.[19] Still, the socially accepted use of alcohol in metropolitan India has evolved significantly over the past two decades.

A lot of people have restrictions in drinking at home. Even in wealthy families who come from certain communities [it was] not really okay to have alcohol at home. They normally will go out of the house to go to a restaurant to have a drink there and that's totally acceptable. So [closure of bars and restaurants during the 2020 lockdown] is something that's probably going to challenge that.[20]

Social Climate Challenges

India's winemakers face unique environmental challenges as well as social ones: The country's extreme climates—hot humid tropical, hot dry desert, hot and cold plains, cold mountain—limit the territory suited to the production of wine grapes. This has not hindered the development of wineries in suitable regions as viticulturists work out how to manage the vines in the prevailing conditions. That there are now more than sixty wineries operating in India, predominantly in Maharashtra and Karnataka, is a testament to their work. Perhaps the more considerable challenge to the development of India's wine industry is bureaucratic. Winemakers can learn to work with soil and climate, but the machinations of government are largely outside their remit. Bottled wine is the most heavily taxed alcohol in India because of its persistent status as an elite beverage, but conversely, the high tax makes it exclusive because it ups the price. Hotels have been permitted to import alcohol duty-free, and most imported liquor was consumed in five-star hotels, and as most wines were imported, it was largely drunk in these upmarket places, further embedding the idea of it as exclusive. It is considerably cheaper to buy a bottle of Indian-made whisky than a bottle of Indian-made wine, and as whisky has up to four times the amount of alcohol, it gives more 'bang for the buck'. Food writer Antoine Lewis pointed to Indian politicians' 'public aversion to alcohol . . . the official wine body is called the Indian Grape Processing Board even though its objectives are to aid the wine industry'.[21] In 2005, Maharashtrian politician and former federal agriculture minister Sharad Pawar put forward a proposal that wine be classified as a food item/ non-alcoholic beverage.[22] The motion didn't succeed, but the fact that this idea—that a beverage with an average of 12 per cent alcohol was not actually alcoholic—got a hearing says much about the complicated socio-political attitude to liquor in India.

Pawar is an exception when it comes to political shyness about alcohol as he is credited with starting the Indian wine industry. His long-held seat of Baramati has been India's largest producer of table grapes since the early twentieth century, since the environmental conditions there are favourable for viticulture. He worked to make the political climate more propitious as well. Maharashtra has the lowest tax regime in India on wine made in that state, hence it has the most wineries. Neighbouring Karnataka also has a more open attitude to wine production. It publicly calls its wine body the Karnataka Wine Board, encourages its farmers to grow wine grapes for local production and export because of the higher return on these, sets lower taxes on it, and actively promotes the state's wineries.

When I flew out of Delhi on my way to Nashik via Mumbai in June 2019, it was a hot, dry summer morning. It was very different 1000 kilometres away in the sky above the Maharashtrian capital where we circled for an hour waiting for a break in the monsoon rain to land. On the ground, squalling wind and rain rocked my Nashik-bound train along the 170-kilometre-long route. From the station there, my auto-driver had to do some nifty manoeuvres through storm water surging across the town's roads to get me to my hotel (winning my gratitude and a generous tip). I felt like I had outrun a tempest. Mother Nature in a turbulent mood might have chased me all the way to Nashik, but she was beneficent when she made this place. Perched on the western edge of the Deccan Plateau, its 986-metre-high elevation bestows it with a milder version of the tropical climate of the lowland it overlooks. In the cool season, the days are warm, the nights fresh and nippy, and the air is bone dry—ideal conditions for growing wine grapes, and more than half of India's wineries are located in this region.

Rajeev Samant, the founder of Sula winery, planted the first vineyard in Nashik in 1996, and his company has since grown into India's most successful wine brand. It made sense to put Sula on the top of my visiting list because of its role as an industry leader; however, my motivation was also personal. I had been enjoying Sula sparkling and chenin blanc for years, and I was curious to see where these wines were coming from, and it turned out to be the perfect place to learn more about the changes in India's contemporary wine culture.

Karan Vasani is the chief winemaker at Sula. After showing me around the production facilities—towering steel holding tanks reached on long ladders, racks of neatly stacked wooden wine barrels, forklifts moving pallets of boxed bottles, the whole place sparkling clean—and talking about the technicalities of the winemaking here, we headed up to the Tasting Room Bar, one of the several public spaces at the winery. As we settled in to taste some wine on the spacious canopied veranda overlooking the vineyards across to the nearby Gangapur Lake, I noticed a large family group at a nearby table. The adults were relaxed, drinking wine, and eating snacks; their children were playing around the area making forays back to the table from time to time to take a bite of some food. I told Karan that I was surprised to see this scene because it was incongruent with my experiences of public drinking in India, i.e., it was not a pastime you saw families doing together. He told me they had deliberately made the bar area casual and approachable because Indians, in the main, are 'already intimidated by wine' as they have had little exposure to it and because it has an 'elitist tag'. 'Indians are becoming more interested in wine, but they need places to come to experience it and feel comfortable in doing this. We have created this venue to offer that. This is helping to change people's attitude to wine.' According to Karan, the Indian palate has been most accustomed to beer and whisky, and people drank to get drunk, or at least to take the edge off things. So drinking wine for its flavour and taking it with food was a 'radical concept': 'India is still a socially conservative country, and we want to help people have an experience of wine as part of their lifestyle, part of spending time with family and not something to just get drunk on.' He also reiterated the Indian preference for sweetness in wines, and as Sula's market is largely domestic, its product needs to cater to this, at least while they, and other winemakers, educate the Indian palate. As an aside, I think wine styles with more 'sweetness' and viscosity pair well with spiced food and complement Indian cuisine.

An advantage of the warm and humid months in India's wine-growing regions is that a large variety of grapes can be grown, allowing for the production of more wine varieties than is usual in a single winery or even in a region. Sula produces sparkling white, rose and shiraz, chenin blanc—in sparkling, still, and dessert styles—riesling, chardonnay, sauvignon blanc, viognier, zinfandel, and grenache rosé. I think there were also others, but as we tasted more wine, I became a bit more relaxed and my note-taking eased off. Karan describes the current state of India's wine industry as the 'American wild west of winemaking . . . there is an amount of freedom to experiment, and we are trying anything and everything . . . being a winemaker in India right now is an interesting, challenging, and fun space to be in'. As Indians are at different stages of wine knowledge, creating a broad range of wine styles allows Sula to cater more broadly and bring people into the wine fold. Over time, they will likely narrow down the range of wine and concentrate on what works best in the climate and in the market. In the meantime, there is a lot of research, learning, testing, and innovation going on here.

It used to perplex me that Indian winemakers predominantly talked and wrote about pairing their wines with European-style food. I thought it would be better if they encouraged Indian consumers to understand wine as something to pair with Indian food if they wanted to expand the domestic market. I shared this opinion with winemakers at a wine show in Mumbai in 2010. Their response was that the Indian market was not ready for that because wine was seen as elite, with a sense of snobbishness about it, and people needed to see it presented as something to pair with foreign foods such that its status was maintained and its high cost could be justified. Happily, this is changing, and Indians are now keen to know how to pair wine with their everyday food. These are some of the great food and wine matches I tried at Sula:

- Sparkling chardonnay with papdi chaat—the crisp fine bubbles of this style pair very well with the tartness and rich textures of this dish.
- Riesling with fish tikka—the lower alcohol and sugar content of this wine makes it a good match for the smoky flavour of tandoor-cooked fish.
- Sauvignon blanc with chilli-garlic paneer—the bright texture and herbaceous palate of this wine stand up to the strong flavours of this dish.
- Sparkling shiraz with chicken in onion gravy—the full-bodied flavour and crisp finish of this red wine act as a counterpoint to the rich gravy.
- Shiraz with salli boti—red meat and red wine is a classic combination in European food culture, and one that is just as good with this traditional Parsi mutton dish.

Women, Wine, and Social 'Bars'

While I was working my way through some of the dishes described above at one of the restaurants on the Sula estate, three women came in to have dinner together. They ordered a bottle of red wine to have with their food and then a bottle of dessert wine to finish the meal. It is not unusual now to see women out on their own for dinner and drinks in restaurants in India's urban centres, but these particular diners caught my attention as they were older, conservative in their dress and demeanour, and looked like women I would not have expected to drink alcohol in public, if at all. They reminded me of the many times when I have been at social functions in India where the women sit together and sip soft drinks and gossip, and the men congregate at a distance and drink whisky and rum and gossip. I usually end up being invited to join the men so I can have a drink, in essence becoming an honorary man because I am a foreigner and not bound by prevailing social norms. I know some of these same women happily enjoy a peg or two or a glass of wine in their own homes but would never be seen taking an alcoholic drink at more public social gatherings. When I mentioned my musings about this to Sula's Disha Thakkar, she told me it is Indian women who buy the most wine.

Drinking alcohol has been especially taboo for women in India. Class, caste, religion, and family influence how true this might be in any individual case. Even so, a social attitude that women should not/do not drink alcohol lingers on. Traditional Indian social norms place demands on women when it comes to what they eat and drink, as they are expected to look after the bodily and spiritual well-being of their families both through cooking and by what they themselves consume, or otherwise, such as the practice of fasting one or two days a week 'for a husband's health and long life'.[23] They have been expected to avoid and disdain alcohol because it is associated with drunkenness, violence, disinhibition, immorality—read between the lines: if women drink, they might become sexually promiscuous—and ill-health.[24] Wine has a 'softer' image, different to the 'hard' liquor more commonly consumed; it is considered a more civilized and sophisticated drink, as well as being 'good for the heart', and as women are supposed to be more concerned with well-being, this makes it appealing to them.[25] Wine as soft, civilized, and healthy makes it socially safer for women to consume it, but the retail environment in which it is available to them can be a barrier to consumption.

> Women are much more comfortable to buy a bottle of wine if they don't have to go to that horrible liquor shop. Um, unfortunately, the way that liquor is treated in India, it's almost worse than hard drugs.[26]
>
> 'Girls can be intimidated at most liquor stores because guys try to letch or just look at you in a weird way,' says a 29-year-old media executive.[27]

A women-only liquor store operates in the Star Mall in suburban Delhi, so women can buy alcohol without being harassed by men. This mall is actually tenanted with a number of liquor stores because it is located close to the Delhi–Uttar Pradesh border in the heavily populated NCR, and as the taxes on alcohol are lower in Delhi than UP, the residents of this state do their booze shopping here.

> India has come a long way in its wine story . . . We now have wine clubs, regular wine dinners, festivals, awards,

competitions, weekly tastings of wines from all over the world . . . People can be seen in restaurants and bars across cities sipping on a glass of wine. They are curious about food and wine pairing. Restaurants and hotels take wine a lot more seriously, not just in terms of what they offer, but how they serve it too. You can see an overhaul in wine retail in some pockets of the big cities as well.[28]

While Sula is at the forefront of the wine revolution in India, Karan said that 'the pace of change with wine [in India] remains slow, even though everything else is really fast', and only 10 per cent of Indians drink wine, averaging a mere one glass each a year between them. Even so, that is more than a 100 million glasses annually, most of which is consumed in Mumbai, Delhi, and Bengaluru in restaurants, cafés, and bars—where I have often observed people drinking more than one glass—and wine is increasingly finding a place as part of a metropolitan lifestyle in India. The country has huge potential as a wine market in the future: There are 700 million Indians above the legal drinking age, and international wine houses, including French icon Moet Hennessy and Pernod Ricard, one of the biggest wine companies in the world, are keenly building partnerships with Indian wine companies to develop this industry.

The Indian consumer palate has evolved significantly from a decade ago. Rapidly changing demographics, increasing access to overseas education, growth in foreign tourism and widening exposure to new cultures have brought upon a very positive impact on the consumption of wine. Even with higher-than-average tariffs.[29]

When I contacted Mumbai-based food writer Rushina Munshaw Ghildiyal in 2019 to arrange an interview with her at her cookery studio, she also organized a dinner there that same evening, inviting a diverse group of 'food people' for me to meet, who each brought a dish for a fabulous potluck dinner. Amongst the guests were Karan Upmanyu, just ranked as a finalist in that year's prestigious international San Pellegrino Young Chef award—who made us 'world class' kachoris that I ate far too many of—archaeologist and food historian Kurush Dalal and his wife Rhea who together run the Parsi catering business Katy's Kitchen, organic farmer, provedore, and environmental activist Gaytri Bhatia, Assamese cookery entrepreneur Gitika Saikia, author and Marathi food expert Saee Koranne-Khandekar, food writer Roshni Bajaj, Authenticook founder Aneesh Dhairyawan, food media specialist Ruchi Shrivastava, writer and producer of Lost Recipes, Shubhra Chatterji, and Shatbhi Basu, whom Rushina introduced as 'India's first female bartender', an introduction suggestive of an interesting story.

It had only been a few years before this meeting with Shatbhi that I had seen female bartenders working in contemporary restaurants in Delhi and Bengaluru, whereas she had been making drinks for others professionally for more than two decades. She told me she came into bar work by accident, discovered she enjoyed it, could see it held opportunity, and decided to pursue a career in it. Shatbhi eventually established her own bartending academy, appeared on three seasons of a television show, consulted for major beverage companies, hotels, and restaurants, and established an industry conference and cocktail competition. I remarked that it must have taken a lot of determination for a woman to do that in India all those years ago. 'Yes,' she said, 'it took quite a bit of persuasion for my family to accept that was what I wanted to do.' Despite the recent appearance of more women mixing up cocktails behind bars, she said change was slow as 'alcohol remains a no-no for girls if they want to get married . . . for a woman to work in a bar in India even now, it requires an evolved family and a passion-driven determination'. Her bar classes are very popular with women, though, eager to learn more about whisky, mixing cocktails, and 'demystifying' wine. Shatbhi believes the attitude to women and alcohol will change over time as younger generations refuse to take on archaic social viewpoints. She is less confident about wholesale changes in alcohol regulation and the 'weird laws that exist from state to state', expecting most governments to continue to toe a conservative line on this to appease constituents who believe liberalization of alcohol will lead to social chaos. She pointed to Goa as a popular place for experimenting with spirits and liquors because the taxes on alcohol are lower there due to the more relaxed, European-influenced sociocultural attitudes and the thriving international tourism industry.[30]

Spirit of India

Spirits and beer remain the most popular alcoholic drinks in India and there is a lot of experimentation and development going on in this sector of the alcohol industry as well. Shatbhi noted a clear trend towards producing liquor products that are distinctly Indian, as exampled by this description of an Indian-made orange liqueur:

> A blend of premium triple distilled Indian grain spirits, pure sugars and the natural essential oils of renowned bitter-sweet oranges from the Nagpur region of India.[31]

Small- and medium-size distilleries are producing distinctive craft whisky, rum, and gin, and reinventing age-old Indian alcoholic drinks such as mahua, arrack, feni, kesar kasturi, and toddy, a trend that will undoubtedly continue in line with the renewed interest in regional food. The northeast states should prove an interesting source in this regard as there are many different fermented and distilled beverages quietly made there yet to be 'discovered' by urbanites. Wanting to reclaim the gin and tonic as a drink of Indian origin, albeit an invention of the British to stave off malaria, and give it a contemporary makeover, Delhi-based Nao produces a Himalayan dry gin flavoured with native juniper and mountain botanicals. When I joined

Rishek Khattar for dinner at Comorin, the restaurant in Gurugram he has been involved in establishing as part of his father's restaurant group, to talk about contemporary food, I was just as impressed with the drinks menu as I was with the regional and nostalgia-inspired food selection. He told me that the regulations around imported alcohol in Haryana were so complicated, randomly changing from year to year, that they had started making their own spirits and liquors at Comorin to ensure supply, experimenting in the process with using local ingredients and flavours to produce products such as khus vermouth and Indian fennel liquor. Alongside of the emergence of all these interesting Indian-made liquors has been the development of a sophisticated cocktail culture utilizing these. I enjoyed several delicious cocktails of this type while I was talking with Rishek at Comorin. Needless to say that the effect of the alcohol I consumed has reduced my memory of this to the overall pleasure of new discovery, but I clearly remember the care taken to ensure the purity, shape, and size of the ice used best complimented the drinks. A very refined touch.

Microbreweries producing small batches of beer and cider are popular with urban youth in places such as Bengaluru and Pune. While attending a writing conference at a university in the former place, I spent a couple of evenings at the Koramangala branch of the Social chain of bar-cafés where patrons are mixed gender, predominantly young, and with what I describe as a global 'tech' vibe—casual, high energy, a bit competitive. This place, and others like it in Indian cities, reflects global trends: Another case of 'You could be anywhere in the world' here.

When I flew into Delhi in July 2019, I landed in the evening and took a taxi to a friend's home near Gurugram. As we drove, we passed several large roadside liquor stores. It reminded me that the last time I had been on this road was eighteen years ago when another friend and I had driven out here on a hot summer night to buy some beer because the only other place we could have gone for a drink was a five-star hotel, and we were too casually dressed and too low on funds to do that. From the liquor vend we drove to a nearby parking spot and sat in the car and drank the beer as we watched planes land at the airport. From my observations, sitting in a vehicle and drinking is a common pastime across India for men, perhaps because they cannot do this at home due to social stigma. Given what I could see of bars, outside of hotels, that I passed by in many of the various towns I have been in in India, these did not appear to be inviting places; for one thing, the windows were often blacked out, and I assumed the intention of this served both as discouragement to enter in the first place (how could you know what was going on inside) and privacy for those who were in there indulging a habit widely considered undesirable.

In my conversations with winemakers, journalists, and restaurateurs, I asked them what they saw as the key influences on the growing interest in wine, the development of local spirits, and the changing attitudes to alcohol and drinking in India. They cited exposure to seeing others drinking more freely on television and social media and experiences of more liberal and relaxed drinking cultures through travel and overseas education as the key drivers of this change. This exposure, both virtual and real, was also influencing the adoption of global trends in drinking, such as microbreweries, and distinctive local flavours in spirits. A younger demographic curious to try new things, socialize more widely and date more freely, along with a higher level of disposable income that gives them the wherewithal to experiment with new flavours and experiences were other salient factors noted as influences.

The restrictions of the COVID-19 crisis sparked a push to legalize home delivery of liquor, a change food delivery companies are eager to see implemented, anticipating this service as an additional source of revenue.[32] However, in 2022, it appears that it is only possible to order alcohol via apps in bigger cities in Orissa, West Bengal, and Jharkhand.[33] Ostensibly, Delhi made some provision in its licensing regulations to allow alcohol to be delivered to private residences if it is ordered and paid for online, but it is unclear whether this was actually implemented; even if it was, I expect this would now be rescinded given the most recent changes in Delhi's liquor laws, but we will come to this a little further on.[34]

While enjoying a Christmas eve drink with a Chennai-based friend there in 2019, I commented that the growth in bars and free-standing (as opposed to hotels) licensed restaurants I had noticed in other major Indian cities was not apparent there. She said Chennai on the whole was 'still really funny about alcohol . . . places get club licenses, but no one knows how long that will stay valid for . . . it is tenuous with each change of government, no one can be sure what the laws actually are'. She said that these circumstances had prevented the development of bars and a more open drinking culture in this city as business owners are reluctant to open venues, concerned that they might have a licence one year and then have it rescinded the next. This is not to suggest that Tamilians are all teetotallers, but public aversion to alcohol has political expediency in this city, which keeps the social enjoyment of alcohol largely confined to homes. Consumption of alcohol carries less social stigma in Kerala. In fact, the state is known for its toddy, the fermented sap extracted from coconut palm made in small batches by families whose traditional work is to make it. This is widely sold across the state from places referred to as 'toddy shops', which are equally known for serving good robust local food to go with the drinks. Visiting a toddy shop for a meal is something many families do together, and it has become a recommended experience for tourists visiting the state.[35] However, the consumption of alcohol in the state is concerningly high, which caused the Kerala government to propose working towards a total prohibition of liquor to counter this in 2015. The announcement of this intention created confusion and chaos in the alcoholic beverage sector, with ongoing changes to what is permitted with respect to the vending of liquor and what is not since then. These restrictions do not appear to have succeeded in diminishing the consumption, resulting in some 'odd' developments to ensure that alcoholic drinks can be sold:

> Now, three years on, the number of bars has gone up by at least 20 times to 540 bar hotels . . . A major development is the increase in the number of clubs licensed to sell alcohol . . . As many as 41 clubs registered under the Charitable Society Act have liquor licence while their number was a mere 19 in 2009 . . . It's strange that clubs registered under Charity Act sell liquor.[36]

One evening in early August 2022, just as I was about to finish the final edit of this chapter, I came across the news that the Delhi government had scrapped its Delhi Excise Policy 2021–22. The implementation of this policy in 2021 had seen the government exiting from retailing of liquor and the closure of government-run liquor stores, such as the one I mentioned I bought wine from, handing over its retail to private enterprise. This, according to a news report, aimed to end 'the liquor mafia and black marketing, increase revenue and improve consumer experience, and ensure equitable distribution of liquor vends across the city'.[37] The newly established private liquor vendors were permitted to set their own prices and took to offering significant discounts, such as two for the price of one on bottles of spirits, to attract customers. Unsurprisingly, this was a very effective strategy to bring in crowds of buyers, which subsequently caused protests against this practice, resulting in stores being prohibited from discounting liquor. Irregularities in the application of this excise policy were also said to have been found—I profess I could not understand the machinations of this—resulting in the announcement on 31 July 2022 that it was to be entirely abandoned. A few days later, the Delhi government then announced that it would be opening 700 liquor outlets, including ' five premium liquor shops that will be set up in posh districts, malls, and large markets'.[38] I am not sure what this means for the private liquor vendors whose licences have been taken away, but it is a powerful demonstration of the complexity of policy and social attitudes with respect to alcohol in India.

Despite all the varied challenges of buying, selling, and consuming liquor in India, a dynamic industry producing wines and spirits uniquely expressing Indian terroir has emerged; educators are helping Indian consumers develop sophisticated palates; and restaurateurs and hoteliers are creating places for people to explore new beverages and pair wine with food in relaxed cosmopolitan surroundings. In his 2020 book *Masala Lab: The Science of Indian Cooking*, author Krish Ashok even encourages Indians to use alcohol as an added ingredient in their cookery to heighten the flavour of Indian dishes.

7

Waste: The End of the Line

The Mountains of Urban India

31 December 2019. R and I are driving back to Delhi from Patiala, Punjab. We have chosen a return route along minor back roads to explore a part of this state neither of us is familiar with, driving for miles alongside fields of winter crops: fledgling green wheat, the sunny yellow of mustard flowers, compact pale green cabbages, creamy cauliflower heads, and low bushes weighed with plump eggplant, sometimes pacing alongside the fast-moving water of the Sirhind canal, winding up in Kurukshetra in Haryana, excited to be in this place of historical-mythic significance—although it relies entirely on imagination to conceive of the events of Mahabharata taking place in this hectic rural conurbation. Out on the main highway, we are slowed by tractors pulling carts bulging with just harvested sugar cane and long lines of traffic backed up at successive tollbooths—never was a road more tolled. The journey

takes several hours longer than expected, and the early winter evening has started to settle in, turning the sky a soft violet-grey by the time we reach the outskirts of Delhi. As we head towards the city, the landscape evolves from sprawling agro-industrial into urban density, twinkling with the light of homes, roadside vendors, and small stores. Suddenly, I notice a distinct change in the atmosphere around us; it feels like we have been plunged into the dark of deepest night. I look out to my left and there seems to be a void—a vast black empty space. Then, I notice a patch of glowing, undulating, deep orange seemingly floating above this abyss. Someone of a more religious orientation might have taken this as a vision, but it was a fire. At the time, Australia was being devastated by bush fires of such magnitude that the situation was dominating international news headlines, so I found this eerie. I asked R, 'What are we driving past?' He looks to my side and says, 'It's a rubbish tip, the Bhalswa landfill.' I looked up this place when we arrived home; it had supposedly been decommissioned a decade before because its capacity was exhausted, yet it has continued to be necessarily used to contain waste generated by the capital's citizens.

The fire I had seen was fuelled by methane gas oozing from the depths of compacted decomposing refuse that had spontaneously combusted, a perpetual occurrence at the site. On the eastern side of Delhi, the Ghazipur landfill has grown so large that it has become infamous, making local and international headlines such as 'The Mount Everest of Trash', 'India's mountain of trash is nearly as tall as the Taj Mahal', and 'Despair over Delhi's deadly rubbish dump'. Inextinguishable methane-fuelled fires burn here almost constantly, spewing toxic smoke and fumes over the surrounding district and up into the atmosphere.[1] These are just two of the massive rubbish tips into which Delhi pours its discards. Every major city in India has similar dumping sites, typically located on its outskirts: Deonar in Mumbai, Dhapa landfill in Kolkata, Perungudi landfill in Chennai—'as high as a two-storey building'. Bengaluru differs in that it dumps its waste around villages twenty kilometres outside the city—out of sight, out of mind.[2] India's rubbish tips are emitting noxious gases, poisoning waterways, and undermining the health of people living in proximity to these.

> Consumption [is] a dynamic, multi-level process that starts with the emergence of needs and desires and comprises the gathering of information about products, purchasing decisions and acts of purchasing, and use and transformation (for example, by cooking) of goods and services, and goes all the way to waste disposal.[3]

Food consumption is intertwined with waste: bodily excretions, compostable refuse, and discarded packaging are the end products of the food production and consumption cycle. The accelerating growth of India's metropolitan rubbish dumps is largely a problem of urbanization: a rapidly growing and densely packed population, lack of commensurate infrastructure, inefficient waste management systems, and a relatively high per capita income that allows people to consume more and, thereby, produce more waste.

> Waste generation increases with increasing income . . . open waste burning increases with increasing prosperity levels, particularly where waste collection systems often fail to keep track with changing consumption habits.[4]

It is the world's wealthiest people who generate the most garbage: Americans send 150 times more waste into tips than the average Indian; Australians produce similar levels. It is completely understandable that Indians who can afford it would want to also enjoy the seeming convenience and comfort afforded by the consumption-focused lifestyle of Americans and Australians, but the sheer number of people in India amplifies the magnitude of waste this type of living generates—Delhi alone houses more people than live across the entire Australian continent—it is this same population statistic that also makes India such an attractive market for producers of consumer goods.[5]

Australia's vast size and small population mean we can hide our waste more easily, and up until the COVID-19 pandemic, we were offloading some of our rubbish and supposed 'recycling' onto places such as China and Indonesia: not something to be proud of.

As more urban Indians adopt a more consumerist way of living and replicate the lifestyle habits of western societies, they are generating more solid waste. The waste disgorged into India's urban tips is made up of all the material that households and businesses dispose of, including organic waste, plastic, glass, paper, e-waste, ash, and metal. Food and food packaging are part of this mix: Wealthier people buy more packaged food and they throw more food away because they can afford to do so.[6] India's plastic consumption has grown twenty times since liberalization, and more than half of all plastic waste is packaging waste—56 per cent compared to 40 per cent in Europe. Not all of this comes from food packaging but given the vastly increased range and availability of convenience foods in India, all packaged in some way to create this affordance, it is making a significant contribution to expanding India's rubbish tips.[7]

Resource-Conservative to Resource-Consumptive

India is going through what is known as a 'nutrition transition', a change in food consumption patterns from traditional diets based on fruits, vegetables, unprocessed cereals, and legumes to a western-style diet increasingly dominated by fats (edible oils), animal products (meat and dairy), and processed packaged food and beverages. There is a long way to go before India replicates the eating habits of the apotheosis of this transition, the USA, and I doubt it will ever come to that. Nevertheless, economic development has made exactly these types of foods more available, which is affecting change in Indian dietary habits—the mounting evidence that eating this type of diet has negative individual, social, and environmental consequences does not seem to be dampening Indian enthusiasm for it. The consumption of these kinds of foods has increased with rising prosperity, and it is in India's cities where there are more higher-income households.

Changing eating patterns are moving India from a resource-conservative country to a resource-consumptive society, in the process wrapping food up into more and more packaging when there was previously very little of it: yoghurt is a good example. Two decades on from my residential stint in Delhi when I had little choice but to make my own curd because of limited commercial availability, there is now a plethora of yoghurt products available, and flavoured yoghurt is one of the fastest-growing retail food categories in India. Go into any metropolitan food store in a prosperous neighbourhood, and there you will see it: rows and rows of yoghurt, most of it sold in plastic containers with foil and/or plastic lids and increasingly in single-serve tubs. Here is a product that most Indians eat every day that has gone from being zero waste, but requiring some effort to produce, to being available in a ready-to-eat form requiring no more effort than its purchase, making it a very 'convenient' food. On the day in 2019, when I had an early afternoon appointment to meet Chef Prateek Sadhu at Masque restaurant in Mumbai, I decided I would spend the morning walking from my Colaba accommodation to Charni Road station from where I would take a train to Mahalaxmi for this meeting. Walking the streets of a city is my favourite way of learning about a place and building an understanding of what the people who live there really eat and drink. I wander and observe what is going on around me, and when something takes my interest, I stop and explore it further. On this day, as I walked through the upmarket residential area of Churchgate, I noticed a Nature's Basket store and decided to go in and have a look around; it was a hot, sticky July day, and the air-conditioned store was a welcome refuge so I took my time inspecting the food products on offer there. At this time, Nature's Basket was marketing itself as a gourmet retailer trading in 'natural', 'healthy' food.[8] The shelves bulged with attractively packaged and labelled organic, sugar-free, gluten-free, and 'superfood' products. When I got to the fresh produce section, I was astounded to find every vegetable tightly wrapped in plastic film, including firm eggplants and cauliflower, hard cabbages, green papaya and mangoes, bunches of drumsticks, onions, garlic, ginger, and potatoes. This seemed like such a contradiction and a huge irony: A store trading on the idea that it sells 'natural' food to Indians concerned with their health, who are wealthy enough to pay the high prices charged here, stocks food that is packaged, often excessively, or, as with the vegetables, unnecessarily—the packaging plays a role in justifying the cost of these food products but has nothing to do with its nutritional value.

Waste produced predominantly for the comfort of the better off will be the critical element in India's relationship with waste.[9]

The Price of Convenience

What makes food convenient? Processing it into ready-to-eat meals, snacks, or meal components that cut down culinary labour is a key aspect. Packaging is another. Food packaging makes it easy for shoppers to pick food and beverage items off the shelf in a food store and carry these away: no mess, no fuss. The same is true for a worker in a warehouse filling an online order: They will be working to a time schedule; so the easier it is to grab items off the shelves, the faster and more efficiently they can work (potentially), and if robots end up doing this warehouse work in the future—which is already happening at Amazon in the USA—packaging will become even more critical when a mechanical device is doing the handling. Food packaging is critical to the supermarket/chain store model of food retail. Packaging is required to ensure items are efficiently and securely packed for transporting over long distances, such as from centralized warehouses. Packaged food is also considered more hygienic and affords further convenience of not having to be concerned about the cleanliness of food. The COVID-19 pandemic has heightened concern around food hygiene and safety in India, and purchasing packaged food will serve to assure consumers in this regard. Ordering home delivery of prepared food via an online platform is the most convenient commercial way to eat (not only do you not have to cook, you also don't even have to make the effort to go out to get it), and each order generates an average of 100 grams of packaging waste—sometimes more, for example, a thali with every individual item in its own receptacle. These services cannot send food out to customers without it being placed in containers and/or wrapped in packaging material, and the more Indians utilize food delivery services, the more waste this will generate.[10] During my conversation with Hyderabad-based tourism operator Jonty Rajagopalan, in that city in 2019, she said that she wished people could use their own containers for home delivered food because the 'waste is crazy. We are living it up without realizing the cost of it'.

Packaging is key to differentiating food products by brand rather than content. Sometimes, it is only the packaging that makes one item all that different from another. Fancy packaging can also upgrade a food and its price. In 1998, I took a course of treatment at a nature cure centre in Bhuj, where I was introduced to khakhra, a thin crisp whole-wheat cracker. I have been eating this traditional Gujarati snack ever since. In 2019, my friend Kavita and I were enjoying a hot drink in a contemporary bakery-cum-café-cum-food store in Chennai when I spotted a brand of khakhra presented in attractive contemporary packaging on one of the store shelves. I bought a box of it. These khakhras were vacuum sealed in the thin metallic packaging material that typically, and singularly, comprises the packaging of these, but the metal package had been placed inside a small cardboard box, like a pizza box, decorated with hip graphics, adding an additional layer of packaging. The khakhra was good but no better than the brand I usually buy for a third of the price without the fancy graphics and box around them. What you got for the extra money was a re-commodification of a food and some additional packaging to dispose of. Nearby this bakery was a modern café-style chai shop, Chai Walle, that I took to frequenting as it served good ginger tea. If you sat in the store to enjoy your chai, it was served in glass cups. The tea could be also delivered, but not, as I observed, by a boy carrying a wire holder of glasses of steaming tea. Instead, it was decanted into a rectangular cardboard box lined with a plastic insert and with a plastic spout through which the tea would be dispensed: I imagine this extensive packaging probably ends up in the garbage later. A glass of delivered Chai Walle chai is three times the price of the same from a street stall. However, the cost includes all the packaging that the kerbside chaiwallah does not offer. This khakhra and tea are just two examples of how commonplace Indian foods are being contemporized, to be charged at higher prices, by wrapping more packaging around these.

> We are treating convenience above everything else; it is a dangerous game we are playing . . . packaged food means a lot of waste.[11]

Food packaging facilitates convenience, novelty, differentiation, and food hygiene and safety; it can also reduce the cost of food because it allows for centralized mass production. But where does all the packing end up? A lot of it is swelling India's rubbish dumps. Any packaging offering the solace of being labelled 'biodegradable' might technically be so, but the process of biodegradation cannot occur in the compressed conditions of municipal rubbish dumps as there is no oxygen in there that is needed to facilitate the process.[12] Biodegradable packaging needs to be sorted out from other household waste going to the tip for it to be treated in a way that would allow it to degrade biologically. Encouragement and initiatives from different levels of government and civic authorities in urban India to get people to sort and separate rubbish and to recycle is certainly developing; I wonder, though, if consumers are choosing food products for their convenience, for the reduced effort these afford, will they then make the effort to sort their domestic refuse? And even if people sort items for recycling, the quality of packaging material used can limit its potential to be recycled. The cost of packaging adds to the price of a food product. If low prices are an attractor for consumers, all input costs need to be reduced, which often results in cheaper, lower quality packaging being used that may not then be able to be recycled because of its poor quality. At least the better-quality packaging used for more expensive food products has the potential to be recycled if the right conditions exist.

The kitchen at the Shree Jagannath Temple in Puri is said to be the biggest in the world. Every day, hundreds of Brahmin cooks work to prepare food for the temple's three presiding deities, and the many thousands of workers and devotees who come here. As a non-Hindu, I am barred from entering the temple or eating in its dining hall; however, I was able to avail of a packing service that allowed me to

enjoy a meal of the consecrated comestibles in my hotel
room on one of my visits to this sacred city. The food came
packed in clay pots covered with banana leaves and tied
down with strips of the same; the basket it came in was also
woven from this natural, and locally abundant, material, a
long-standing system of low-waste food packaging. India
holds vast knowledge about conserving resources, including
food, the type of practices recognized by the contemporary
environment movement as those the world needs to look
towards to make our existence more sustainable.

It reminds us that the wisdom of the past, as much as the
ingenuity of the present, can help us survive the future.[13]

India's domestic cooks have typically been very careful
with food, painstakingly using up rice-and-grain cooking
water, fruit and vegetable peels, leaves, stalks and seeds,
and leftover cooked cereals, to produce other dishes,
creating little, if any, waste. While the food habits of an
increasing number of Indians are changing towards the
type of consumer lifestyle that generates substantial waste
and sends much of it off to fester in dumps, it seems,
fortunately, that not all of it ends up there.

Households, itinerant waste merchants and garbage
collectors in India jointly recover 1.2–2.4 million tonnes
of newspapers, 2.4–4.3 million tonnes of cardboard and
mixed paper, 6.5–8.5 million tonnes of plastic, more
than 1.3 million tonnes of glass, more than 2.6 million

tonnes of metal waste and 4–6.2 million tonnes of other
recyclable material per year. Overall, 30–60% of all paper
and cardboard, 50–80% of all plastic and close to 100%
of all glass bottles produced in India are recycled.[14]

That India recycles so much of its waste is an admirable
track record, far exceeding that of many wealthy
industrialized countries. It is poor migrant workers who
do much of the work of sorting rubbish for recycling in
India's cities. If large numbers of these people continue
to stay out of cities after the pandemic-inspired exodus of
rural workers in 2020, I wonder who will do this work?
(Whether people should be working picking rubbish from
tips given the serious health consequences is another
issue). And if Indian consumers continue to grow their
consumption of packaged foods, and other goods, will the
system be able to cope? According to a 2021 report, there
are already not enough people, plants, or dealers in India's
separation and recycling system to cover all the recyclable
waste generated.[15]

In my conversation with Chef Sadhu, he cited food
waste management as a key challenge for contemporary
chefs, and he has installed a compost plant in his
restaurant's backend. Like Sadhu, there are many people
doing different things across urban India to reduce and
manage waste more effectively, but greater India faces
the collective challenge of balancing consumer spending
power with environmental imperatives. Weighing up
the ecological as well as the social and cultural costs of

'convenience' food against its benefits is part of this challenge for contemporary Indians.

> Hence, the role of the [cities'] middle classes, as consumers and as citizens, in shaping the politics of ecological transformation in post-liberalisation India merits scrutiny. For if double-income middle-class households with high disposable incomes and a consumerist lifestyle are responsible for the generation of large amounts of solid waste, the same class (though not necessarily the same sections of it) has developed sensitivity towards urban (and often also rural) environmental issues.[16]

What to do with food packaging waste should not necessarily only be the sole concern of the end-user, the consumer. There is growing expectation on producers to take more responsibility for the waste their products generate, and India is implementing a legislative approach to this known as the extended producer responsibility (EPR), 'to promote recycling and upcycling of non-biodegradable waste [such as plastics] . . . to prevent emissions from spiralling out of control with increasing prosperity levels and consumption', but 'the global experience on EPR in [plastic waste management] has been that large producers typically delay, distract, and derail promulgation and implementation of EPR regulations through a variety of tactics that influence consumers and policy makers'.[17]

Solving the problem of overall waste management in India will require 'joint initiatives from an array of entities such as the government, corporates, retailers, and of course the general public'.[18] Acknowledging again that food packaging is only a part of the waste generated, and that my observations about the low- or no-waste food system I experienced in India twenty years ago might well be considered 'romantic', it still seems that one of the more simple contributions that the 'general public' could make is to limit the amount of packaged food they purchase—'zero packaging' stores are now being suggested as a solution to food packaging waste in Australia.[19] But perhaps that is really romantic thinking: That would require a return to preparing meals from scratch or actually going out to a restaurant to eat a restaurant meal (less OTT time) or taking our own containers to be filled when purchasing pre-prepared food, but the convenience food genie is now well and truly out of the bottle in India, and industry and consumers will not want to put that particular djinn back inside. Let's hope someone out there is developing edible packaging.

8

Food for the City

December 2020. On an early summer day, my mother and I set out from her home in rural Victoria to drive 180 kilometres to the nearest coast. The route, from beginning to end, passed through some of the best agricultural lands in Australia, producing wheat, sheep (for meat and fleece), and milk. We were taking a day trip and passed back through the same landscape on our return. Across all those hours of travelling through many hundreds of thousands of hectares of prime farmland, I saw one person doing agricultural work, and that was someone sweeping out a stall at a large dairy. There are various possibilities as to why we did not see any persons working the land: time of day, season and cycle of planting–harvest, or they may have been working on sections of the property some distance from where we passed by, but the one worker I did see is reflective of the percentage of the Australian population engaged in the agricultural sector, less than 3 per cent. Agriculture in Australia is predominantly mono-cropped and mechanized, it is also disconnected from urban life. Very few Australians have a personal connection to a farm, procuring most of our food from intermediary supermarkets. Despite my professional and personal interest in cooking and eating, I, in common with the majority of my countryfolk, had little direct experience of the agricultural work that went into producing our food, and I admit I had little curiosity about it until I came to India.

On another road trip some twenty years prior, my friend Amar, Suresh, a mutual friend from our Melbourne alma mater, and I had set out from south Delhi at 5 a.m. to drive to Rudrapur in rural Uttarakhand, 250 kilometres northeast of the capital, to visit Amar's family on their farm there. We had started early to avoid traffic, and there were few other cars on the road as we slipped out of the city in the emerging dawn. The day was well underway by the time we reached the Ganga at Garhmukteshwar, where an ancient temple attracts devotees in their thousands on auspicious days, at which time the bridge there becomes a static entanglement of cars, bullock carts, trucks, bicycles, and tractors, and it can take an hour or more to traverse from one side to the other. Fortunately, this day was of no particular spiritual merit, and we crossed over in a fast few minutes. At Gajraula, the halfway point, we stopped for a breakfast of slow-cooked rajma, home-made curd, and hot tandoori roti at a roadside dhaba. It was lucky that we ate this substantial meal because the day then turned somewhat inauspicious. As we came to the outskirts of Moradabad, we were diverted off the highway due to major roadwork, sending us in an arc counter to our intended direction. What should have been a five-hour drive turned into a ten-hour endurance challenge along the back roads and by-ways of Uttar Pradesh. Instead of arriving for lunch, it was time for an evening drink when we finally piled out of the car at the farm. I felt shattered after this journey spent slowly bumping along kutcha roads riddled with potholes and ruts, often stuck behind a tractor or bullock cart. But for all its discomfort, it was an experience that gave me my first sense of how deeply connected India is to agricultural life.

The very roots of Indian culture and society lie in agriculture; that rural agrarian India is 'invariably referred to as Bharat', suggests that it is understood as elemental to the nature of the subcontinent.[1] Primary production of foods and other natural materials is the broadest and most important sector of India's economy, and more than half the population is engaged in agricultural work. Agricultural production is diverse, ranging from traditional farm villages to larger mechanized farms, and the practices and seasonal rhythms of farming underlie most Indian festivals and play a major role in the social fabric of India. Our unexpected meandering through the farmlands of central Uttar Pradesh took us through a patchwork of small fields of wheat, rice and sugar cane, winter vegetables and mango orchards, places busy with human activity: People and bullocks were doing the type of manual labour machines had replaced in Australia. I recognize the physical hardship of this work and the arguable inefficiency of land ceilings that limit the size of farms to small-scale landholdings on which the return is commensurately small, preventing farmers from investing in equipment that might ease their labour and enhance productivity. Even so, coming from a continent-sized island where the production of our food is almost hidden, happening 'out there in the country' detached by long distance from the majority urban population, observing the activity of Indian rural life was fascinating for me.

Two years later, I came to live in south Delhi, where apart from a large tract of city forest, it was unrelentingly urban. In the small market across from my apartment, there was an atta chakki, a miller, where whole grains were ground into fresh flour. Most days, I went to this chakkiwallah and bought a small portion of wheat berries from him, which he ground into atta that I made into roti: I had never eaten freshly ground wheat before, and the flavour of this was so nutty and delicious that the bread I made from it was tasty enough to be eaten on its own. While I was waiting for my portion of flour to be ground, other local residents would come in carrying bags of wheat or corn, procured from a family farm, to be milled. This, and my subsequent discovery that millers were commonplace around the city, was a visible manifestation of the connection many urban Indians retain with agriculture.

Some small-scale agriculture still operates in India's cities, but most of the food Indian urbanites eat is produced on the outskirts or hinterlands and further into the countryside proper. India's urbanites are enjoying the material and social benefits of India's economic development (perhaps not the congestion and pollution that has come with it), but the rural communities producing their food are not doing as well: Farmers have been marching towards parliaments from around the country to demand fair prices for their crops that would make them worth growing;[2] environmental change is being keenly felt by farmers;[3] the rate of farmer suicides in India is unconscionably high;[4] and in 2020, Indian farmers blocked the main highways out of Delhi protesting against the introduction of new farm bills they are concerned will leave them worse off—a protest writ large in international news.[5] Slow growth in agricultural development has been driving people off their lands and into cities to seek better economic opportunities there, swelling urban populations. It is not a dismal scenario for all agriculturists; some are doing very well meeting the increasing demand for meat, fish and seafood, milk, fruits and organic and niche produce.

The focus of this book is food in India's cities, but I could not conceive of it without exploring agriculture in India; and, above all else, the production of food connects urban and rural India in a material sense. With this in mind, I eagerly bought a hardback copy of Feroze Varun Gandhi's 2018 publication, *A Rural Manifesto: Realizing India's Future Through Her Villages*, from a Bengaluru bookshop. At 848 well-proportioned pages, it took up a sizeable corner of my luggage when I travelled back to Australia with it. When I got home and sat down to read it, I found the size and weight of it made it difficult to handle and that its physicality embodied the magnitude of its subject, leading me to consider 'What could I possibly offer to this critical field populated by scholars, economists, journalists, and writers with decades of dedicated focus on India's agrarian sector?' I purposefully went in search of stories about agriculture, following my own interests and instincts and taking up serendipitous opportunities when they arose, such as travelling to rural Jharkhand. I spoke with Indians who grow food across the socio-economic spectrum: wealthy, subsistence, middling, producing various crops including millet, wheat, sugar, mushrooms, shrimp, cocoa, milk, vegetables, and fruits in mountain, coastal, and inland areas. I also continue to have conversations with friends who are farmers and take an interest in media reports and research on India's primary food production. Some of these stories are told in other chapters where they were illustrative of a particular theme. My singular experiences of Indian agriculture are fragments of a colossal system in constant motion producing food to feed the largest population of people in the world. I decided the best I could do in this dedicated chapter was to simply share these experiences and trace further connections with the evolving foodscape of urban India.

Urban Farmers

In recent years, there has been a global trend to 'urban farming' in big cities around the world, with people growing food on rooftops, in vertical farms and highrise hot houses, on old factory sites, in disused railway tunnels, and re-purposed shipping containers.

> Urban farming seeks to bring food production right into the city. It eliminates the need for long transport distances and refrigeration, thereby helping to preserve the environment, and promising fresh produce for the megacities of tomorrow.[6]

India is no exception to contemporary urban farming development: '*Ghar ka khana* is best, and what about *ghar ka khana* WITH *ghar ki sabzi*!' proclaims the Edible Routes Foundation, a Delhi-based organization that promotes and develops urban farming through workshops, renting out suburban farmlets and helping people turn their city terraces, domestic gardens, and unused lands over to food production.[7] Earthoholics, Urban Leaves, and iKheti are helping Mumbaikars transform their terraces, balconies, and common areas into food-producing gardens; Swayam Krishi Self Farming rents suburban plots to Bengalurians and supports them grow their own food on these, or they can call on Square Foot Farmers to help them create a harvestable terrace; Hyderabad-based Homecrop sells urban gardening units for rooftops and educates clients to grow food in these, and Urban Kissan helps clients establish hydroponic systems for growing fresh produce in small spaces.[8] All these urban farming services are entrepreneurial start-ups, but governments and NGOs are also leading projects to help urban Indians grow more of their own food: The

Government of Tamil Nadu has produced a 'do-it-yourself kit', *Guidelines on the Promotion of Nutrition Garden on Roof Top*, as part of their Urban Horticulture Development Scheme to guide people on growing vegetables on open terraces of houses and apartment buildings;[9] Pune City Corporation runs a City Farming Project as part of their 'smart city' development; the municipal government in Hyderabad offers a subsidized kit, including portable beds, earth, manure, and seeds, to create a home vegetable garden. The COVID-19 pandemic amplified interest in urban food production, although the percentage of urbanities growing their own food is miniscule, and it is common for the initial enthusiasm for the work involved in growing *ghar ki sabzi* to wane.[10] All of these urban farming services and projects are predominantly concerned with helping people to grow food for their own consumption on a micro-scale, although surpluses might certainly be shared or traded. Urban agriculture is the production of food, plant, and animals in urban areas for commercial purposes; an enterprise growing food specifically to sell it, which might be of small to medium size—noting that any urban agriculturist will undoubtedly grow food for their own consumption as well. Urban farming is considered a subset of urban agriculture, but the two terms tend to be used interchangeably as the two practices overlap. Urban agriculture has long been practised in Indian cities, but we will come to this further on.

Before Keith Goyden became a professional baker and began baking bread in the Uttarakhand Hills, he worked in the development sector in India for more than thirty years. Goyden is an informed advocate of sustainability and a practitioner of an environmentally sound way of living. I met him on his food-producing property, where we had a long and wide-ranging conversation about all sorts of food-related matters, including urban farming in India. He believes that it will not be possible for India's megacities to ever be self-sustaining in food production. However, 'cities that don't exist yet [have a] real opportunity to experiment with urban agriculture and build it into city planning . . . they have an opportunity to think about the environment they want to live in', potentially utilizing advanced technology, such as hydroponic towers, to create enough food to feed a large urban population, although this would require high capital investment. In India's established cities, the value of land has become so inflated that the choice is usually to convert productive peri-urban farmland for housing and commercial development. I can recall when the area covered by ultra-urban Gurugram—a hard surface vista of concrete, glass, and asphalt—still had large swathes of farmed land and some trees, and the outskirts of Noida, south-east of Delhi, were farmed fields, since lost under towers of apartments and sprawling shopping malls stretching over hundreds of kilometres to create the Greater Noida region, extending the reaches of the NCR.

A different kind of people used to live in Gurgaon [just a few years ago] leading a very different life. They were farmers who used to grow grain, millets and mustard. Then the builders made them an offer they could not refuse. Hectares of land were sold to the builders transforming villagers into sudden millionaires.[11]

It is rare that I am in India without making a visit to my friends Kini and Gogi on their Rudrapur farm. The route there traverses the Gangetic plain in eastern Uttar Pradesh, some the most intensely farmed areas in the world because the land is some of the most fertile in the world. Travelling through here in different seasons, you still see fields of sugar cane, rice, wheat, mustard, peas, peanuts, eggplants, cabbages and cauliflower, kohlrabi, fenugreek, potatoes and carrots, and mango and guava orchards. But I have watched the peri-urban border where this agriculture begins being pushed further out year on year by the spatial expansion of the NCR and the subsequent encroachment of housing and industrial development on this fecund food-producing land.

The other agricultural work I noted with interest on these long road trips out of the city was in the earliest part of the journey when we crossed the Delhi–Noida Bridge, from where I could see farmers at work growing crops along the banks of the Yamuna River. As the Delhi Metro developed, and I took to travelling around the city on it, I discovered that there was a large area of urban agriculture at Mayur Vihar on the river floodplains. The Yamuna farmers I could see were not urbanites latterly come to growing vegetables for their own meals—they had been engaged in producing fresh food for the city for many decades, often over several generations.

> From preliminary research, one comes under the impression that there is little to no significant urban agriculture in Delhi. But as one goes deep inside you will find out that there is in fact extensive urban agriculture in Delhi . . . [y]et, urban agriculture in Delhi exists in such a way that it is both intensively practiced and decidedly irrelevant.[12]

When I decided that I wanted to explore the cultivated areas along the Yamuna and learn first-hand about the farmers working there, I knew that I would need an escort/translator to accompany me. I asked several friends if they would do so; I was surprised at how reluctant they were, suggesting that such a visit might be dangerous—something I didn't believe. Finally, I got a keenly positive response when I asked Anubhav Sapra, founder of Delhi Foodwalks, if he would come with me. Not only did he assent to this, he said that it was something he was also interested in knowing more about and went ahead to request permission from some riverside farmers near Old Delhi for us to visit them. They agreed, only asking that we come later in the day when they had finished their work.

It was late afternoon on a warm autumn day when my auto dropped me into a boisterous tangle of scooters, bicycles, street stalls, pedestrians, and dogs at the entrance gates to Majnu Ka Tilla, a densely populated residential colony adjacent to the Yamuna in North Delhi, where Sapra and I had arranged to meet. We took a convoluted path along narrow overhung lanes through the colony's interior until a dark sloping passageway delivered us out to its rear, facing the riverside and taking me by surprise. It was a bucolic scene before us: an unmade road ran adjacent to the external wall of the built colony and on its other side was open space running all the way down to the river. The sky here was expansive over the water, sparking blue and gently streaked with thin wispy strands of cirrus; intermittent sounds from children playing ball games on the soft sand of the riverbank drifted up to us in the absence of traffic noise. We met with Dashrath who has been growing food here for nearly thirty years and his adult son Bableu, one of four, who have all joined their father in his urban agricultural work. We talked for a while in the makeshift home the family occupy and then Bableu took us for a tour of the family farm. We walked along narrow raised paths dividing the small fields into sections where various types of spinach, mustard, coriander, fenugreek, spring onions, and white radishes are grown. The respective leaves, bulbs, and taproots of these plants are picked, bunched, and sold in the Azadpur mandi if the crop is large, otherwise the produce is sold directly to small street vendors. On the other side of the river, the family cultivates cucumbers and tomatoes for the market on a piece of land they rent there, taking themselves across the water on a small boat to work it. There were also okra, eggplant, and chillies growing just for the family to eat. We came up to a couple of small goats,

happy to let me scratch their knobbly heads, belonging to
the family, kept only for their milk and considered as pets.
As we stood on the bank of the river and chatted, it was
clear that Bableu's family were experienced cultivators of
food on this fertile 'mithi' river soil—using clean municipal
water on the crops, not river water. They work alongside
another twenty-five to thirty related families, all originally
from the Allahabad region of Uttar Pradesh, who have
migrated to Delhi because growing vegetables for the city
earns them a better livelihood than growing cereal crops in
rural India. Given that their lives in this city are amongst
the most challenged and marginalized, their preference for
it says something about the conditions being experienced
by many Indian farmers.

The positive media interest in urban farming tends to
focus on the projects undertaken by people wealthy enough
to have a terrace or patch of land in a city, rarely extending
to people such as Delhi's riverside agriculturists—little
attention is paid to them, besides the unwanted notice
of the authorities, and they are 'conspicuously invisible',
most likely because they are poor.[13] The land Bableu and
his family, and the others alongside them, are working is
public property; they do not own it nor do they pay rent.
Depending on your viewpoint, you could see this as illegal
squatting or use of common land as has been customary
in village societies. Local authorities regularly bulldoze the
farmers' dwellings to try and force them to leave, hence
the makeshift nature of the family's home. They have
limited access to civic services and no electricity: They can

only charge a mobile phone by paying a local shopkeeper, sitting in his well-appointed store on the adjacent colony side of the road, ten rupees to use his power. Their children attend the local government school but have to study by candlelight at night. Their housed neighbours are keen to see them gone so they can use the land to park their vehicles. Water is regularly released from the nearby Wazirabad barrage, flooding the riverbanks and washing away any crops; this also happens during the monsoon, at which time it becomes difficult for the farmers to earn a livelihood.[14] They must also contend with urban dairy farmers who bring their cows here to feed on the scrub-covered areas; left unattended, the animals leave this tough fare and make a beeline to devour the more tender vegetables growing nearby. Bableu said his family do not have the money to pay for these hungry bovines to be kept away from their crops. The farmers working on the banks and floodplain of Delhi's Yamuna, in common with poor urban farmers in other Indian cities, are fighting to sustain their farming activities, and they may not be there for much longer. If urban agriculture is one of the 'solutions to meet the demand of the urban population', it will be interesting to see who does the work of this if the people currently doing it are forced out.[15]

In spite of its seeming simplicity, urban agriculture does not just happen. To foster the development and growth of urban agriculture, a city may have to consider implementing techniques that include zoning ordinances, comprehensive plans and, in some cases, state legislation . . . [but] people's livelihoods have to be at the center of any discussion about sustainability and making changes.[16]

Rural Splendour?—A Convenience-Free Life

It was mid morning on a mid-October day when we walked through the village of Saitoli in Nanital District, Uttarakhand, under a cloudless cerulean sky; the air was clear and crisp, the sun luxuriantly warm, ideal weather for post-harvest food processing in preparation for the impending winter months. The stone courtyards of most of the village homes we passed were filled with millets, various dals, some still in their pods, lobia (black-eyed beans), rajma, chillies, and local sweet potato drying in the sun. Most houses sported at least one voluptuous haystack on the roof, and the work of making these was still taking place as piles of hay were carried up to the roof and forked into shape. Cows and their calves, buffaloes, and goats, all kept for milk and manure, were out of their pens and chomping on the same hay being stored for their winter feed. In one yard, a young woman was threshing millet with a large wooden baton, rhythmically swinging it over her head in an elegant arc to bring it down on a tumble of sun-dried millet to dislodge the cereal seeds from their heads. The fruit trees were bare at this time of year, but I imagined their bounty being enjoyed in season. The pumpkin vines growing on walls and trellises were also bare, having been harvested earlier in the year and stored away. Several homes had vibrant green patches of turmeric plants, and I identified vegetables and herbs growing in small garden beds, against fences and in nooks of earth. We came across a mother and son sitting before a pile of just-harvested hemp, rolling the resinous seed heads of this plant between the palms of their hands to form the intoxicating bhang they would consume to celebrate Holi. Their hands were covered in green residue from their work, and they were very cheerful and happy to chat with us. They talked of how they produced most of the food they ate, only buying a few items such as tea and sugar from the local store. On this day, under this sky, in the warm sun, it seemed an idyllic existence. Here was a food 'lifestyle' that ticked all the buzzwords and aspirational boxes: seasonal, local, organic (natural fertilizers and pesticides are made and used here), simple, low-sugar, additive-free, artisanal, antibiotic-free animals producing pure milk, clean, unprocessed, and waste-free food—little convenience food is purchased, so there is little packaging, and any excess organic matter is fed to the animals—that required the sort of physical effort to grow, produce, and cook that made it unnecessary to go to the gym to 'exercise' one's body. For wellness-focused urbanites who espoused food as health, and who were paying high prices for exactly the type of food eaten by the residents of Saitoli, this was the lifestyle that would offer just that, and nobody here was overweight, and probably did not have any food 'allergies' either.

If my musings on the seemingly idyllic food system of an Indian village were a scene in a film, complete with my gazing out across the majestic mountain scenery, the soundtrack would have abruptly ground to a halt at this point, as I pondered the reality of it. Realizing that I was well into the territory of what Indian journalist and writer Manu Joseph calls 'village romantic', someone who holds a 'quaint adoration' for India's rural life that is not shared by its 'impoverished' farmers. According to Joseph, India's rural agricultural sector has low productivity and the Indian village a 'perpetually miserable place'.[17] I am not sure how Indian villagers might feel about this description of their lives. Undoubtedly, some would agree, but it is hard to imagine that the people I chatted with in Saitoli, and in other villages around them, do not have some enjoyment in their lives. On the other side of this argument are those who believe that 'thriving villages are key to India's success'.[18] I had conceded my 'rural romanticism' to myself on that October day before I had even read Joseph's work and learnt that term, acknowledging that the way these villagers feed themselves requires a lot of physical work, all year round, most days of the year. They also had to contend with the vagaries of the elements, such as drought, pests, and lack of rain, which might damage or destroy crops or cause them to fail. And there was little, if any, convenience in food in this model of living, requiring as it did, constant labour in order to eat, which did not leave too much time for other creative or leisure pursuits (noting the craft work of women has always been evident in village homes I have been in). Was this a lifestyle a perpetual urbanite such as myself would really want to live? Would I even know how?

The hills of Uttarakhand have become increasingly populated with the alternative residences of urbanites. City folks are building huge homes here, designed to maximize mountain views that take up most of their land. Few are growing any food. The villages of Sitla and nearby Mukteshwar have transformed since I first visited here in 2001, with restaurants lining the roadside, serving all sorts of food from pizza to seafood (transported from Delhi) to Kumaoni cuisine—you could hardly get this local food outside a home ten years ago, and it bespeaks the urban trend to regional cuisine—new grocery stores have opened to cater to city preferences: The foodways of these villages are altering to suit the tastes and desire for convenience of urban escapees, not the other way around, and the increased amount of rubbish I noticed as I walked around was mainly food packaging. Goyden told me how one Saturday during the summer just past, he had set off to sell his fresh loaves of bread at a farmer's market in Nainital town fifty kilometres away, only to turn back, because the narrow local roads were so blocked with traffic that it wasn't moving: a replication of one of the most unpleasant aspects of urban life, i.e., road congestion, in this beautiful rural region.

Farming Shrimp to Feed the World

When R and I were planning our trip to Visakhapatnam, the 'executive' capital of Andhra Pradesh, he asked me if I would like to see a shrimp factory there for my research. A friend of his traded seafood and said he could arrange for us to visit a crustacean processing plant if I was interested. I unhesitatingly said yes. Two years previously, I had travelled to Yanam, a coastal district 180 kilometres south from Visakhapatnam, and on the return journey to the city, we took the ocean road along which there were many aquaculture enterprises. On that occasion, I only observed these in passing, but the presence of all these fish and seafood farms caught my interest, and I noted it as something for further research. The opportunity to get a first-hand look at an aspect of this industry was an exciting prospect to me. We arrived mid-morning at the shrimp factory on the outskirts of the city. From the outside, it was an enormous nondescript white industrial facility with no indication as to what went on inside it. The sun beat on our backs as we bent down to remove our shoes, placing them on the external racks provided, in exchange for a pair of knee-high rubber boots. It was a relief to get inside the cool interior where we were handed a hair cap and knee-length protective coat that we were required to wear to enter the factory proper— kitted up in this disposable PPE, we looked just like the health professionals who had become a feature of our lives a few months later when the COVID-19 pandemic began. We waded through a corridor deliberately flooded with chlorinated water, to ensure that our shoes were clean, and thoroughly washed and sanitized our hands at one of the many washing stations. We then proceeded to follow the processing route of the fresh shrimp: To begin, these are deposited via a loading bay from temperature-controlled refrigerated trucks into large blue tubs filled at aquaculture farms within a 100-kilometre reach north and south of Visakhapatnam; these tubs were upended to spill piles of shrimp onto stainless steel tables where teams of women, dressed in the same protective gear as we, worked with small scissors to snip the shells open and sort out any duds; next, the shrimp were submerged in vats of salted water for a measured time before being iced to prevent dehydration. A conveyor belt transported them into another section of the factory, which was sealed off from the place where the work of cleaning the shrimp was done. This necessitated us sploshing along another corridor filled with ankle-deep chlorinated water and washing our hands again before we could enter the inner sanctum of the factory where the shrimp roll through a series of automated processes: First these are steamed, then peeled—this work done by hand— chilled, snap frozen, coated with a layer of water to further prevent dehydration and maintain product quality, frozen again, packaged, boxed, and stored in commercial freezer units until ready to be shipped out. This facility is world class: modern, spotlessly clean, efficient, the large workforce all kitted out in clean uniforms and provided with good facilities. I hardly felt like I was in India here, which is perhaps not surprising as nobody in India is eating any of these shrimps. Every one of the 8000 tonnes of shrimps processed annually in this plant are exported to America to fill the freezers of several major chain store brands. On the day we were there, the frozen shrimps were being packaged for the biggest food retail chain in the USA where they are sold at $5.34 for 500 grams of frozen shelled flesh. The waste shells and heads are sold to a Japanese company to be used in medical and vitamin products.

Aquaculture is a thriving industry in India, predominantly on the eastern seaboard. The country is the second largest producer of farmed fish (carp and catfish) in the world, and Andhra Pradesh India's biggest producer of farmed shrimp (giant tiger shrimp, or *Penaeus monodon*) and fish. More than 90 per cent of India's cultivated aquatic produce is exported to the USA, Europe, China, and Japan, bringing an estimated $5 billion in foreign exchange into the economy, with farmed shrimp earning the higher percentage of this.[19] All together, it is an economically impressive integrated farming and processing industry, employing more than 1.2 million Indians and offering better wages and conditions for workers, particularly women, than any other rural-agricultural employment. Farmers in coastal areas of Andhra Pradesh who have turned their land over to ponds to raise fish and shrimp are enjoying a greater return than traditional paddy farming; others have benefitted by selling unproductive land to aquaculture companies. The standard of living has generally improved in areas where aquaculture is practised.[20]

Indians are not yet as keen as the rest of the world on eating frozen prawns and fish. People in India's coastal cities and regions generally favour seafood and fish—enjoyed in an extensive variety of preparations—but they prefer it to be fresh. Given its output is primarily exported, the

COVID-19 crisis caused a significant disruption for Indian aquaculture, resulting in the estimated loss of around $1.5 billion in foreign exchange and local jobs, leading the Central government to declare aquaculture an essential activity to ensure that its operations continue. This situation brought into focus the industry's over-dependence on external markets and renewed consideration of how the domestic market might be expanded. Supplying the domestic market has been hampered by the lack of supply chain infrastructure for safely transporting and storing frozen produce within the country—it is easier to ship it to the other side of the world. Indians might buy more frozen foods in the future if improved logistics systems allow these to be kept in better conditions and make them more widely available.[21] The peeled frozen shrimp shipped off to America from Andhra is a convenience food (it is all meat with no work required to clean it) and is cheap (relative to paying market price for fresh ones), qualities that are increasingly influential on Indians' food choices. A nationwide marketing campaign funded by global investors could do the trick in persuading Indians to eat more farmed fish and seafood, just as it has persuaded them to use food delivery.

India's commercial fish and seafood farmers—as different to the harvest of fisherman—have enjoyed success and profitability by producing food for the rest of the world; even so, their gain has potential consequences for the local environment. As I drove past the fish farms along the Andhra coast, I assumed, given the location, that seawater was used in their operations. It was a false assumption.

Most aquaculture requires the use of large volumes of fresh water, drawn from the ground or bore sources, which must be changed at each stage of the process: hatching, growing, harvesting, and cleaning the ponds. Even though shrimps require saline water to grow in, the necessary level of salinity is achieved by pumping water in from other sources, not from the ocean. The salty water in the shrimp ponds can seep into ground water, water reservoirs, and canals. Research has shown that groundwater levels have dropped, and fresh-water aquifers are more salinized in areas where aquaculture is practised compared to areas where it is not. Wastewater from aqua farms is high in nitrogen, phosphorous, carbon compounds, organic matter, shrimp and fish faeces, plankton, and some chemical and antibiotic residues—I recall seeing workers standing ankle-deep in a thick black sludge of fish poo and food residue at the bottom of a small aquaculture pond on a friend's farm after the water had been drained to clean it. This contaminated water is often released untreated from aquaculture ponds into other waterways and has been shown to pollute drinking water and negatively impact coastal habitats, destroying mangroves, causing fish deaths, and disturbing natural fisheries, leading to conflict between aquaculturists and fishermen in some areas. Researchers have expressed concern that 'intensive ecosystem exploitation' by [India's] aquaculture industry threatens ecological, economic, and social problems and conflicts in the longer term if rules and regulations, including requirements for proper water treatment systems, are not put in place to create a balance between an industry that is a 'promising agent of economic welfare and a good source of foreign exchange' and environmental sustainability.[22] A technological 'leap', of the type India is known for, could ensure aquaculture can continue to be economically advantageous for India as well as sustainable.[23]

Milk: Food of the Gods

Manek Chowk is a civic square in the old city precinct of Ahmedabad.[24] By day, it is a busy vegetable market; at night, it transforms into a vibrant street food precinct. I had last come here in 2009 and visiting again ten years later, I found it little changed. Food vendors set up their stalls, serving local specialities; street food from around the country, all of it vegetarian, around the edges of the square. The central area is laid out with tables and chairs for patrons to sit and enjoy until late into the night. Many of the stalls have signs proclaiming 'only Amul butter used', one of which was advertising 'pineapple sandwiches' and 'chocolate ice-cream sandwiches'. This sounded interesting, and I stepped in closer to see what these items were made from. I watched with bemusement as the stall keeper spread melted Cadbury chocolate on two slices of white bread, laid these on a plate, took a scoop of chocolate ice cream—having sent another staff member to obtain this from a nearby ice-cream vendor—placed this on top of one slice of bread, picked up a large block of Amul cheese, and grated this over the ice-cream, sandwiching this with the other slice of bread, grating more cheese over the lot, before finishing it off with a sprinkling of chocolate drops. This was definitely a novelty for me. I ordered one: It was delicious, and I revelled in enjoying this unusual food combination. Judging from the disbelief, sometimes bordering on disgust, with which most people later responded to my description of this sandwich, it seems that this combination was equally curious to others, and perhaps a step too far for some.

Gujaratis are very fond of dairy products. They are the biggest consumers of ice-cream in India, and as the signs displayed at Manek Chowk market indicate, dedicated consumers of butter and cheese produced by Amul, a company of local origin. Amul is also one of the largest and most successful dairy cooperatives in the world, bringing 10 million litres of milk to Indian consumers every day of the year through a nationwide network of small farmers. In my experience, two things are ubiquitous in Indian kitchens: a pressure cooker and Amul Dairy products. I would even venture to suggest that if India has a national food, it is Amul butter—Chef Manish Mehrotra told me he considers it so integral to Indian cookery that he buys it at a much higher cost than the best French butter to ensure the food served at the Indian Accent restaurants in New York and London accurately reproduce the flavours of its origins. As I wrote in Chapter 5, I had held an aspiration to visit Amul for many years and decided that it was time to act on that for this book, coming to Ahmedabad with the intention to travel to the company headquarters in Anand, a small rural city eighty kilometres away, along what a roadside sign deemed the 'Expressway to Prosperity', the following day.

> Since milk and other dairy products (butter, yogurt) have been central to the Indian diet for a long time, it also has deeper meanings. Cow worship has been an integral part of Hinduism and milk has mythological importance, which can be traced back to Lord Krishna's epics. In a culturally derived dairy building, which strives to be Indian, it cannot escape the mythological and sacred connections or its rural associations.[25]

The Amul factory in Anand, is located in a towering modernist building designed by architect Achyut Kanvinde—the quote above refers to the Dudhsagar Dairy complex in Mehsana that he also designed for Amul— where I discovered that my interest in the workings of this place was far from original. Taking a tour of this dairy complex is apparently a popular political undertaking— the corridor walls hung with photographs of the many visiting luminaries who have walked this same route— and a tourist attraction. As we moved around the various areas of the complex, we peered through wide windows to take in different aspects of the factory operations, where fresh milk, collected from numerous small farmers, is delivered from tankers each morning to be processed into milk powder and the company's famed butter, which I saw being extruded from a wide-mouth pipe into portions to be packaged up.

This was as much as I got to see of the production at Amul as most of it happens inside huge industrial machinery with the inputs moving around the factory in a system of streamlined pipes, such as the one I saw the butter coming out of. My tour concluded in the visitor's room where I watched a short film about Amul and was offered the choice of a range of packaged drink products to enjoy. The visit wasn't quite what I had expected; I had imagined it would more 'farm' like, say with herds of cows chewing their cud contentedly while being milked, rather than the mechanized industrial factory I was shown around. These were expectations entirely of my own making, and reflecting on the actual experience, I was glad that I had travelled to Anand. If nothing else, it satisfied my curiosity and took me to a part of India I had not visited before.

Something that caught my interest on my tour of the Amul factory with respect to the subject of this book was the display of products the company now produces: flavoured milk drinks, ghee, yoghurt, ice cream, paneer, chocolate confectionery, biscuits, and many more varieties of milk than the pouches of fresh Amul Gold and Amul Taaza I was familiar with, and more cheeses than the iconic processed style that was grated over my ice-cream sandwich the night before. I will deal with the milk first and then the cheese. Noting that other Indian dairy companies such as Mother Dairy are also producing a similar wide range of value-added dairy-based foods, which speaks to the popularity of these items. The contemporary Indian consumer can choose Amul milk in the following varieties:

Desi A2 cow milk, Cow milk, Camel milk, Lactose-free milk, Amul T-Special and Chai Maaza milk—both of which 'do not form cream layer when tea is prepared from same'—Amul Skim-Trim Milk, Amul Shakti milk, and Diamond milk. What a choice: The milk market in India was getting complicated, reflecting both global trends and unique cultural aspects of India.

India is the world's largest producer of liquid milk, most of which is consumed in the country, making Indians the largest consumers of dairy in the world, enjoying more than twice that of the European Union, and becoming increasingly selective about it, evidenced by the diversified products produced in India now.[26] A2 milk has a slightly different amino acid profile to regular or 'A1' milk, and all sorts of health claims have been made for it, for which there is no reliable evidence. Nonetheless, people around the world, including Indians, are paying more for what is essentially a marketing strategy rather than a product with any more benefits than 'regular' milk.[27] It has been known for many decades that a significant number of Indians, around 60 per cent of south Indians and 27 per cent of north Indians cannot tolerate lactose[28]—somewhat ironic given the significant role milk and milk products play in India's food culture, strongly linked to socio-medical beliefs about the benefits of milk—yet, lactose-free milk has only recently appeared in the market in India. In my observation, this coincided with lactose-free milk becoming widely available in the West as people started to believe that the culprit causing their 'gut' problems was milk and the lactose it contains—ignoring other factors such as the amount of coffee or alcohol they drink and/or their stress levels. Plant-based 'milks' such as almond milk are gaining popularity in India as an alternative to dairy milk, in line with other heath-focused consumers around the world. These 'milks'—there is a dispute as to whether they should be able to be called as such—are more costly than cow milk, and the commercial varieties are predominantly water.[29]

Regardless of any problem Indians might have digesting lactose, cow milk, especially that from indigenous cow breeds is the most prestigious, and, therefore, expensive, milk product. There is a niche market for organic cow milk in Indian cities, including online delivery services bringing 'country fresh milk' from 'farm to table'. Home delivery of milk is far from a new service in urban India. In the central Delhi suburb where R resides, a milkman delivers fresh milk every morning from cows kept somewhere near the city—perhaps the ones munching on foliage and vegetables alongside the Yamuna—to a number of households, dispensing it from stainless steel milk cans carried on his motorbike, something he has been doing so for years—a service that was standard practice before milk came in plastic pouches and he would not be the only 'traditional' milkman still operating in an Indian city. There has been a contemporary revival of milk delivery services in India's cities via online platforms, allowing consumers to order organic, 'farm fresh' milk, free from adulteration, hormones, or pesticides to be delivered to their doorstep.[30]

Most commercial milk in India is a mixture of cow and buffalo milk, unless it is labelled otherwise. When we met, journalist and food writer Vikram Doctor described the existence of a 'buffalo prejudice' in India, saying that it partly stems from an enduring conception of these animals as 'low caste', compared to the venerated *Bos Taurus*, and a belief that consuming their milk will cause a person to become 'slow and lazy' like these large beasts. Conversely, buffalo milk fetches a higher price because it has a higher fat content, a key factor in deciding the market value of all milk. In Australia, buffalo milk products sell at a much higher price than those made from cow milk because of the superior taste, health, and nutritional benefits claimed for these. In Italy, buffalo milk is an important food as it is used to make authentic mozzarella cheese.[31] The varied conceptions of buffalo milk serve as another example of how beliefs about the value of any food, or otherwise, often has little to do with its material qualities.

Milk plays an important role in the life of Mumbai-based food importer Jehangir Lawyer, albeit in a preserved form, as he is a lauded expert on cheese. Lawyer is a vibrant, effusive conversationalist, and our interview went well over its allotted time, ranging over many topics, some more related to food than others. When I asked him about trends in India's consumer food market, the first thing he said was: 'Dairy is what talks, [particularly] value-added dairy such as flavoured yoghurt.'[32] He said that this style of product had taken off in India because it was 'not a big step for people to try these' as sweetened yoghurt is a familiar concept in Indian's taste vocabulary. Somehow, we didn't get around to talking about cheese, even though that is also a value-added dairy product in which he trades. I had noticed the increasing availability of different cheeses in upmarket food stores in Delhi, but I didn't think too much about this until several months after my conversation with Lawyer when I visited Amul and discovered that they were producing Gouda and Emmental cheese. If this large company serving the pan-Indian market was producing mild European-style products, then there must be a reasonable demand for it. However, these cheeses were mainly sold in gourmet food stores in metropolitan India, revealing that the demand for these products is predominantly from urban consumers.

For many years, I was under the impression that the only cheese produced in India was the firm paneer used in vegetarian cooking; the soft cheese called chhenna which is used to make a range of Bengali sweets; and Amul processed cheese for sandwiches and any western-style dishes requiring cheese. On occasion, I would bring different cheeses from Australia to share with Indian friends, who often recoiled from the taste of European varieties with more pronounced flavours that were unfamiliar to them and for which they had not developed a taste. Certainly, there were Indians who were familiar with a wider variety of cheese and enjoyed eating it; somebody had to be buying the cheese that Lawyer has been importing for decades, but it was more of a 'super niche' taste.

For a country that is said to be one of the world's largest dairy producers, Indians' taste for cheese, especially the artisanal variety, has been guarded.[33]

It was not until I travelled extensively to all corners of the subcontinent to deeply investigate regional food that I discovered that India had more indigenous cheeses than I had been aware of: There was kalari, a cooked curd cheese referred to as the 'mozzarella of Jammu and Kashmir' that becomes moreishly gooey and stringy when fried; across the Himalayan region, in Spiti, Sikkim, and Arunachal Pradesh, I ate churpi/churpe, a pungent hard cheese made from yak's milk used to add flavour to food in the same way as Italian parmesan, along with a soft curd cheese also called churpe made with the whey left over from making butter; in Kolkata, I tried crumbly smoked Bandel and Kalimpong cheese, originating from the hill town of the same name in West Bengal. It is not a long list, and you can see from their origins that Indian cheese making has been largely confined to the cooler hill and mountain areas—with the exception of the Bandel style, which originated in the Portuguese settlement of that name on the Hooghly River where it was smoked to preserve it as the tropical climate would not allow for a slow curing process. So, a more everyday taste for the cheese had perhaps been confined to Indians in these regions.

Consumer demand for value-added dairy products such as ghee, butter, and curd/yoghurt is ever increasing in metropolitan India.[34] These dairy products are, by the very

nature of having 'value' added to them, more expensive.
The high/er incomes of a larger section of urban Indians
allow them to enjoy more diversity in their diets; Indians,
generally, like dairy products—which is why they hold the
number one global ranking on milk consumption—and are
willing to spend money on these foods, so dairy companies
are creating more products for them to buy—a commercial
virtuous circle. Since the pandemic lockdown, I have noticed,
via the social media feeds of the Indian food folk I follow,
a trend towards home-delivered 'curated' cheese plates.
The year before the pandemic took hold, I had enjoyed a
long conversation with Chef Manu Chandra in Bengaluru,
during which he mentioned that he was in partnership in
a cheese making venture called Begum Victoria, making
cheese right in the centre of this city, an enterprise that
developed because there was no good local cheese available.
If Chandra was making cheese, then it was a sign there was
something underway with this dairy product: I delved into
this to discover that artisanal cheese making was thriving
across the country, in Sikkim, Mumbai, Delhi, Kashmir,
Goa, Coonoor, Kodaikanal, Puducherry, Kerala, Chennai,
and the Kumaon hills. India's new cheese makers are often
self-taught, making European style cheeses that are at
the same time uniquely Indian—'Cheese that Screams of
India'—because its raw material, milk, carries the flavour of
the land on which the animals have grazed.[35]

From cheese made in the highlands of Kashmir to
monks churning out fresh buffalo milk cheese in South

India, the country's artisanal cheese revolution has truly taken off.[36]

It turned out that the cheese on those home-delivered cheese platters was largely produced in India. Cheese production in India is moving out of its 'super niche' to supply for more mainstream consumption. Visiting Darima farms, an artisanal cheese making facility in the Uttarakhand hills, in October 2019, we were shown around the small production unit and the temperature-controlled cheese room filled with roundels ripening on wooden shelves by co-founder Arvind Chawla, who then took us through a tasting of their products. During this, we talked about the business and its beginnings in 2016. It was a new undertaking for everyone: Chawla and his partner had no experience making cheese; the village women they employed had never tasted it before; and the local dairy farmers were sceptical about the whole thing, but now prefer to sell their milk for cheese making, because they get a better rate than what the government dairy offers. Expectations for growth in consumer demand for Indian cheese is such that indigenous cheese producers such as Chawla are concerned about obtaining enough milk to satisfy it.

Punjab: Sugar and Wheat

28 December 2019. R and I are travelling from Delhi to Kapurthala, a small city in the Punjab. Our long road journey is prolonged by having to constantly slow down, or

in some cases halt altogether, as groups of Sikh men, dotted at intervals along the highway, flagged down cars to hand the occupants slices of soft white bread, pakoras, halwa, and cups of tea. Some people pulled off the road altogether to join in the langar being served in tented dining halls temporarily installed by the roadside. The Punjab region is one of the most fertile places on earth; the Indian portion of this land, the state of Punjab, is the third-most productive agricultural area in the country, producing wheat, rice, sugar cane, vegetables, fruits, and milk. The region's God-given rivers and alluvial soil, its extensive irrigation canal system built by the British prior to Independence, and the adoption of the techniques and seeds of Green Revolution in the 1960s—which was actually reliant on the availability of plenty of good old-fashioned water despite its proclamation as advanced technology—brought prosperity and development to Punjab. Its success as an agricultural producer has meant farming food has remained the predominant industry there. If I had not been with R, who could explain what this gifting of food to all passers-by was about, I might have interpreted it as symbolic of the prosperity of the land we were on. However, what we were witnessing was part of an annual festival commemorating the martyrdom of the two younger sons of Guru Gobind Singh, who at the ages of six and eight chose death over forced conversion to Islam. The two young boys, along with their grandmother, came into the capture of their executioner, Wazir Khan, after being betrayed by the family cook. Fortunately, this treacherous incident has not besmirched the good reputation of Punjabi cooks, and they dominate the food service industry in India.

I wanted to make this trip to Punjab because of the region's agricultural significance, imagining us driving through endless farmland vistas and stopping along the way to talk to farmers about their crops and the general state of local food production. On this halting drive to Kapurthala, the day was weighed down with a damp heavy fog, which veiled the fields and made it seem as if we were looking at a white wall for most of our day-long drive. The only signs of agricultural activity we could see was when we found ourselves sitting behind slow moving tractors pulling loads of sugar cane to nearby mills. We had chosen Kapurthala as a destination as it was of mutual interest to both R and I: He wanted to see its historic buildings, and I thought it might serve as a juxtaposition to India's mega-metros as it is one of the least populated cities in the country. We spent our time looking at architecture and investigating the food offerings available there. In the local supermarket, I found a range of different flours available including a gluten-free mix for baking, a possible sign that food trends were filtering in here. Pizzas and burgers (vegetarian) and coffee and cake were available in popular local eateries. That was about it. I couldn't turn out anything more relevant to this work there, but we enjoyed the place and the more traditional local fare.

Our return journey via Patiala was somewhat more elucidating. The prevailing fog lifted around midday, and we could see what was going on around us beyond the immediate side of the road. We stopped and talked to a family of farmers making winter gur, squeezing the juice form their own cane and reducing it to a firm fudge-like consistency via a series of evaporating pits that were heated by burning the pulverized cane stalk refuse. People driving by pulled off the road and bought kilos of this unrefined mineral-rich sweetener. Further on, we pulled off the main highway and drove along a quiet rural by-way until we saw a farmer working close to the roadside. We stopped, introduced ourselves, and asked if he would be willing to have a chat with us about his farm. His name was Pravinder—a young man dressed in tight, branded sportswear, looking identical to his urban generational counterparts who spend their time lifting weights in front of the mirror in a gym. He had a small holding of 3.5 hectares on which he grew wheat and rice. He said he was able to plant and harvest three crops a year, making the farm productive enough for him to earn a living from. However, the land needs to be cleared quickly between each crop for this to happen. As a small farmer, he cannot afford to purchase machinery that can clear fields expediently. The government lends shared farm equipment to small landholders to raze their fields, but with the average farm size in the district around four hectares, there are many farmers who need to access this machinery. Pravinder said that he often cannot afford to wait his turn if he wants to get a new crop in on time, necessitating the burning of stubble in his fields instead. The smoke from this burning contributes to the pall of pollution that blankets Delhi from the autumn harvest time, lingering well into the winter, causing urbanites to complain about the practices of the people who grow their food. Pravinder said that he could force more from his farm by using more chemical inputs but did not want to do that. He was satisfied with the income he earned, loved farming and the culture of his community, and was content with rural life.

A Youth-Led Agrarian Revival?

Young farmer Pravinder might be an exception. Owning and working his own land gives him autonomy, independence, and satisfaction—essential aspects of human existence that money does not necessarily buy—but not being able to earn a decent living from agricultural work is driving many young people out of rural areas:

> Working on an Indian farm is amongst the least paying jobs in India. Not surprisingly, the aspiration of young rural Indians is to find liberation from farming. In fact, it is the lack of good opportunities in agriculture that is driving millions of young Indians to seek their future in the cities.[37]

Prateek Sadhu is one of India's best contemporary chefs; in 2020, he was also rated as one of the country's 'most exciting *young* chefs [my italics].'[38] When we met in his simultaneously slick and earthy Mumbai restaurant, Masque, he shared his observations on how food was changing in India and where it might be going, declaring that the 'future of Indian food is about farming'. This could be taken as an obvious statement; food has to be grown to be available for chefs to work with—or perhaps not if it can be manufactured in test tubes—but that is not what he was getting at. He was talking about using raw ingredients and taking these to 'another level' by applying modern techniques to treat these foods such that their flavours spoke of their inherent qualities rather than any clever 'innovation' of a chef. For example, by eating a dish prepared from morels gathered in Kashmir or greens grown in the Sahyadri hills, you would taste the place the food is grown in and the way it is grown as a key element of it.[39] Locale has been instrumental to the development of India's regional cuisines; the distinctive tastes of the locale emerging from whatever foods could be farmed, caught, or foraged in the environment of a particular area—so his idea mirrors time-tested precedent.

I was introduced to Abhishek Dhawan, a researcher at the Agricultural Development Trust, Baramati, with a background in computer science, as one of his areas of interest is food and lifestyle and its impact on health. Without having inquired as to his age, I am confident he would qualify in the same 'young' category as Prateek. He has an interesting perspective on his generational contemporaries working in the information technology industry in metropolitan India, saying that the combination of the long working hours, expectations of performance, and commuting in heavy traffic or on overcrowded public transport has forced many of them to adopt a less than optimal 'convenience food lifestyle', such as ordering in fast food from take-outs or online delivery services, because they have no time, or inclination, to cook for themselves. He actually sees a hopeful future for rural India arising from these conditions, predicting that the 'burden of this work' will trigger a reverse in the outflow of labour, capital, and technologies from farming. He explained he believed young people working in cities will return to live in rural areas and become involved in agriculture or associated work, as it is the only labour that 'gives time for proper rest and relaxation', allowing people to create a more sustainable lifestyle that includes time to prepare home-made food. The return of this educated and technologically skilled workforce to rural living will bring the skills and knowledge to solve a whole host of problems, leading to an 'agro-friendly revolution'. For this to happen, he said that there has to be a 'breaking [of] the existing order to create a gap in which opportunities emerge'.

Dhawan's vision of rural India might be dismissed as idealistic, improbable, or 'village romantic', but he shared it with me prior to the COVID-19 pandemic, an event that triggered a historic reverse migration of millions of Indians from big cities back to small towns and rural villages. This unforeseen occurrence might just be the 'break' in the existing pattern needed to revitalize rural India. A large number of migrants, many of them young people who had left to seek their future in the city, have, in one example, returned to the state of Himachal Pradesh, where the government has been quick to provide support to them to start farming ventures 'to revive rural economies that suffered when young people left to work in cities . . . some have started modest ventures to raise cattle and goats, while some are reclaiming forgotten patches of land' and growing vegetables:[40]

> Chamba district authorities hope returning migrants will boost the rural economy by looking beyond traditional farming of staple crops to starting horticulture projects that bring in higher income.
>
> [Bhatt's] life took a complete U-turn during the COVID-19 pandemic . . . when he lost his job at a call-center in the city of Chandigarh. After returning to his village in Chamba Valley in the Himalayan state of Himachal Pradesh, he built a cattle shed, hoping dairy farming would yield a decent income.[41]

It would be naïve to suggest that the type of small farming ventures reported above have the capacity to transform India's agriculture sector; it is the agro-industrial enterprises of India's big corporates, such as Adani and Godrej, that will do that. Only time will tell if reverse migrants will stay on and persist with their small farming enterprises, but if they do, perhaps they might create a micro revolution in food production. If they are familiar with digital technology and urban food trends, they might connect with chefs like Sadhu to build partnerships to directly sell their produce to them; or they might provide high-quality milk to local artisanal cheese makers, or become cheese makers themselves, or revive indigenous grains and become artisanal bakers, or grow vines and become boutique winemakers. Perhaps tech-savvy returned migrants might create new forms of cooperatives to assist small food producers to directly reach urban consumers and earn a better return for their work.

Conclusion: The Future of Indian Food

In our past lies our future. This is not about just the hotel industry but about reimagining 'Tourism India' in its entirety. Yoga, Ayurveda, knowledge of balanced and healthy life . . . ancient wisdom of healthy eating and our cuisine's evolution have the potential to make us a holistic hub of the world.

—Natkal Anand, Executive Director ITC,
24 January 2021.

Twenty-two years ago, I read Salman Rushdie's *Midnight's Children*. While I remember that I loved reading it, I recall little of the storyline except that the protagonist, Saleem Sinai, fights in the India–Pakistan war and ends up with some connection to a pickle factory. Even so, there are two fragments of this work clearly lodged in my memory. One is the scene during the premiere of Uncle Hanif Aziz's film when the lights suddenly come on during its showing and a man walks onto the stage to announce Gandhi's assassination; the movie is forgotten in the shock and clamour, effectively ending Aziz's movie career. I expect Rushdie intended this as an allegory of some aspect of Indian political or cultural life that went over my head, but it has stayed with me as a poignant reminder of how our lives can be derailed by events outside our control, such as a global pandemic. The other potent recollection of the book was that at a place called the Breach Candy Swimming Club, there was a pool in the shape of a map of undivided India. I found the name of this place charming as much as it seemed preposterous, and I assumed it was made up, only to later realize it wasn't, which only added to its magic.

When I contacted A. D. Singh, managing director of the Olive Group of restaurants, to ask if we might meet for a conversation for this book, he invited me to come to the Breach Candy Club, completely unaware of my literary connection to it: I was excited to see this place I had long held in my imagination in its actuality. Unfortunately, the sky was pouring dense monsoonal rain on that evening, and while our corner table looked out over the famed pool, I could barely see it; a trifling disappointment, nothing career-shattering like the lights coming up on Uncle Aziz's masterpiece. Singh has had some tough moments in his three decades of hospitality entrepreneurship, although these have not undone him, far from it—he is one of India's most successful restaurateurs. Described as 'the man who changed the way India eats out', introducing Indians to a more informal cosmopolitan dining style via the Mediterranean-cuisine-focused Olive Bar and Kitchen restaurants in Mumbai, Delhi, and Bengaluru—an enduring concept that has grown branches in other major cities—he now heads up a company with fifteen restaurant brands.[1] I have referred to my conversation with Singh and the observations he shared with me on India's changing foodscape throughout this book, and I am going to draw on my meeting with him in a different way here.

I was not feeling very well when I met Singh; unusually, I had picked up a stomach bug in Mumbai. It had been a long time since I had been unwell like this; I had thought my years of eating in India had inured me to the predations of digestive nasties, obviously this was not true. When Singh invited me to choose what I would like to eat, I suggested that he decide to suit his appetite as I would be unlikely to eat much of anything. He chose a 'classic' meal of butter chicken, dal, and roti. It was a choice partly driven by knowledge of what was best out of the club kitchen; but for a man who had been instrumental in introducing western-style food to India through his restaurants, it spoke to me of how Indians will never relinquish their unique cuisine no matter the incursions of global corporations. Singh ate with his hand, but rather than hunching over the plate to reduce the distance between his hand and mouth, he sat perfectly straight and lifted the food with a subtle twist of his wrist—it was very graceful. Of course, I have eaten with many other Indians who eat their food as elegantly with their hands, but it really struck me on this occasion. I think it was in part because I have another interest in the history of western eating etiquette—and the lack of it now. While I can't fully explain the connection my food-history-laden synapses brought forth, it seemed to me that Singh's eating pointed to the future of India's food: that it would continue to absorb external, global influences that will change the country's food culture, yet, at the same time, remaining a distinctive embodiment of all that India is.

> [The] locational and demographic diversity of India's people ensures [that] how they choose to produce, cook and eat their food will always be unique. India's food culture will never be a slavish copy of any other.[2]

India's foodways have always been dynamic, evolving over many thousands of years, absorbing new foods, cookery techniques, and food ideas from her neighbours to the north, the east, and the west (not a lot has come in from the ocean void directly south) through trade, migration, and colonization. What is different now is the rapidity and weight of influence enabled by media networks, internet technology, and the attractiveness of India as a market to multinational corporations, international investors, and governments,[3] due to the size of her population and the increased economic capacity of a larger segment of Indians to consume goods and services paired with their enthusiasm to do so. Even more so, Indian food producers and companies are ever expanding the retail and product choices available to Indian consumers. There is no doubt that the changes in the types of foods and food products available, the blossoming of restaurants, cafés, and other eateries offering food styles from around the world, online food delivery, and new food retail concepts are as exciting, interesting, and enjoyable for Indians with the means to afford these as they are to people in affluent societies around the globe: Discovering new things to eat is a universal human pleasure.

On my seminal visit to India in 1997, what first alerted me to differentiation in Indian food—before I ate a meal in Hospet, before I ate chaat, before eating home food—was that as I travelled the country on long-distance trains, I noticed the food sold by railway food vendors was often quite different as we moved along the line, such that the Indian-American academic and author Tulasi Srinivas described 'train travel in India [as a] culinary tasting journey with stations stocking local delicacies'.[4] I understand Srinivas to be referring more to purchasing durable foods such oranges in Nagpur and petha in Agra, whereas I am referring to perishable meals, snacks, and hot sweet chai; nonetheless, train travel was equally a 'culinary journey' for me, with emphasis on *was*. The quality and variety of food available on Indian trains and stations on major train routes has become dismal. A tea bag in a plastic cup submerged in tepid milk and pre-ordered meals picked up along the line from a factory that dispenses these in a tray under a vacuum-sealed layer of thick plastic that is so hard to pull off that the exertion required to remove it usually causes me to spill the food. I understand these meals are potentially more hygienic than those produced in the dark infernos of on-board catering kitchens—although I have never been ill from eating train food—or individual stations or itinerant vendors. Station food concessions are also increasingly serving the same foods across the country. The intention in changing the railway food system is to offer rail passengers hygienic food of assured quality, and I expect there have been cost benefits in this process; however, the standardization and homogenization of railway food has diminished its variety, and in my opinion, also its flavours and appeal, making it nondescript and unappetizing. As much as this has detracted from my experience of train travel, it is probably not of particular concern to most Indians, nor of any consequence to the country's food system; I mention this, though, to illustrate the unintended consequences of a change in the way food is prepared and distributed no matter how well intentioned.

Food trends will always come and go. What is the most super superfood now will be replaced by a new one a few months on, while the broader contemporary concept of healthism and eating commercially prescribed foods for individual 'well-being' will continue to exert influence on Indians' food choices, typically from the top down. The need to 'save time' will be one of the most, if not the most, influential factors on the food choices of urban Indians in the future. The availability of convenience foods that require little to no effort to be ready to eat—partly pre-prepared meal components, fully-prepared meals and snacks, and packaged products such as flavoured yoghurt—and easily plucked from a store shelf are a boon for women, offering them liberation—to whatever extent they want or are able to take up—from the work of feeding their families. The availability of convenience foods could potentially increase India's productivity levels by freeing women to take up more formal work, and in doing so, allow them more financial independence and political and social influence. Using more convenience foods could also result in detrimental environmental (more rubbish from packaging and food waste), nutritional (diminished quality through industrialization), and social impacts (less family engagement, loss of cooking skills, and cultural connection). The 'variety' offered by food retailers and online food delivery services may diminish differentiation in India's food, i.e., the same food choices will be more uniformly available across the country, pushing out more localized foods. Before the Industrial Revolution, Britain had regionally differentiated foods, but these largely disappeared with the concomitant industrialization of the food system, even as new foods were being brought in from the colonies of the empire.

One of the questions I asked the people I interviewed for this book was 'what they would like to see for India's food future'. Several chefs expressed hope for the development of a national food logistics system to improve access to the country's diverse fresh produce. Chef Manish Mehrotra said that it was often easier to have mushrooms flown in from Italy than procure them from the northeast because of poorly joined-up transport. Chef Prateek Sadhu regularly travels to Kashmir and Ladakh to seek out and bring back indigenous produce from this region for his Mumbai restaurant, because there is no reliable way to access these foods otherwise. As much as 30–40 per cent of the fruits and vegetables Indian producers currently grow go to waste because the transport system is so poor. Lack of cold storage facilities means fresh produce either rots waiting to be moved or is in such bad condition by the time it arrives at a metropolitan market that it must be thrown away.[5] Their hope for an improved internal logistics system is being addressed by projects such as the Delhi–Mumbai highway and associated industrial hubs. On the other hand, the lack of adequate transportation has played some part in the development of India's diverse regional cuisine, precisely because cooks had to make do with what was available in the local area. An improved infrastructure system that makes certain types of food, those that are produced commercially, and/or by dominant industry players, more widely available across the nation could eventually contribute to a flattening out of India's foodscape. As an example, Australians eat the same food all around the country, in part because we have an advanced road-logistics system.

A Global Culinary Superpower

India has not only absorbed external influences into her food, but she has also equally, if not more so, exerted influence on the food habits of foreigners. Spices traded from India—not necessarily native to the place, but that did not matter in the global understanding of the origin of these—were a major ingredient in the medieval cookery of Europe, and the Anglo-Indian cookery born of Britain's colonization of India was arguably the world's first 'East–West' cuisine, with the British experience of Indian food carried 'home' going on to exert a major influence on contemporary food preferences in that country, such that the cultural hybrid 'chicken tikka masala' was famously nominated in 2021 as the United Kingdom's 'true national dish'.[6]

I like to imagine my personal food connection with India replicates a much older one between India and Australia. In 1788, the British initially settled themselves on this remote island continent to use the place as a penal colony, a prison at the ends of the earth where the most 'depraved' people of Britain—largely petty thieves and political agitators—could be banished, hopefully never to be seen again in the mother country. As these first colonists were either 'guests of the Crown' or officials sent to mind them, it was the responsibility of the British government to provide their food. By 1791, some three years into this project, the government-supplied rations carried over on the first two convict fleets were almost exhausted, and their attempts at farming the shallow soil around Sydney Cove had failed to return anything more than a small harvest of maize and stunted vegetables. The spectre of starvation was looming large for this latterly arrived European population. When the transport ship Atlantic arrived in October of that year, Governor Arthur Phillip sent it off to Calcutta with orders to fill it up there with as much foodstuff and stores as the ship could carry as soon as it had dispatched its cargo of criminals. Seven months later, in June 1792, the Atlantic returned, stuffed to the gunwales with provisions as ordered. Phillip's secretary, David Collins, wrote that India offered 'the only hope for replenishing the [colony's] stores', but when the shipment of 'soujee', rice, 'dholl', dried peas, and wheat arrived, it was declared to be 'scarcely fit for consumption'; regardless, it was met with joy by the hungry colonists. 'That,' wrote Collins, 'people of all ranks were thrown into raptures by the arrival of a vessel loaded with unpalatable food, the situation of the colony may be understood.' While the colonists might have endured the Indian comestibles due to their grim circumstances, they enthusiastically consumed the Bengal rum sent out on the same ship. The convict population were not allowed alcohol, but they surreptitiously swapped their government-issued clothes and blankets for rum with the Bengali lascars crewing the Atlantic, because these natives of a tropical clime were freezing in the mild southern hemisphere spring.[7] This initial exchange opened the trade route between the eastern seaboard of Australia and Calcutta, and for the next fifty years, food supplies and rum were regularly sent out to the Antipodean population along with all manner of goods and people from India. Commercial and cultural food exchanges between India and Australia have continued since this time. In the twentieth century, the direction reversed, and Australia started to send bulk supplies of cereals and pulses to India.

More recently, India has become a significant market for Australian fresh produce, meat, dairy, processed food—jams, cheese, honey, pasta, ready-to-eat food, canned meats and vegetables, breakfast cereals—and wine. The potential size of the Indian market has many Australian food and wine producers keenly interested in selling their products in India.

India's traditional food practices and food knowledge have also been co-opted and commercialized by outsiders of more recent times, including attempts to copyright turmeric and a small industry producing packaged instant masala chai and haldi dudh re-packaged as 'turmeric latte' mixes. Fasting and eating fermented foods are also currently touted as having significant benefits for well-being in the global 'wellness-sphere': Indians have long done both.

> It's also jarring to see how the language around Indian food has changed over time, with new recipes branded as Ayurveda, vegan, and cleansing in order to seem more approachable. Ghee, which I grew up thinking was an indulgence, is now a superfood. Khichdi, one of my childhood comfort foods, has been co-opted as kitchari, the latest detox cleanse.[8]

The theme of the 2018 Tasting India Symposium was 'Making India the next global culinary superpower'. The specific question addressed by the various presenters and panellists was: 'What will get the world to eat and drink in India?' The discussions on how to achieve this were largely focused on gastronomic tourism and how India's diverse food culture could be developed as a major domestic and international tourist drawcard, and how India might have a bigger impact on the global culinary stage like that of France and Italy. Amongst the ideas put forward to achieve this were developing safe 'street food' precincts around the country and creating a food museum in Delhi to showcase India's culinary history and living food heritage. I had a brief, spontaneous, ten-minute slot on the podium at this event to talk about 'how India can become the next big gastronomic magnet'; quite an undertaking to be tasked with, let alone in such a short time. I can't recall now exactly what I said on this occasion in more than general terms, expressing my opinion that India has the most interesting regional food culture in the world, that was, at the time, not understood to even exist by most foreigners, and only recently come into interest for many Indians, and therefore held enormous potential as food-focused travel was becoming a major driver of choice of travel destination. I also mentioned the image problem India had with food hygiene and how tourists' fear of becoming ill stopped them from experimenting with unknown foods when in the country, radically truncating their experience to selecting the type of 'greatest culinary hits' dishes they were familiar with from Indian restaurants in their home countries, or not touching local food at all and insisting on eating western-style dishes—something that is becoming increasingly easier to do as this book attests. The audience clapped politely when I finished, but I didn't flatter myself to think that I had offered anything particularly useful to the subject under question. Having spent much time since then discovering more about a changing India, I will try and offer something more constructive here.

When I started writing this book I was 'locked up' in Australia—quite ironic given that the European settlement here started as a prison—as our government had shut our borders tight (except the Indian cricket team was let through), and I did not know when I would be able to return to India or when anyone would be able to travel. Indeed, there was much speculation as to whether the pandemic meant the end of global tourism. Fortunately, that is not what happened, but it was a two-year hiatus before I was able to be in India again in April 2022. Travelling to the Uttrakhand hills and into central India, I noticed a few westerners amongst all the local holiday makers, so I expect international tourism will eventually return to pre-COVID numbers, maybe even increase. In the meantime, that leaves Indians with their own culinary backyard to explore amongst themselves; the opportunity to encourage the development of food-based destinations and experiences with their curiosity and patronage; and influence broader understanding of India's unique food system, if they care to.

Now I'm back in India . . .I finally feel like I can learn without judgment, and have already warned various aunties that I'm coming over to cook after quarantine ends. I'm wanting to sink my feet into the spaces my

ancestors created, to unconditionally love where I come
from and give myself permission to explore it. It's always
going to be a process, but I want to decolonize my mind
and take my power back.[9]

Indians might be more under the sway of global food trends
than ever before, yet ultimately what happens in India will
have a huge impact on the world as the country moves
from a resource-low to a resource-intensive model of food
production. India's internal economy is large enough to
sustain itself. It is a powerful nation. Global corporations,
and the Indian companies mimicking their products and
methods, want to get into the Indian market because of the
numbers, and this could lead to a different colonization,
that of the food system and ideas of what should be valued
in food. Food companies have the power to change food
for good or otherwise, but it is individuals who give them
this licence by buying their products.

India still has an intact diverse food culture of
many different established cuisines, reflecting the
varied environmental and human geography of the
subcontinent, connected by broadly shared philosophical
and social concepts, integrating agriculture, health, and
the environment. It is a food culture operating with many
of the elements considered ideal for sustainability: local,
seasonal, self-reliant, diversified, and minimum waste
generation. That India has maintained such a food system
is, in part, a product of her economic circumstances, but the
country's contemporary condition allows for opportunity

for the best of both worlds: Indians can draw on their rich culinary heritage as it remains easily accessible to them, and they can use technology to enhance their food system to ensure that it develops in ways that are economically and socially beneficial, health-supportive, and equitable. India has the potential to have a huge impact on the planet by leading the way on sustainable food systems—as it is doing on renewables in the energy sector—and show us the way to the future.

Acknowledgements

Over the past twenty-five years, I have been supported, cared for and well-fed by a number of people in India with whom I have built enriching and enduring relationships. My love and gratitude to Kini and Gogi Sandhu, Bhuwan Kumari, Bharti Kumari, Vishu Vardan Singh, Kamini Prakash, Kavita Chessetty, Amrita and Ranjeet Batra, Rajesh Luthra and Daleep and Joan Majithia—vale Joan who sadly left us in 2021 at the age of 100. Without you, I would not have come to know the 'inside' workings of India's kitchens or her complex social and cultural systems to the extent that I felt I could write this book and offer some considered reflections on a changing India.

Many thanks and gratitude to Radhika Mishra and Fiona Caulfield for your generosity in making so many introductions for me in support of this book with some of the best restaurateurs, chefs, food writers and journalists, and other food people in India. The conversations I had with these people made a significant and important contribution to this work (acknowledged individually below). A note of thanks also to Dr Hemangi Raul in Baramati.

Appreciation and thanks to my editorial team at Penguin Random House—Richa Burman, Tarini Uppal, and Shaoni Mukherjee.

I want to acknowledge and thank the following people and institutions, who shared their time, experiences, and observations of changes in India's food system with me for this book.

Agricultural Development Trust (Baramati)	www.agridevelopmentrustbaramati.org
Avantika Bhuyan	https://lifestyle.livemint.com/author/avantika-bhuyan
Karen Anand	http://karensfarmersmarkets.in
Roshni Bajaj	https://www.vogue.in/author/Roshni-Bajaj-Sanghvi
Shatbhi Basu	Stir Academy of Bartending https://indulgeindia.com/shatbhi-basu-stir-academy-of-bartending/
Avni Biyani	https://www.foodhallonline.com
Gaytri Bhatia	www.vrindavanfarm.com
Sourish Bhattacharyya, India Food Symposium	https://www.linkedin.com/in/sourish-bhattacharyya-5a385256/. https://www.tastingindiasymposium.com
Tanushree Bhowmik and Om Routray	https://forktales.in

Fiona Caufield	https://www.lovetravelguides.com
Manu Chandra	https://www.instagram.com/begumvictoriacheese/?hl=en
Shubhra Chatterji	https://www.historywali.com/about
Shubhangi Choudhan	https://trivenioilandfoods.com
L. Nitin Chordia	www.cocoatrait.com
Kurush Dalal	kurushdalal@gmail.com
Phorum Dalal	https://www.linkedin.com/in/phorum-dalal-35b48711/?originalSubdomain=in
Ritu Dalmia	https://divarestaurants.com/chef
Aneesh Dhairyawan	https://www.linkedin.com/company/authenticook/?originalSubdomain=in
Vikram Doctor	https://economictimes.indiatimes.com/blogs/author/vikramdoctor/ or contact Vikram via his Instagram page.
Anahita Dhondy	Chef and author of *The Parsi Kitchen* @AnahitaDhondy
Rushina Munshaw Ghildiyal	https://rushinamunshawghildiyal.blogspot.com
Keith Goyden (Pao Bakery)	paochatola@gmail.com
Prachi Joshi	https://deliciouslydirectionless.com/about/
Rohit Khattar	https://indianaccent.com/newdelhi https://www.oldworldhospitality.com/our-brands/
Rishek Khattar	https://www.comorin.in/
Saee Koranne-Khandekar	https://www.saeekhandekar.com
Megha Koli	https://www.linkedin.com/in/megha-kohli-0406a14b/?originalSubdomain=in

Jehangir Lawyer	https://fortunegourmet.com/
Antoine Lewis	https://antoinelewis.com
Joanna Lobo	https://www.linkedin.com/in/joanna-lobo/?originalSubdomain=in
Ahbhay Mangaldas	https://houseofmg.com/
Manish Mehrotra	https://indianaccent.com/chef-manish-mehrotra.php
Sudhir M. Pai Food & Beverage Consultant	www.chefsudhirpai.com
Jonty Rajagopalan	https://www.detoursindia.com
Dr Dayakar Rao B.	https://www.millets.res.in
Marryam H. Reshii	https://marryamhreshii.com
Ashwin Rodrigues	https://gooddropwine.com
Prateek Sadhu	https://www.masquerestaurant.com/
Abhijit Saha	https://chefabhijitsaha.in/about/
Gitika Saikia	https://www.indiafoodnetwork.in/author/gitika-saikia
Sameer Seth	https://thebombaycanteen.com/
Rajeev Sethi	www.asianheritagefoundation.org
Vishal Shetty, Bengaluru Oota Company	www.bengaluruootacompany.com
Ruchi Shrivastava, Food Media	ruchi@greedgoddess.com
Shilpa Sharma	http://mustardrestaurants.in
Jashan Sippy, Food Architect	www.sugarandspace.in
A. D. Singh	https://olivebarandkitchen.com/management.html

Rahul Singh	https://thebeercafe.com/
Dr Syed Shakir Ali, Head and Senior Scientist	Agricultural Science Centre www.kvkbaramati.com
Shreya Soni	https://www.linkedin.com/in/ shreyasoni/?originalSubdomain=in
Priyank Sukanand	Bangelore Connection 1888 www.thebc1888.in
Anubhav Sapra	http://www.delhifoodwalks.com/
Disha Thakkar	https://sulavineyards.com/
Karan Upmanyu	https://www.woodstreetsauceco.in

Notes

Introduction

1   A listing at the end of this book includes the names of all the people who generously shared their experiences and insights with me.

2   In his 2022 book, *Ten Cities That Led the World*, author Paul Strathern includes a chapter titled 'Mumbai: A Vision of Our Future', so I am not the only one who thinks the future of city life is there to be experienced in India.

3   R. Tannahill, *Food in History* (London: Penguin, 1973), p. 393.

4   R. Krishnendu and T. Srinivas, eds., *Curried Cultures: Globalization, Food, and South Asia* (Berkeley: University of California Press, 2012), p. 8.

5   T. Srinivas, 'Exploring Indian Culture through Food', *Education about Asia* 16, no. 3 (2011): 38.

6   J. M. Parsons, 'When Convenience is Inconvenient: "Healthy" Family Foodways and the Persistent Intersectionalities of Gender and Class', *Journal of Gender Studies* 25, no. 4 (2016): 383. DOI: 10.1080/09589236.2014.987656.

7   A. Appadurai, 'How to Make a National Cuisine: Cookbooks in Contemporary India', *Comparative Studies in Society and History* 30 (1988): 3.

8   S. Harris, *Metabolic Living: Food, Fat, and the Absorption of Illness in India* (Durham: Duke University Press, 2016), pp. 109–12.

9   Ibid.

Chapter 1: The Rise of Regionalism

1   V. Jones and S. Pokharel, 'Is This the World's Best Indian Restaurant?', *CNN*, 27 March 2020, Available at https://edition.cnn.com/travel/article/indian-accent-best-indian-restaurant.

2   I noted down all that Mehrotra said, and as I know something of this history myself, I have fleshed out his rendition a little further in the paragraphs that follow. The quotations are his exact words.

3   The use of white tablecloths in a public dining room per se was not original to Moti Mahal. These have been used in Europe since the middle ages as a symbol of wealth and refinement in homes. In a restaurant setting, white table linen sets expectations of a superior standard of food and service and a higher price. Moti Mahal's innovation was to present its style of 'north Indian' food in a more westernized setting, complete with white tablecloths.

4   The indigenous peoples who had inhabited the continent for tens of thousands of years before this colonization took place in 1788 ate a widely variated and region-specific diet.

5   Anoothi Vishal, 'How will the pandemic change the long tradition of "cookbooks" from the kitchens of India?' *Scroll.in*, 25 August 2020. Available at https://scroll.in/article/971267/how-will-the-pandemic-change-the-long-tradition-of-cookbooks-from-the-kitchens-of-india

6   As I wrote in *The Penguin Food Guide to India*, it would require an encyclopaedic endeavour to faithfully document all the foodways of India . . . and I am still hoping someone might take up my invitation to fund such a project one day.

7   Circumstances prevented my visiting Tripura, Mizoram, and Manipur—as yet.

8   T. Srinivas, 'Exploring Indian Culture through Food', *Education about Asia* 16, no. 3 (2011): 38–41.

9   K. Karmakar, 'Thirteen Types of Puris from Eleven States', *Finely Chopped*, 26 January 2019. Available at https://www.finelychopped.net/2019/01/thirteen-types-of-puris-from-eleven.html.

10   A. Appadurai, 'How to Make a National Cuisine: Cookbooks in Contemporary India', *Comparative Studies in Society and History* 30 (1988): 3.

11   T. Srinivas, 'Exploring Indian Culture through Food', *Education about Asia* 16, no. 3 (2011): 38–41.

12   A. Krishna, R. Dsouza-Prabhu, and S. Unakar, 'Godrej Food Trends Report 2020', *Vikhroli Cucina*, 13 March 2021. Available at https://www.vikhrolicucina.com/resources/godrej-food-trends-report/godrej-food-trends-report-2021.

13   K. Katrak, 'Food and Belonging: At "Home" in "Alien-Kitchens"', in *Through the Kitchen Window: Women Explore the Intimate Meanings of Food and Cooking*, ed. Arlene Voski Avakian (Boston: Beacon Press, 1997), p. 270.

14   Ibid., 270.

15   A. Vishal, 'In the Popularity of Delhi Food, the Far Superior Dehli Food is Being Forgotten', *Scroll.in*, 17 August 2020. Available at https://scroll.in/magazine/970270/as-delhi-loses-its-syncretic-culture-it-is-forgetting-its-great-legacy-dehli-food.

16   K. Bamzai and L. G. Bhutia, 'The Art of Eating: How Pandemic Has Changed Our Food Habits', *Open*, 6 August

2021. Available at https://openthemagazine.com/cover-stories/the-art-of-eating/?fbclid=IwAR0GBBKN9LtL8bOPOJ6zHAiqWnv5zhAuIp4OhLiOx07aeBug86mb66UYMCk.

17 Dr Vibha Varshney addressing hospitality students at a forum at the Indian Culinary Institute in Noida, December 2019.

18 K. Bamzai and L. G. Bhutia, 'The Art of Eating: How Pandemic Has Changed Our Food Habits', *Open*, 6 August 2021. Available at https://openthemagazine.com/cover-stories/the-art-of-eating/?fbclid=IwAR0GBBKN9LtL8bOPOJ6zHAiqWnv5zhAuIp4OhLiOx07aeBug86mb66UYMCk.

19 In *Consuming Passions: The Anthropology of Eating*, the flavour principles of fifteen different world cuisines are listed, most of which have six to seven distinguishing flavours; Indian food has twelve! P. Farb and G. Armelagos, *Consuming Passions: The Anthropology of Eating* (Boston: Houghton Mifflin Company, 1980).

20 J. Lobo, '40 Under 40: India's Most Exciting Young Chefs', *Condé Nast Traveller*, 10 February 2020. Available at https://www.cntraveller.in/story/best-indian-chefs-under-40-bangalore-delhi-mumbai-goa-pune.

Chapter 2: Software Eats India

1 'The Strong Growth of India's Food Delivery Sector Will Likely Continue', APAC, *GLG*, 30 June 2021. Available at https://glginsights.com/articles/the-strong-growth-of-indias-food-delivery-sector-will-likely-continue/.

2 Uma Kanan, 'No Takers for 10-Min Food Delivery', *NRAI*, 24 March 2022. Available at https://nrai.org/no-takers-for-10-min-food-delivery/; 'India 21.41 Billion Online Food Delivery Market to 2026: Focus on Bangalore, Delhi NCR, Mumbai, Hyderabad & Pune', *GlobeNewswire*, 17 May 2021. Available at https://www.globenewswire.com/

news-release/2021/05/17/2230423/28124/en/India-21-41-Billion-Online-Food-Delivery-Market-to-2026-Focus-on-Bangalore-Delhi-NCR-Mumbai-Hyderabad-Pune.html.

3   All these terms were drawn from a recent article on the National Restaurant Association of India's website: Vindu Goel and Ayesha Venkataraman, 'India's Restaurants Rebel Against Food Delivery Apps', *NRAI,* 30 August 2019. Available at https://nrai.org/indias-restaurants-rebel-against-food-delivery-appsvindu-goel-and-ayesha-venkataraman/.

4   Vijay Govindarajan and Anup Srivastava, 'What Zomato's $12 Billion IPO Says About Tech Companies Today', *Harvard Business Review*, 6 August 2021. Available at https://hbr.org/2021/08/what-zomatos-12-billion-ipo-says-about-tech-companies-today.

5   Vindu Goel and Ayesha Venkataraman, 'India's Restaurants Rebel Against Food Delivery Apps', *New York Times*, 29 August 2019. Available at https://www.nytimes.com/2019/08/29/technology/india-restaurants-logout-delivery-zomato.html.

6   Ananya Bhattacharya, 'Indian Restaurants Have Forced Zomato to Change Its Recipe—And Customers Are Left With A Sour Taste', *Quartz*, 22 August 2019. Available at https://qz.com/india/1691902/indias-zomato-swiggy-eazydiner-may-end-food-discounts-soon/.

7   Kritti Bhalla. 'FHRAI Calls Out Zomato, Dineout Over Protests By Restaurants; Backs #LogOut Campaign', *Inc 42*, 19 August 2019. Available at https://inc42.com/buzz/fhrai-calls-out-zomato-dineout-over-protests-backs-logout/.

8   Aditi Shrivastava and Patanjali Pahwa, 'Zomato, Swiggy, UberEats Reduce Discounts As Food Delivery Market Grows Cold', *Economic Times*, 29 November 2019. Available at https://economictimes.indiatimes.com/small-biz/startups/newsbuzz/zomato-swiggy-ubereats-reduce-discounts-as-food-delivery-

market-grows-cold/articleshow/72286430.cms?from=mdr; 'Online food Aggregators to Soon Face Fresh Blow From NRAI', *Mint*, 25 August 2019. Available at https://www. livemint.com/companies/news/online-food-aggregators-to-soon-face-fresh-blow-from-nrai-1566708145796.html.

9   Ratna Bhushan, 'To Detox Consumers From Discount Addiction, 300 Eateries To Opt Out Of Aggregator Menu', *Economic Times*, 15 August 2019. Available at https://economictimes.indiatimes.com/industry/services/hotels-/-restaurants/to-detox-consumers-from-discount-addiction-300-eateries-to-opt-out-of-aggregator-menu/articleshow/70685144.cms?from=mdr.

10 Suneera Tandon, 'The Revolt Against Food Delivery Apps', *Mint*, 21 August 2019. Available at https://www.livemint.com/companies/start-ups/the-revolt-against-food-delivery-apps-1566324255842.html.

11 Ratna Bhushan, '8000-Strong Hotels Body To Shun Zomato Gold Delivery', *Economic Times*, 25 November 2019. Available at https://economictimes.indiatimes.com/industry/services/hotels-/-restaurants/8000-strong-hotels-body-to-shun-zomato-gold-delivery/articleshow/72215761.cms.

12 Patanjali Pahwa, 'Zomato CEO Deepinder Goyal Logs Out Of Talks With Restaurants', *Economic Times*, 23 August 2019. Available at https://m.economictimes.com/small-biz/startups/newsbuzz/zomato-ceo-deepinder-goyal-logs-out-of-talks-with-restaurants/articleshow/70797457.cms.; 'Zomato Offers To Restructure Gold Scheme But Restaurants Stick To Guns', *Times of India*, 21 August 2019. Available at http://timesofindia.indiatimes.com/articleshow/70776326.cms?utm_source=contentofinterest&utm_medium=text&utm_campaign=cppst; Ratna Bhushan, '8000-Strong Hotels Body To Shun Zomato Gold Delivery', *NRAI*, 25 November 2019. Available at https://nrai.org/8000-strong-hotels-body-to-shun-zomato-gold-delivery.

13 Sanchita Dash, 'Zomato CEO Deepinder Goyal Responds To The 'Logout' Movement – Restaurant Owners Mock Him On Twitter', *Business Insider*, 19 August 2019. Available at https://www.businessinsider.in/zomato-ceo-deepinder-goyal-responds-to-the-logout-movement-restaurant-owners-mock-him-on-twitter/articleshow/70731971.cms; Gaurav Gupta, 'Introducing Infinity Dining –An All-New Way To Dine Out', *Zomato*, 26 July 2019. Available at https://www.zomato.com/blog/infinity-dining.

14 Ratna Bhushan, 'Food Firms Feast On Binge Watching', *Economic Times*, 14 December 2019. Available at https://economictimes.indiatimes.com/industry/cons-products/food/food-firms-feast-on-binge-watching/articleshow/72576298.cms?

15 Some readers will have recognized that the title of this chapter is a play on tech entrepreneur Marc Andreessen's famous comment: 'Software is eating the world'.

16 Shyamak R. Tata, 'Here's How Technology Is Shaping India's Workforce', *Go Global Consulting Group*, 24 February 2020. Available at http://www.goglobalconsultinggroup.com/blog/heres-how-technology-is-shaping-indias-workforce/.

17 Internationally, FSAs have fought hard legal battles to keep things this way.

18 V. Govindarajan and A. Srivastava, 'What Zomato's $12 Billion IPO Says About Tech Companies Today', *Harvard Business Review*, 6 August 2021. Available at https://hbr.org/2021/08/what-zomatos-12-billion-ipo-says-about-tech-companies-today;

     N. Sharma, 'In India, Delivery Riders Are Taking to Social Media to Talk About Their Long Hours and Low Pay', *Scroll.in*, 19 September 2021. Available at https://scroll.in/article/1005628/in-india-delivery-riders-are-taking-to-social-media-to-talk-about-their-long-hours-and-low-pay;

     S. Tandon and V. Bansal, 'The Loneliness of the Delivery Man', *Mint*, 18 September 2019. Available at https://www.

livemint.com/news/india/inside-the-lives-of-food-delivery-riders-1568800031736.html;

S. Nanisetti, 'Poor Wages, Punishing Hours, and Lack of Labour Rights Make Food Delivery a Thankless Gig', *The Hindu*, 21 August 2021. Available at https://www.thehindu.com/society/poor-wages-punishing-hours-and-lack-of-labour-rights-make-food-delivery-a-thankless-gig/article36012013.ece.

This plethora of reading about the abysmal working conditions of delivery riders made me wonder why there was so much attention on them. After all, there are plenty of other workers who do low-paid, onerous, and even unsafe work. Was it because the riders are the only visible human manifestation of the online food delivery sector? Or was it the lingering, erroneous idea that technology companies are more disruptive and socially minded than other corporates? Maybe it was the contrast between the look and feel of their slick communication channels, clever graphic design, and focus on community 'feel' and the reality of the deliverers' work life.

19 S. Mukerji, *Times Food & Night Life Guide* (Delhi: Times Group Books, 2018), pp. 202–205.

20 Rashi Varshney, 'Zomato Hints Its New Focus On Farm-To-Table Concept', *Medianama*, 11 July 2018. Available at https://www.medianama.com/2018/07/223-zomato-hints-its-new-focus-on-farm-to-table-concept/

21 Vindu Goel and Ayesha Venkataraman, 'India's Restaurants Rebel Against Food Delivery Apps', *New York Times*, 29 August 2019. Available at https://www.nytimes.com/2019/08/29/technology/india-restaurants-logout-delivery-zomato.html.

22 Ashish Rukhaiyar, 'Cash Burning Zomato Has Immense Potential, Says Aswath Damodaran', *Business Today*, 23 July 2021. Available at https://www.businesstoday.in/markets/

company-stock/story/cash-burning-zomato-has-immense-potential-says-aswath-damodaran-302158-2021-07-23.

23 Laxitha Mundhra, 'Foodtech Zomato Shares Open At 4% Rise Post Q4 Results; Market Cap At $6.19 Bn', *Inc 42*, 24 May 2022. Available at https://inc42.com/buzz/foodtech-zomato-shares-open-at-4-rise-post-q4-results-market-cap-at-6-19-bn/;

Kaushlendra Singh Sengar, 'IPO Scanner: Is Grey Market Premium The Holy Grail Indicator?', *Money Control*, 17 July 2021. Available at https://www.moneycontrol.com/news/business/ipo/ipo-scanner-is-grey-market-premium-the-holy-grail-indicator-7185051.html;

V. P. Tammiraju and S. Chu, 'Swiggy: Optimizing Cash Burn till Next Funding Round', *NUS*, 15 August 2018, Available at http://courses.nus.edu.sg/course/bizchucl/swiggy.pdf;

Anjali, 'How Much Cash Zomato, Paytm, Ola, and Swiggy etc. Are Burning in India?', *FinnovationZ*, Available at https://www.finnovationz.com/blog/how-much-cash-zomato-paytm-ola-swiggy-are-losing-in-india;

Dharna, 'Not Pitting Ourselves Against Anyone Else's Cash Burn: Swiggy CEO', *InShorts*, 22 November 2019. Available at https://inshorts.com/en/news/not-pitting-ourselves-against-anyone-elses-cash-burn-swiggy-ceo-1574419646504;

TNN, 'Cash Burn Battle May Return In Online Food Delivery Business', *Times of India*, 29 August 2019. Available at https://timesofindia.indiatimes.com/business/cash-burn-battle-may-return-in-online-food-delivery-biz/articleshow/77818462.cms.

24 R. Narayanaswamy, *Financial Accounting: A Managerial Perspective* (Delhi: PHI Learning Pvt. Ltd, 2022), p. 483.

25 Carsten Hirschberg, Alexander Rajko, Thomas Schumacher, and Martin Wrulich, 'The Changing Market For Food

Delivery', *McKinsey & Company*, 9 November 2016. Available at https://www.mckinsey.com/industries/technology-media-and-telecommunications/our-insights/the-changing-market-for-food-delivery.

26 Aditi Shrivastava, 'Taking The Fight To Swiggy & Zomato, Amazon Joins Food Delivery Business In Bengaluru', *Economic Times*, 28 February 2020. Available at https://economictimes.indiatimes.com/small-biz/startups/newsbuzz/amazon-joins-at-food-delivery-business-in-bluru/articleshow/74327763.cms?from=mdr

27 Consumer Foods-to-Go, 'What Can Restaurants Do with the Rise of Delivery?', *Apple Podcasts*, Available at https://podcasts.apple.com/au/podcast/consumer-foods-to-go/id1450161970?i=1000516263041

28 Consumer Foods, 'Podcast: Ghost Kitchens in India and Southeast Asia Explained', *Rabobank*, September 2020, Available at research.rabobank.com/far/en/sectors/consumer-foods/podcast-ghost-kitchens-in-india-and-southeast-asia-explained.html?utm_medium=RSS

29 J. Barman, 'Entrepreneurs Wanted—Part 2', Rebel Foods, 21 November 2020. Available at https://www.rebelfoods.com/blogs/topic/entrepreneurs-wanted-part-2.

30 Aditi Shrivastava, 'Fine-Dining Chains Smell The Money In Delivery-Only Brands', *Economic Times*, 14 January 2020. Available at https://tech.economictimes.indiatimes.com/news/startups/restaurant-chains-launches-new-delivery-only-brands-to-sell-on-swiggy-and-zomato/73232853.

31 J. Barman, 'A Unique Take on Food Tech', *Rebel Foods*, 11 June 2017, Available at https://spirit.rebelfoods.com/a-unique-take-on-food-tech-dcef8c51ba41

32 M. Chanchani, 'Online Food Delivery Wars Are Moving from India to Bharat', *Times of India*, 17 March 2019. Available at http://timesofindia.indiatimes.com/articleshow/68447011.

cms?utm_source=contentofinterest&utm_medium=
text&utm_campaign=cppst

33 N. D'Souza, 'Speciality Restaurants to Open 15 New Cloud
    Kitchens; Eyes Rs 500–550 Cr Revenue', *CNBC TV-18*,
    25 February 2022. Available at https://nrai.org/speciality-
    restaurants-to-open-15-new-cloud-kitchens-eyes-rs-500-550-
    cr-revenue/

34 A. D. Singh, 'Fine Dining Died in the Past Decade': AD
    Singh', *Forbes India*, 10 January 2020. Available at https://nrai.
    org/fine-dining-died-in-the-past-decade-ad-singh/

35 Phorum Dalal, 'Mumbai: NRAI Bootcamp to Help Restaurants
    Become Less Dependent on Food Delivery Apps', *NRAI*, 7 May
    2021. Available at https://nrai.org/mumbai-nrai-bootcamp-to-
    help-restaurants-become-less-dependent-on-food-delivery-apps/

36 Vijay Govindarajan and Anup Srivastava, 'What Zomato's $12
    Billion IPO Says About Tech Companies Today', *Havard Business
    Review*, 6 August 2021. Available at https://hbr.org/2021/08/
    what-zomatos-12-billion-ipo-says-about-tech-companies-today

37 Ankit Arora, 'India Food Delivery Market - Evolution & the
    Road Ahead...', *LinkedIn*, 24 September 2020. Available at
    https://www.linkedin.com/pulse/india-food-delivery-market-
    evolution-road-ahead-ankit-arora

38 Prateek Munjal, '#Logout Campaign - A Deep Discounting
    Massacre', *LinkedIn*, 1 September 2019. Available at https://
    www.linkedin.com/pulse/logout-campaign-deep-discounting-
    massacre-prateek-munjal

39 Andrew Alexander, 'The Pros and Cons of Online Food Delivery
    Services', *Fridge Agency*. Available at https://thefridgeagency.
    com/blog/pros-cons-online-food-deliery-services/

40 Vijay Govindarajan and Anup Srivastava, 'What Zomato's $12
    Billion IPO Says About Tech Companies Today', *Havard Business
    Review*, 6 August 2021. Available at https://hbr.org/2021/08/
    what-zomatos-12-billion-ipo-says-about-tech-companies-today

41 Both Swiggy and Zomato operate impressive social sites to keep their customers engaged and informed.

42 Deepinder Goyal, 'Say No to Cutlery in Food Delivery', *Zomato*, 30 August 2021. Available at https://www.zomato.com/blog/say-no-to-cutlery-in-food-delivery

43 Deepinder Goyal, 'Say No to Cutlery in Food Delivery', *Zomato*, 30 August 2021. Available at https://www.hotelierindia.com/fb/14844-nrai-conducts-a-second-bootcamp-for-restaurateurs-on-enabling-direct-ordering-with-dotpe;

BW Hotelier, 'NRAI's First-Ever Cloud Kitchen Convention Witnesses Successful Fruition', *NRAI*, 19 April 2022. Available at https://nrai.org/nrais-first-ever-cloud-kitchen-convention-witnesses-successful-fruition/

44 Prabalika M. Borah, 'Why the NRAI Wants to Cut Out the Middleman of Aggregator Platforms Like Swiggy and Zomato', *The Hindu*, 10 May 2021. Available at https://www.thehindu.com/life-and-style/food/nrai-townhall-webinar-4-2021-report-cutting-out-middleman-aggregator-swiggy-and-zomato/article34526801.ece

45 Shilpa Nair Anand, 'All About Rezoy, One of India's First Food Delivery Apps by a Restaurant Association', *The Hindu*, 1 June 2021. Available at https://www.thehindu.com/life-and-style/food/rezoy-food-delivery-app-by-kerala-hotel-restaurant-association/article34689158.ece

46 Rabobank Podcasts, 'What Can Restaurants Do With the Rise of Delivery?', Consumer Foods to Go on Apple Podcasts, 8 April 2021. Available at https://podcasts.apple.com/au/podcast/consumer-foods-to-go/id1450161970?i=1000516263041

47 Shilpa Nair Anand, Prabalika M. Borah, and Meghna Majumdar, 'The Great Indian Food Delivery Tussle', *The Hindu*, 9 June 2021. Available at https://www.thehindu.com/life-and-style/food/indian-restaurants-go-for-direct-delivery/article34770229.ece

48 Jaydeep Barman, 'Entrepreneurs Wanted—Part 3', *Medium*, 13 February 2020. Available at https://jaydeep-barman.medium.com/entrepreneurs-wanted-part-3-167e798992fa

49 Corey Mintz, 'Do Homes Without Kitchens Mark the End of Human Civilization?', *TVO Today*, 13 August 2019. Available at https://www.tvo.org/article/do-homes-without-kitchens-mark-the-end-of-human-civilization

50 Shyamak R. Tata, 'Here's How Technology is Shaping India's Workforce', *Go Global Consulting Group*, 24 February 2020. Available at http://www.goglobalconsultinggroup.com/blog/heres-how-technology-is-shaping-indias-workforce/

51 'Delhi Emerges as the Dining Capital of India with 32% Diners, Bangalore 2nd with 18%: Dineout Trends Report 2021', *Hotelier India*, 9 January 2022. Available at https://www.hotelierindia.com/business/delhi-emerges-as-the-dining-capital-of-india-with-32-diners-bangalore-2nd-with-18dineout-trends-report-2021

52 Anirban Chowdhury and Arijit Barman, 'Modi Has More Vision Than Many Western Politicians: Frank Appel, CEO of Deutsche Post DHL Group', *Economic Times*, 24 April 2017. Available at https://economictimes.indiatimes.com/opinion/interviews/modi-has-more-vision-than-many-western-politicians-frank-appel-ceo-of-deutsche-post-dhl-group/articleshow/58332798.cms?from=mdr

Chapter 3: Women: Agents of Change

1 Rudrapur became part of Uttarakhand in 2000 and it was a town more than a city when I first came here.

2 Krishnendu Ray, 'Culinary Culture in Colonial India. A Cosmopolitan Platter and the Middle-Class', *Global Food History* 4 (2018): 98.

3   'Only 6.1% Indian Men Participate in Cooking, Reveals Time Use Survey', *Money Control*, 13 October 2020. Available at https://www.moneycontrol.com/news/india/only-6-1-indian-men-participate-in-cooking-reveals-time-use-survey-5958921.html

4   Tulasi Srinivas, 'Masala Matters', in *Curried Cultures: Globalization, Food, and South Asia*, ed. Tulasi Srinivas and Krishnendu Ray (Berkeley: University of California Press, 2018) 220.

5   My editor observed that it is often men who bring non-vegetarian snacks into a vegetarian household to eat alone or share with their children.

6   Kodandarama Chandramouli, 'Women Domestic Workers in India: An Analysis', *International Journal of Innovative Technology and Exploring Engineering* (IJITEE) 8 (2018): 1–5.

7   An attitude that is not exclusive to India: Australian women still do more unpaid domestic work than men.

8   M. Mahadevan, D. Blair, and E. R. Raines, 'Changing Food Habits in a South Indian Hindu Brahmin Community: A Case of Transitioning Gender Roles and Family Dynamics', *Ecology of Food and Nutrition* 53 (2014): 596–617.

9   My own work, 'The Devil at Work', demonstrates that the desire to gain the status of employing servants overrode the strong prejudices colonial Australians held about having to employ convicted criminals, poor Irish girls and educated unmarried English women as domestic cooks as these were the only workers available to them. See: O'Brien, C. 'The Devil at Work', in *The Routledge Companion to Food in Literature*, ed. by Donna Lee Brien, and Lorna Piatti-Farnell (United Kingdom: Routledge, 2018).

10 Sidney Mintz, *Sweetness and Power: The Place of Sugar in Modern History* (New York: Penguin Books, 1985), pp. 128–129.

11 Rujuta Diwekar, *Indian Superfoods* (New Delhi: Juggernaut, 2016).

12 Ibid.

13 Rachel Berger, 'Between Digestion and Desire: Genealogies of Food in Nationalist North India', *Modern Asian Studies* 47 (2013): 1622–1643.

14 Anoothi Vishal, 'Pinch of Irony: As Indian Restaurants Embrace Home Food, Home Cooks Are Recreating Restaurant Dishes', *Scroll.in*, 30 November 2020. Available at https://scroll.in/magazine/979004/pinch-of-irony-as-indian-restaurants-embrace-home-food-home-cooks-are-recreating-restaurant-dishes.

15 Dipti Nagpaul, 'How the Pandemic Struck Businesses of Women Home Chefs in India', *HuffPost*, 8 August 2022. Available at https://www.huffpost.com/archive/in/entry/home-chef-women-cooking-covid-pandemic_in_5f2ecb92c5b64d7a55f42123.

16 Sandhya Keelery, 'Alternatives to Home Cooking in India 2021', *Statista*, 30 May 2022. Available at https://www.statista.com/statistics/1236179/alternatives-to-home-cooking-in-india/.

17 Aashna Dhiman, 'Food & Drink: How Home Chefs Are Shaking Up the Food Industry in India', *Outlook*, 14 November 2022. Available at https://www.outlookindia.com/travel/how-home-chefs-in-india-are-shaking-up-the-food-industry-news-197499

18 Sindhu Kashyap, 'With Over 60 Home Chefs, This Startup Aims to Bring Ghar ka Khaana to Your Doorstep', *YourStory*, 24 December 2019. Available at https://yourstory.com/2019/12/mumbai-startup-curryful-chefs-homecooked-food-delivery

19 Solomon Harris, *Metabolic Living: Food, Fat, and the Absorption of Illness in India* (Durham: Duke University Press, 2016), p. 110.

20 Marryam H. Reshii. Facebook post January 24, 2021.

21 Sean Colin Young, 'In a man's world', *Asian Age*, 8 March 2019. Available at https://www.asianage.com/life/food/080319/in-a-mans-world.html

22 Prerna Shah, 'Indian men, cooking and kitchen chores – Covid-19 and beyond', *The Good Story* Project, 2 September 2021. Available at https://thegoodstoryproject.com/2021/09/02/indian-men-cooking-and-kitchen-chores-covid-19-and-beyond/

23 Joanna Lobo, '40 under 40: India's most exciting young chefs', *Condé Nast Traveller*, 10 February 2022. Available at https://www.cntraveller.in/story/best-indian-chefs-under-40-bangalore-delhi-mumbai-goa-pune/

24 Ibid.

25 Ibid.

26 'India's top 10 young chefs,' *Mint Lounge*, 23 April 2022. Available at https://lifestyle.livemint.com/news/big-story/indias-top-10-young-chefs-111650622709158.html

27 Samar Halarnkar, 'The dilemma of celebrating men who cook,' *Mint Lounge*, 21 November 2021. Available at https://lifestyle.livemint.com/food/cook/the-dilemma-of-celebrating-men-who-cook-111637298197513.html.

28 Prerna Shah, 'Indian men, cooking and kitchen chores – Covid-19 and beyond', *The Good Story* Project, 2 September 2021. Available at https://thegoodstoryproject.com/2021/09/02/indian-men-cooking-and-kitchen-chores-covid-19-and-beyond/.

Chapter 4: New Influences on Indian Food

1 In 2022, I noted several more cake and ice-cream stores added to the ranks of confectioners operating in this market.

2 S. Mintz, *Sweetness and Power: The Place of Sugar in Modern History* (New York: Penguin Books, 1986), p. 20.

3   I am referring to natural whole cow milk here. The fat content
     of the milk of desi cows is lower than that of Jersey cows
     commonly milked in European countries. These days, there is
     so much modification of milk that it is hard to know what is
     what though.

4   Kimi Dangor and Kaveree Bamzai, 'Urban India picks up taste
     for eating out', *India Today*, 17 November 2011. Available
     at https://www.indiatoday.in/magazine/society-the-arts/
     story/20050711-indain-food-industry-growing-as-indians-
     eating-out-more-than-787348-2005-07-11.

5   Sourish Bhattacharyya, 'Sassy restaurateur and pastry chef
     Rachel Goenka ramps up the oomph factor of Indian sweets',
     Indian Express, updated on 3 November 2019. Available
     at https://indianexpress.com/article/lifestyle/books/rachel-
     goenka-adventures-with-mithai-book-review-6100094/.

6   I use the term 'social media' to refer to all platforms that allow
     people to share content.

7   Reece Robertson, 'Why You're Addicted to Social Media—
     Dopamine, Technology, and Inequality', *Medium*, 19 December
     2017. Available at https://medium.com/@Reece_Robertson/
     why-youre-addicted-to-social-media-dopamine-technology-
     inequality-c2cca07ed3ee

8   'How the Changing Food Habits of Millennials are Impacting the
     Restaurant Business', *Restaurant Times*. Available at https://www.
     posist.com/restaurant-times/resources/millennials-changing-
     food-habits-and-impact-on-restaurant-business.html

9   Aatish Nath, 'Are Food "Influencers" Wearing Out
     Their Usefulness in India?', *HuffPost*, 18 January 2020.
     Available   at   https://www.huffingtonpost.in/entry/are-
     food-influencers-wearing-out-their-usefulness-in-india_
     in_5e233836c5b6321176148cce

10   I understand the percentage of Indians who eat a 'pure veg' diet
     is not as great as perceived, although it is the highest in the

world. However, even when a domestic meal includes a meat/fish/chicken component it will typically be accompanied by 'plant' based dishes and condiments.

11 Vir Sanghvi, *The Game Changers: Transforming India* (New Delhi: Westland Publications, 2019), p. xi.

12 Aatish Nath, 'Are Food "Influencers" Wearing Out Their Usefulness in India?', *HuffPost*, 18 January 2020. Available at https://www.huffingtonpost.in/entry/are-food-influencers-wearing-out-their-usefulness-in-india_in_5e233836c5b6321176148cce

13 Despite the pandemic enforced shut down of travel across 2020–21, the industry has rebounded, demonstrated by the fact that the international and internal flights I took to and from and within India in April 2022 were all packed to capacity.

14 Kimmy Dangor and Kaveree Bamzai, 'Urban India Picks Up Taste for Eating Out', *India Today*, 17 November 2011. Available at https://www.indiatoday.in/magazine/society-the-arts/story/20050711-indain-food-industry-growing-as-indians-eating-out-more-than-787348-2005-07-11

15 Although Chowdury is actually of Bangladeshi descent, Bengali cuisine would be similar in both countries, with regional differences in flavours.

16 Chidanand Rajghatta, 'In America, Indian Cuisine Gets a Big Bite of Recognition and Reward', *Times of India*, 14 June 2022. Available at https://timesofindia.indiatimes.com/nri/us-canada-news/in-america-indian-cuisine-gets-a-big-bite-of-recognition-and-reward/articleshow/92211101.cms

Chapter 5: Supermarkets and Superfoods

1 C. Lutringer and S. Randeria, 'How Not to Waste a Garbage Crisis: Food Consumption, Solid Waste Management and

Civic Activism in Bangalore/Bengaluru, India', *International Development Journal*, DOI: https://doi.org/10.4000/poldev.2476.

2   Foodhall website: https://www.foodhallonline.com/pages/about-us

3   Or it was: At the time of writing, Future Group was in the process of selling their food retail holdings to Reliance Group.

4   Europeans introduced avocadoes into India in the nineteenth century, but they did not take off in any significant way, except in the Kumaon hills garden of my friend Bhuvan, where a beautiful *Persea americana* produces an abundant crop of fruit annually that only the monkeys eat because nobody else likes them. Avocados are also commonly eaten by people of the Sikkim hill tribes.

5   C. Finney, 'End of the Avocado: Why Chefs Are Ditching the Unsustainable Fruit', *Guardian*, 1 November 2021. Available at https://www.theguardian.com/food/2021/nov/01/end-of-the-avocado-why-chefs-ditching-the-unsustainablefruit?CMP=fb_gu&utm_medium=Social&utm_source=Facebook&fbclid=IwAR3PNIH1M_CyGB4B4ry XBCfzgcizg-mSAvp-MEzv0l4uSo_aBAEPvYN2GF0# Echobox=1635768171.

6   S. Levin, 'Millionaire Tells Millennials: If You Want a House, Stop Buying Avocado Toast', *Guardian*, 15 May 2017. Available at https://www.theguardian.com/lifeandstyle/2017/may/15/australian-millionaire-millennials-avocado-toast-house.

7   https://www.abc.net.au/news/rural/2022-07-26/farmers-beg-aussies-to-eat-avocado-avolanche/101268396

8   S. Jain, 'The Myth of Big Retail', *DNA India*, 19 September 2012. Available at https://www.dnaindia.com/analysis/column-the-myth-of-big-retail-1741787.

9   A. Baviskar, 'Consumer Citizenship: Instant Noodles in India',
     Gastronomica: The Journal of Critical Food Studies, 18(2018):
     1–10.

10   'Indian Online Grocery Market Outlook (2019–2023)
     with Historic Analysis (2016–2019)', *Business Wire*, 29 July
     2019.   Available   at   https://www.businesswire.com/news/
     home/20190729005605/en/Indian-Online-Grocery-Market-
     Outlook-2019-2023-with-Historic-Analysis-2016-2019---
     ResearchAndMarkets.com.

11   Ibid.

12   M. Singh, 'Indian Online Grocery Startup Bigbasket Raises
     $60M', *Tech Crunch*, 9 April 2020. Available at https://
     techcrunch.com/2020/04/09/indian-online-grocery-startup-
     bigbasket-raises-60m/

13   H. Razdan, 'The 'New Normals' for Consumer-Retail-
     Relationship: Short-Term and Long-Term', *Economic
     Times*, 6 July 2020. Available at https://retail.economictimes.
     indiatimes.com/re-tales/the-new-normals-for-consumer-
     retail-relationship-short-term-and-long-term/4369.

14   'Indian Online Grocery Market Outlook (2019–2023)
     with Historic Analysis (2016–2019)', *Business Wire*, 29 July
     2019.   Available   at   https://www.businesswire.com/news/
     home/20190729005605/en/Indian-Online-Grocery-Market-
     Outlook-2019-2023-with-Historic-Analysis-2016-2019---
     ResearchAndMarkets.com.

15   A. R. Naik, 'Amazon Partners with Indian Farmers to Deliver
     Fresh Produce', *Inc 42*, 18 December 2019. Available at https://
     inc42.com/buzz/amazon-partners-with-indian-farmers-
     to-deliver-fresh-produce/. 'Amazon shuts down Pantry, to
     consolidate grocery delivery instead', Retailing.com, 10 January
     2021.   Available   at   https://indiaretailing.com/2021/01/10/
     amazon-shuts-down-pantry-to-consolidate-grocery-delivery-
     instead/.

16 R. Nader, '11 Ways Amazon Is Crushing the Competition, In Order to Rule Over the Ways We Consume Virtually Everything', *Salon*, 15 July 2017. Available at https://www.salon.com/2017/07/15/11-ways-amazon-is-crushing-the-competition-in-order-to-rule-over-the-ways-we-consume-virtually-everything_partner/.

17 C. Finney, 'End of the Avocado: Why Chefs Are Ditching the Unsustainable Fruit', *Guardian*, 1 November 2021. Available at https://www.theguardian.com/food/2021/nov/01/end-of-the-avocado-why-chefs-ditching-the-unsustainablefruit?CMP=fb_gu&utm_medium=Social&utm_source=Facebook&fbclid=IwAR3PNIH1M_CyGB4B4ryXBCfzgcizg-mSAvp-MEzv0l4uSo_aBAEPvYN2GF0#Echobox=1635768171; A. Abraham, 'Environmentalist Vandana Shiva Explains Where The Food We Eat Really Comes From', *Refinery 29*, 23 August 2016. Available at https://www.refinery29.com/en-gb/who-really-feeds-the-world.

18 There are genuine farm-to-fork enterprises operating in India, but the logistics of giant food retail chains do not allow this concept in the way consumers might imagine it.

19 S. Yasmin, 'Can the Farm Bills Promote Agricultural Prosperity?', *LEAD, Krea University*. Available at https://ifmrlead.org/can-the-farm-bills-promote-agricultural-prosperity/.

20 Indian retailer Bureau, 'Demystifying Women's Shopping Behaviour Pre v/s Post COVID-19', *Indian Retailer*, 28 April 2021. Available at https://www.indianretailer.com/article/retail-business/retail-trends/demystifying-women-s-shopping-behaviour-pre-v-s-post-covid-19.a6988/.

21 H. Razdan, 'The 'New Normals' for Consumer-Retail-Relationship: Short-Term and Long-Term', *Economic Times*, 6 July 2020. Available at https://retail.economictimes.

indiatimes.com/re-tales/the-new-normals-for-consumer-retail-relationship-short-term-and-long-term/4369.

22 P. Mehta, '5 Things to Keep in Mind While Venturing into Organic Food Business in India', *Your Story*, 14 April 2018. Available at https://yourstory.com/2018/04/organic-food-business-india.

23 J. Kearney,' Food Consumption Trends and Drivers', *Philosophical Transactions of the Royal Society B* 365(2010): 2793–2807.

24 'Americans' Views About and Consumption of Organic Foods', *Pew Research Center*, 1 December 2016. Available at https://www.pewresearch.org/science/2016/12/01/americans-views-about-and-consumption-of-organic-foods/.

25 Kearney, 2010: 2793–2807.

26 N. C. Sharma, 'The New Food Factories Inside India's Organics Trade', *Mint*, 14 January 2019. Available at https://www.livemint.com/Industry/RoxfUb6XwV2Qbq7qDaLhqL/The-new-food-factories-Inside-Indias-organics-trade.html.

27 K. Prasher, 'How Organic is Organic Food in India?', *Weather Channel*, 6 December 2018. Available at https://weather.com/en-IN/india/health/news/2018-12-06-organic-food-india.

28 'Health and Wellness: Organic Packaged Food Market to Cross INR 871 Million by 2021', *Progressive Grocer* [India Edition] (23 May 2018).

29 N. C. Sharma, 'The New Food Factories Inside India's Organics Trade', *Mint*, 14 January 2019. Available at https://www.livemint.com/Industry/RoxfUb6XwV2Qbq7qDaLhqL/The-new-food-factories-Inside-Indias-organics-trade.html.

30 Ibid.

31 K. Prasher, 'How Organic is Organic Food in India?', *Weather Channel*, 6 December 2018. Available at https://weather.com/en-IN/india/health/news/2018-12-06-organic-food-india.

32 R. Rau, 'Say Cheese Desi-Style', *India Today*, 18 August 2019. Available at https://www.indiatoday.in/mail-today/story/say-cheese-desi-style-1581889-2019-08-18.

33 'No Chemical Fertilisers, No Cripping Loans: What Exactly is Zero Budget Farming?', *DNA India*, 5 July 2019. Available at https://www.dnaindia.com/business/photo-gallery-no-chemical-fertilisers-no-cripping-loans-what-exactly-is-zero-budget-farming-2768579.

34 Finn, 2017.

35 Cocoa and cacao are both used when describing chocolate but cacao is more often used to refer to raw cacao butter. However, I am going to use cocoa throughout this chapter unless directly quoting.

36 'City Landmark—The Oriental Fruit Mart, Connaught Place', *The Delhi Walla*, 11 October 2016. Available at https://www.thedelhiwalla.com/2016/10/11/city-landmark-the-oriental-fruit-mart-connaught-place/.

37 A. Verma, '15 Indian Candies That Have Disappeared from Our Nukkad Shops Over The Years', *Huffpost*, 19 October 2016. Available at https://www.huffingtonpost.in/2016/10/19/15-indian-candies-that-have-disappeared-from-our-nukkad-shops_a_21586707/.

38 I learnt from Nitin that it is the high quality of the milk used in Swiss chocolate, produced by cows chewing on this country's rich cold-climate uplands grass, that gives this famed product its distinctive creamy texture and taste rather than the quality of the cocoa used.

39 N. Fleming, 'The Dark Truth about Chocolate', *Guardian*, 25 March 2018. Available at https://www.theguardian.com/lifeandstyle/2018/mar/25/chocolate-the-dark-truth-is-it-good-for-you-health-wellbeing-blood-pressure-flavanols.

40 Ibid.

41 Ibid.

42 D. Yu, 'India "Defying The Odds" as a Fast Growing Chocolate Confectionery Market, Mintel', *Confectionery News*, 2 May 2017. Available at https://www.confectionerynews.com/Article/2017/05/02/India-is-one-of-the-fastest-growing-chocolate-markets-Mintel.

43 O. Nieberg, 'Mars Develops Heat Resistant Chocolate With Polyol Mix', *Confectionery News*, 10 April 2014. Available at https://www.confectionerynews.com/Article/2014/04/10/Mars-heat-resistant-melt-free-chocolate-method.

44 S. Menon, 'Made in India: 25 Indian Food Brands That Are World Class!', *Condé Nast Traveller*, 14 May 2020. Available at https://www.cntraveller.in/story/made-in-india-25-indian-food-brands-local-vocal-pm-modi-chocolate-cheese-coffee-honey-beverage/; P. Krishna, 'Indians Love Cadbury Chocolate. These Rivals Would Love to Woo Them Away', *New York Times*, 9 November 2020. Available at https://www.nytimes.com/2020/11/09/dining/india-cadbury-chocolate-diwali.html.

45 Vikram Doctor, 'Garam Masala – Bhicoo Manekshaw, A Tribute', *Economic Times*, 17 April 2013. Available at https://economictimes.indiatimes.com/blogs/onmyplate/garam-masala-bhicoo-manekshaw-a-tribute/.

46 R. Crawford, 'Healthism and the Medicalization of Everyday Life', *International Journal of Health Service* 10, no. 3 (1980): 365–388; J. Germov and L. Williams, 'The Epidemic of Dieting Women: The Need for a Sociological Approach to Food and Nutrition', *Appetite* 27, no. 2 (1996):97–108.

47 'People Moving Towards Experiences. Cooking at Home Will Be a Big Part', *FnBNews*, 20 April 2020. Available at http://www.fnbnews.com/Interview/people-moving-towards-experiences-cooking-at-home-will-be-a-big-part-54638.

48 Sonali Acharjee, 'Gluten Free? Think Again', *Open*, 19 October 2016. Available at https://openthemagazine.com/health/gluten-free-think-again/.

49 This diagnosis requires a jejunum biopsy, not a guess.

50 This quote comes from an article titled 'Going gluten-free just because here's what you need to know' originally published on the Harvard Health blog on 8 January 2018. The link to this article is no longer active but it has been referenced extensively in other online articles including this one: https://abigailsoven.com/blogs/abigails-oven/the-gluten-revolution-and-you.

51 Jutie Upton, 'The Vast Majority of People Who Think They Are Sensitive to Gluten Are Wrong', *Insider*. Available at https://www.businessinsider.com/gluten-sensitivity-is-usually-not-real-2015-6?IR=T&r=MY.

52 Lachmi Deb Roy, 'Orthorexia Nervosa | Eating Disorder - Indian Scene', *MedIndia*, 6 September 2014. Available at https://www.medindia.net/patients/patientinfo/orthorexia-nervosa-indian-scene.htm

53 'Orthorexia', *NEDA*. Available at https://www.nationaleatingdisorders.org/learn/by-eating-disorder/other/orthorexia

54 Bee Wilson, 'Why We Fell for Clean Eating', *Guardian*, 11 August 2017. Available at https://www.theguardian.com/lifeandstyle/2017/aug/11/why-we-fell-for-clean-eating.

55 Jane E. Brody, 'Should You Be Eating Eggs?', *New York Times*, 22 April 2019. Available at https://www.nytimes.com/2019/04/22/well/eat/should-you-be-eating-eggs.html.

56 Rakesh Kalshian, 'Good or Bad? When It Comes to Food, It's Not That Simple', *Down to Earth*, * June 2020. Available at https://www.downtoearth.org.in/news/food/good-or-bad-when-it-comes-to-food-it-s-not-that-simple-71621.

57 Wansink, B., and Chandon, P., 'Can "Low-Fat" Nutrition Labels Lead to Obesity?', *Journal of Marketing Research* XLIII, (2006): 605–617.

58 Askegaard et al, 2014.

59 Appetite, Vol. 104, 1996. This edition is focused on recent psychological research on eating and pleasure; Wansink, B., and Chandon, P., 'Can "Low-Fat" Nutrition Labels Lead to Obesity?', *Journal of Marketing Research* XLIII, (2006): 605–617.

60 Jessica Knoll, 'Smash the Wellness Industry', *New York Times*, 8 June 2019. Available at https://www.nytimes.com/2019/06/08/opinion/sunday/women-dieting-wellness.html.

61 'India Weight Management Market: Industry Trends, Share, Size, Growth, Opportunity and Forecast 2022–2027', *IMARC*. Available at https://www.imarcgroup.com/india-weight-management-market; Suparna Sharma, 'India's Weight-Loss Guru Rujuta Diwekar on Why Grandma Knows Best', *Al Jazeera*, 23 July 2021. Available at https://www.aljazeera.com/economy/2021/7/23/indias-weight-loss-guru-rujuta-diwekar-on-why-grandma-knows-best.

62 Sharda Purwar and Ajay Karkare, 'A Study of Eating Disorder in Indian Women on the Basis of Their Socio-Economic Status', *International Journal of Physical Education, Sports and Health* 6, no. 5(2019): 150–151. Available at https://www.kheljournal.com/archives/2019/vol6issue5/PartC/6-5-9-813.pdf.

63 'Top 10 Health Bloggers and Influencers of India To Follow', *InfluGlue*, 24 July 2020. Available at https://www.influglue.com/blog/top-10-health-bloggers-and-influencers-of-india; This quote comes from the section on the blog 'The Picky Eater'.

64 Rebbeca Gregson, Jared Piazza, and Ryan L. Boyd. 'Against the cult of veganism: Unpacking the social psychology and ideology of anti-vegans'. *Appetite*, 178 (2022). Available at: https://doi.org/10.1016/j.appet.2022.106143

65 K. T. Achaya, *Indian Food: A Historical Companion* (Delhi: Oxford University Press, 1994). (There are numerous

references in this work to the cultivation and consumption of millets throughout India's long history); B. Venkatesh Bhat, B. Dayakar Rao, and Vilas A. Tonapi, *The Story of Millets* (Karnataka State Department of Agriculture, 2018).

66 Ann Raeboline Lincy Eliazer Nelson, Kavitha Ravichandran, and Usha Antony, 'The Impact of the Green Revolution on Indigenous Crops of India', *Journal of Ethnic Foods* 6 (2019). Available at https://journalofethnicfoods.biomedcentral.com/articles/10.1186/s42779-019-0011-9.

67 Daisy A. John and Giridhara R. Babu, 'Lessons from the Aftermaths of Green Revolution on Food System and Health', *Frontiers*, 22 February 2021. Available at https://www.frontiersin.org/articles/10.3389/fsufs.2021.644559/full.

68 The first millet recipe I came across in a widely available Indian cookbook was in Madhur Jaffrey's *Taste of India*.

69 https://www.geographyandyou.com/agriculture/a-critical-review-of-the-green-revolution-in-india/The potential for exactly these 'unintended consequences' were raised alongside the implementation of the new agricultural technology. See: K. Sebby, 'The Green Revolution of the 1960s and Its Impact on Small Farmers in India', *Environmental Studies Thesis* (2010). Available at https://digitalcommons.unl.edu/envstudtheses/10.

70 Ibid.

71 Shruti Bhogal, Adam S. Green, Cameron Andrew Petrie, and Sandeep Dixit, 'Young Indian Farmers Are Turning to an Ancient Crop to Fight Water Stress and Climate Change', *Conversation*, 11 May 2022. Available at https://theconversation.com/amp/young-indian-farmers-are-turning-to-an-ancient-crop-to-fight-water-stress-and-climate-change-179248.

72 Sebby, 2010.

73 Comment made by Dr Varshney at a forum at the India Culinary Institute in Noida in December 2019 where we were both guest speakers.

74 N. Lothungbeni Humtsoe, 'From Weight Loss to Strong
    Bones, Health Benefits of Millets', *India New England News*,
    20 May 2021. Available at https://indianewengland.com/from-
    weight-loss-to-strong-bones-health-benefits-of-millets/.   I
    have referenced just one example of the claims made for the
    'health benefits of millets'. An Internet search on the same will
    provide you with materials for days of reading.

75 Stacey Wilcox, '2023 Will be the International Year of
    Millets', *Foodbank*. Available at https://foodtank.com/
    news/2019/03/2023-will-be-the-international-year-of-millets/.

76 B. Dayakar Rao, Vishala A. D., G. D. Arlene Christina, V. A.
    Tonapi, *Millet Recipes – A Healthy Choice*, ICAR. Available at
    https://millets.res.in/m_recipes/Millets_Recipes-A_Healthy_
    choice.pdf.

77 While I can't pinpoint when this began, my sense is that the
    understanding that millets are healthier emerged from the
    environmental movement in the first place and then 'superfood'
    has been grafted on as a more acceptable/popular way of
    commercializing this grain.

78 J. P. Singh, 'Process Millets with Low-Cost Dehuller
    Machines and Earn 2–10 Times Profit', *Rural Voice*, 24 July
    2022. Available at https://eng.ruralvoice.in/technology-16/
    process-millets-with-low-cost-dehuller-machines-and-earn-
    2-10-times-profit.html.

79 Søren Askegaard, Nailya Ordabayeva, Pierre Chandon, et al.
    'Moralities in Food and Health Research', *Journal of Marketing
    Management* 30 (2014):1800–1832.

80 This information comes from the curriculum I was taught when
    I attended a course on Ayurveda at The Sivanada Institute
    of Health at the Dhanwantari Ashram in Kerala in 2013.
    'Ayurveda Wellness Course', Neyyar Dam Sivananda Yoga
    Vedanta Dhanyantari Ashram. Available at https://sivananda.
    org.in/neyyardam/ayurveda-wellness-course/.

81 T. Srinivas, 'Exploring Indian Culture through Food', *Education About Asia*, (2022):38. DOI: https://www.asianstudies.org/publications/eaa/archives/exploring-indian-culture-through-food/.

82 D. D. Arnold, 'The Good, the Bad, and the Toxic: Moral Foods in British India'. In *Moral Foods: The Construction of Nutrition and Health in Modern Asia*, ed. M. L. Caldwell, A. Ki Che Leung, and C. R. Yano (Hawaii: University of Hawaii, 2019), pp. 111–129. https://doi.org/10.1515/9780824879570.

83 Bee Wilson, 'Why We Fell for Clean Eating', *Guardian*, 11 August 2017. Available at https://www.theguardian.com/lifeandstyle/2017/aug/11/why-we-fell-for-clean-eating.

84 Ananya Barua, 'Rice Tea to Millet Momos: This Woman Is Reviving India's Tribal Culinary Gems', *Better India*, 9 January 2020. Available at https://www.thebetterindia.com/208683/ajam-emba-ranchi-tribal-cuisine-slow-food-organic-jharkhand-india-ana79/.

85 A. Magrach and MJ Sanz, Environmental and social consequences of the increase in the demand for 'superfoods' world-wide', *People Nat.* 00 (2020):1–12. https://doi.org/10.1002/pan3.10085

86 'What Makes Superfood So Super?', *UC Davis*. Available at https://www.ucdavis.edu/food/what-makes-superfood-so-super.

87 This take on superfoods is not uncontested. See: J. Loyer, 'The Social Lives of Superfoods, (PhD Thesis, University of Adelaide, 2016). Available at https://digital.library.adelaide.edu.au/dspace/handle/2440/101777.

88 Marion Nestle, 'Superfoods are a Marketing Ploy', the *Atlantic*, 23 October 2018. Available at https://www.theatlantic.com/health/archive/2018/10/superfoods-marketing-ploy/573583/.

89 M. Nestle, 'How Sweet It Is: Sugar and Candy as Health Foods', in *Unsavory Truth: How Food Companies Skew the Science of What We Eat* (New York: Basic Books, 2018).

90 P. Anbukkani, S. J. Balaji, and M. L. Nithyashree, 'Production and Consumption of Minor Millets in India-A Structural Break Analysis', *Annual Agriculture Research New Series* 38, no. 4 (2017): 1–8.

91 Jeremy Cherfas, 'Your Quinoa Habit Really Did Help Peru's Poor. But There's Trouble Ahead', *NPR*, 31 March 2016. Available at https://www.npr.org/sections/thesalt/2016/03/31/472453674/your-quinoa-habit-really-did-help-perus-poor-but-theres-trouble-ahead; 'Overproduction Threatens Andes Superfood Haven', *Phys.org*, 25 March 2018. Available at https://phys.org/news/2018-03-overproduction-threatens-andes-superfood-haven.html.

92 Chethana Prakasan, 'Health Benefits of Makhana: 7 Amazing Benefits Of Fox Nuts', *India.com*, 7 February 2018. Available at https://www.india.com/lifestyle/health-benefits-of-makhana-7-amazing-benefits-of-fox-nuts-2882256/.

93 Swathi Chaganty, 'First Food Authors on Food Habits in the Changing Dietary Landscape of India', *Foodtank*. Available at https://foodtank.com/news/2017/05/first-food-authors/.

94 Ibid.

95 'How Cooking Can Change Your Life – Michael Pollan', RSA, 4 September 2013. Available at https://www.youtube.com/watch?v=TX7kwfE3cJQ&t=7s.

Chapter 6: India's Drinking Style

1 Chidanand Rajghatta, 'Christopher Hitchens, Intellectual Who Took on God & Gandhi, Dead', *Times of India*, 17 December 2011. Available at https://timesofindia.indiatimes.com/world/us/Christopher-Hitchens-intellectual-who-took-on-God-ampamp-Gandhi-dead/articleshow/11137698.cms.

2   Christopher Hitchens, 'There Will Always Be an India', *Vanity Fair*, February 2012. Available at https://www.vanityfair.com/news/1997/08/hitchens-199708.

3   Vindu Goel, 'India's Wine Country: A Charming Work in Progress', *New York Times*, 2 March 2020. Available at https://www.nytimes.com/2020/03/02/travel/nashik-india-wine-country-grapes.html?action=click&module=Editors%20Picks&pgtype=Homepage.

4   K. T. Achaya, *A Historical Dictionary of Indian Food* (New Delhi: Oxford University Press, 1998), pp. 25–28.

5   Ibid.

6   R. L. S. Sikarwar, 'Oceans in Hindu Mythology', Uttar Pradesh State Biodiversity Board. Available at https://www.upsbdb.org/pdf/Souvenir2012/ch-21.pdf.

7   S. Ottilingam, D. V. Raghavan and A. G. Tejus Murthy, 'Drinking Habits in Ancient India', *Indian Journal of Psychiatry* 58, no. 1 (2016): 93–96.

8   Ibid.

9   Achaya, *Historical Dictionary*, 26; Ottilingam et al, 'Drinking Habits', 95.

10 K. T. Achaya. *Indian Food: A Historical Companion* (New Delhi: Oxford University Press, 1994), p. 143.

11 Ibid., 51, 58.

12 Ibid., 57–60.

13 H. K. Sharma, B. M. Tripathi and Pertti J. Pelto, 'The Evolution of Alcohol Use in India', *Aids Behaviour* (2010): 8.

14 K. T. Achaya, *A Historical Dictionary of Indian Food* (New Delhi: Oxford University Press, 1998), p. 27; also see K. T. Achaya. *Indian Food: A Historical Companion* (New Delhi: Oxford University Press, 1994), pp. 157–159.

15 H. K. Sharma, B. M. Tripathi and Pertti J. Pelto. 'The Evolution of Alcohol Use in India', *Aids Behaviour* (2010): 11.

16 Babu Rajendra Prasad, 'Teachings Of Mahatma Gandhi',
    Interet Archive. Available at https://archive.org/details/
    in.ernet.dli.2015.219057. This archive of Gandhi's teachings
    contains several references to the 'evil' of alcohol and clearly
    demonstrates his beliefs about the detrimental social impact of
    the use of alcohol in India.

17 Bill Chappell, 'Bootleg Liquor Kills 100 In India's Worst
    Outbreak In Years', *NPR*, 11 February 2019. Available at
    https://www.npr.org/2019/02/11/693516595/bootleg-liquor-
    kills-100-in-indias-worst-outbreak-in-years; 'Over 80 Killed by
    Bootleg Alcohol in Indian State', *Bangkok Post*, 2 August 2020.
    Available at https://www.bangkokpost.com/world/1961287/
    over-80-killed-by-bootleg-alcohol-in-indian-state.

18 H. K. Sharma, B. M. Tripathi and Pertti J. Pelto. 'The
    Evolution of Alcohol Use in India', *Aids Behaviour*, (2010): 12.

19 'India Bootleg Alcohol Death Toll Crosses 100, Dozens
    Arrested', *Al Jazeera*, 3 August 2020. Available at https://
    www.aljazeera.com/news/2020/8/3/india-bootleg-alcohol-
    death-toll-crosses-100-dozens-arrested. Note: This chapter
    focuses on the optimised use of alcohol—as a taste and social
    pleasure—by India's more prosperous and privileged, while
    acknowledging that its overconsumption can bring problems
    across all classes.

20 Kamiya Jani, 'Covid-19 Impact On India's Wine Industry With
    Sula CEO', *Curly Tales*, 10 June 2020. Available at https://
    curlytales.com/the-last-thing-we-want-to-do-is-reopen-right-
    now-rajeev-samant-founder-ceo-sula-vineyards/.

21 Comment in response to an email I sent to Lewis in 2020. As
    of August 2022, the IGPB seems to have been disbanded.

22 'Red Wine In A Paan Shop, Howzat! - Pawar Pops Populist
    Proposal', *Telegraph*, 28 August 2005. Available at https://
    www.telegraphindia.com/india/red-wine-in-a-paan-shop-
    howzat-pawar-pops-populist-proposal/cid/860713.

23 The man can hardly be gaining any physical benefit from this; it is possible that it might help his wife live longer though.

24 Women have been the driving force behind anti-alcohol activism in India as they, and their children, are the ones who suffer most from its availability.

25 Indians buy more red wine than white, influenced by the idea that it has health benefits.

26 Kamiya Jani, 'Covid-19 Impact On India's Wine Industry With Sula CEO', *Curly Tales*, 10 June 2020. Available at https://curlytales.com/the-last-thing-we-want-to-do-is-reopen-right-now-rajeev-samant-founder-ceo-sula-vineyards/.

27 Vishakha Saxena, 'This Women-Only Liquor Store In East Delhi Provides Women A Safe Alcohol-Buying Environment', *Indian Express*, 29 December 2015. Available at https://indianexpress.com/article/lifestyle/life-style/this-women-only-theka-in-east-delhi-provides-women-a-safe-alcohol-buying-environment/.

28 '20 Inexpensive Wines', *Upper Crust India*. Available at https://uppercrustindia.com/2019/posts/383/20-good-indian-and-international-wines.

29 https://londonwinecompetition.com/en/blog/insights-1/how-to-successfully-export-wine-and-increase-sales-in-india-510.htm

30 This comment refers to the influence of tourists pre-COVID. I am sure foreigners will eventually return to Goa in the same significant numbers over time.

31 'Orange Liquers', *Desmondji*. Available at https://desmondji.com/orange-liqueurs/.

32 Satviki Sanjay, 'Home Delivery of Alcohol May Be a Reality Soon', *Vice*, 8 May 2020. Available at https://www.vice.com/en/article/jgxe3y/home-delivery-of-alcohol-in-india.

33 '5 Alcohol Delivery Apps In India That Offer A Great Selection', *Lifestyle Asia*, & December 2020. Available at

https://www.lifestyleasia.com/ind/food-drink/drinks/5-alcohol-delivery-apps-in-india-that-offer-a-greats-selection/.

34 Shuchi Bansal, 'Home Delivery of Liquor Requires Safeguards', *Mint*, 10 June 2021. Available at https://www.livemint.com/opinion/columns/home-delivery-of-liquor-requires-safeguards-11623266860429.html.

35 I am talking about families visiting 'toddy shops' where the food is known to be really good and the atmosphere and amenities conducive to family outings, not necessarily to drink toddy.

36 Anil S., 'Kerala Guzzled Liquor Worth Rs 45,000 Crore In The Last Three-And-A-Half Years, Data Show', *New Indian Express*, 29 October 2019. Available at https://www.newindianexpress.com/states/kerala/2019/oct/29/kerala-guzzled-liquor-worth-rs-45000-crore-in-the-last-three-and-a-half-years-data-show-2054207.html.

37 Gayathri Mani, 'What Is The Controversy Surrounding Delhi Government's Liquor Policy?', *New Indian Express*, 19 August 2022. Available at https://indianexpress.com/article/explained/explained-controversy-surrounding-delhi-governments-new-liquor-policy-8061391/.

38 'Delhi Govt To Resume Selling Liquor After Controversies Around Private Licenses, To Open 700 Vends Including 5 Premium Stores', *OpIndia*, 6 August 2022. Available at https://www.opindia.com/2022/08/delhi-govt-to-open-700-liquor-vends-after-controversies-on-private-stores/.

Chapter 7: Waste: The End of the Line

1   Hridayesh Joshi, 'Mountain of Waste in Aravallis Casts a Shadow in Villages Nearby', *Mongabay*, 18 October 2019. Available at https://india.mongabay.com/2019/10/mountain-of-waste-in-aravallis-casts-a-shadow-in-villages-nearby/.

2   Akshatha M., 'Bengaluru Dumping Its Garbage in Nearby Villages', *Economic Times*, 9 August 2019. Available at https://economictimes.indiatimes.com/news/politics-and-nation/bengaluru-dumping-its-garbage-in-nearby-villages/articleshow/70599664.cms?from=mdr.

3   C. Lutringer and S. Randeria, 'How Not to Waste a Garbage Crisis: Food Consumption, Solid Waste Management and Civic Activism in Bangalore/Bengaluru, India', *International Development Journal* (2017). DOI: https://doi.org/10.4000/poldev.2476.

4   G. Sharma, S. Annadate, and B. Sinha, 'Will Open Waste Burning Become India's Largest Air Pollution Source?', *Environmental Pollution* (2021). DOI: https://doi.org/10.1016/j.envpol.2021.118310.

5   A. Doron and R. Jeffrey, *Waste of a Nation: Garbage and Growth in India* (Boston: Harvard University Press, 2018); Australians are the second-most resource-consumptive people after Americans.

6   C. Law, I. Fraser, and M. Piracha, 'Nutrition Transition and Changing Food Preferences in India', *Journal of Agricultural Economics* 71 (2020):118–143.

7   Saroj Kumar Pani and Atul Arun Pathak, 'Managing Plastic Packaging Waste in Emerging Economies: The Case of EPR in India', *Journal of Environmental Management* 288 (2021): 1–9.

8   In August 2022, Nature's Basket was marketing itself as 'online supermarket and premium grocery' where you 'taste the world' as well as enjoy 'not just the gourmet but the opulent life too'. https://www.naturesbasket.co.in

9   A. Doron and R. Jeffrey, *Waste of a Nation: Garbage and Growth in India* (Boston: Harvard University Press, 2018).

10 'Growing Plastic Pollution in Wake of COVID-19: How Trade Policy Can Help', *UNCTAD*, 27 July 2020. Available

at https://unctad.org/news/growing-plastic-pollution-wake-covid-19-how-trade-policy-can-help.

11 Personal conversation with Bengalaru-based Chef Abhijit Saha.

12 ABC Podcasts, 'Plastic Addiction', *ABC* Podcasts, 5 February 2020. Available at https://www.abc.net.au/radionational/programs/latenightlive/plastic-production-set-to-increase/11929440

13 A. Little, *The Fate of Food: What We'll Eat in a Bigger, Hotter, Smarter World* (London: One World Publications, 2019), p. 259.

14 Biplob Nandy and Gaurav Sharma, et al., 'Recovery of Consumer Waste in India – A Mass Flow Analysis for Paper, Plastic and Glass and the Contribution of Households and the Informal Sector', *Resources, Conservation and Recycling* 101 (2015):167–181.

15 Jeevaraj Pillai, 'Managing Plastic Waste – What Emerging Economies like India Can Learn from Developed Nations', *Reinforced Plastics* 65 (2021): 10.

16 C. Lutringer and S. Randeria, 'How Not to Waste a Garbage Crisis: Food Consumption, Solid Waste Management and Civic Activism in Bangalore/Bengaluru, India', *International Development Journal* (2017). DOI: https://doi.org/10.4000/poldev.2476.

17 Saroj Kumar Pani and Atul Arun Pathak, 'Managing Plastic Packaging Waste in Emerging Economies: The Case of EPR in India', *Journal of Environmental Management* 228 (2001): 7.

18 Jeevaraj Pillai, 'Managing Plastic Waste – What Emerging Economies like India Can Learn from Developed Nations', *Reinforced Plastics* 65 (2021): 11.

19 Sabrina Chakori and Amar Abdul Aziz, 'Recycling Is Not Enough. Zero-Packaging Stores Show We Can Kick Our Plastic Addiction', *The Conversation*, 17 January 2019.

Available at https://theconversation.com/recycling-is-not-enough-zero-packaging-stores-show-we-can-kick-our-plastic-addiction-106357.

Chapter 8: Food for the City

1   A. Gunvald Nilsen, 'How Can We Understand India's Agrarian Struggle Beyond "Modi Sarkar Murdabad"?' *Economic & Political Weekly* 53 (2018): 50.

2   Mayank Bharadwaj, 'Angry Indian Farmers March on Parliament to Denounce Their Plight', *Reuters*, 30 November 2018. Available at https://www.reuters.com/article/us-india-farmers-idUSKCN1NZ0MO

3   Mayank Aggarwal and S. Gopikrishna Warrier, 'Environmental Issues in Agriculture A Silent Reason Behind Farmers' Protests', *Mongabay*, 8 December 2020. Available at https://india.mongabay.com/2020/12/environmental-issues-in-agriculture-a-silent-reason-behind-farmers-protests/.

4   Gunisha Kaur, 'The Country Where 30 Farmers Die Each Day', *CNN*, 17 March 2022. Available at https://edition.cnn.com/2022/03/17/opinions/india-farmer-suicide-agriculture-reform-kaur/index.html; Rajit Sengupta, 'Every Day, 28 People Dependent On Farming Die By Suicide In India', *Down To Earth*, 3 September 2020. Available at https://www.downtoearth.org.in/news/agriculture/every-day-28-people-dependent-on-farming-die-by-suicide-in-india-73194.

5   Mujib Mashsal, Emily Shmall, and Russell Goldman, 'What Prompted the Farm Protests in India?', *New York Times*, 19 November 2021. Available at https://www.nytimes.com/2021/01/27/world/asia/india-farmer-protest.html; 'Farm Laws: India Farmers End Protest After Government Accepts Demands', *BBC News*, 9 December 2021. Available at https://

www.bbc.com/news/world-asia-india-59566157;   Stephen
Stockwell and Meghna Bali, 'Why Are Tens of Thousands
of Farmers Protesting in India?', *ABC*, 8 February 2021.
Available at https://www.abc.net.au/triplej/programs/hack/
india-farmer-protests-explainer-hack/13132968.

6   'Mega Trend Urban Farming', *Future Markets Magazine*.
Available   at   https://future-markets-magazine.com/en/
markets-technology-en/urban-farming/.

7   'Home-made food is best but what about home-made food
with home grown vegetables!' https://edibleroutes.com/about-
edible-routes/

8   See: Lekshmi Priya S., 'Live Green: 5 Startups That'll Help
You Set Up An Organic Urban Farm From Scratch!', *The Better
India,*30 April 2019. Available at https://www.thebetterindia.
com/180575/how-to-do-urban-farm-organic-city-weekend-
diy-india/.

9   http://tnhorticulture.tn.gov.in/horti/sites/default/files/doitkit/
operational_manual.pdf

10   P. Awasthi, 'Urban Agriculture in India and Its challenges',
*International Journal of Environmental Science: Development
and Monitoring* 4, no, 2 (2013): 48–51; D. T. H. Lintelo, F.
Marshall, and D. S. Bhupal, 'Urban Food: The Role of Urban
and Peri Urban Agriculture in India: A Case Study from Delhi',
Food, Nutrition and Agriculture 29 (2002): 4–13.

11   Manu Joseph, 'Falling for the Village Romantics', in *India Now
and In Transition*, ed. A. K Thakur (New Delhi: Niyogi Books,
2017), p. 254.

12   Joseph Redwood-Martinez, 'Urban Agriculture in Delhi:
Thousands of Invisible Farmers', *Huffpost,* 8 May 2013.
Available   at   https://www.huffpost.com/entry/urban-
agriculture-in-delhi_b_3231174.

13   Joseph Redwood-Martinez, 'Urban Agriculture in Delhi:
Thousands of Invisible Farmers', *Huffpost,* 8 May 2013.

Available at https://www.huffpost.com/entry/urban-agriculture-in-delhi_b_3231174.

14 'Delhi: Yamuna Rises Again, Water Woes to Ease', *Times of India*, 17 July 2021. Available at https://timesofindia.indiatimes.com/city/delhi/yamuna-rises-again-water-woes-to-ease/articleshow/84487333.cms.

15 D. T. H. Lintelo, F. Marshall, and D. S. Bhupal, 'Urban Food: The Role of Urban and Peri Urban Agriculture in India: A Case Study from Delhi', *Food, Nutrition and Agriculture* 29 (2002): 4–13.

16 Joseph Redwood-Martinez, 'Urban Agriculture in Delhi: Thousands of Invisible Farmers', *Huffpost*, 8 May 2013. Available at https://www.huffpost.com/entry/urban-agriculture-in-delhi_b_3231174.

17 Manu Joseph, 'Falling for the Village Romantics', in *India Now and In Transition*, ed. by A. K Thakur (New Delhi: Niyogi Books, 2017), p. 259.

18 Harry Dillon, 'Thriving Villages Are Key to India's Success', *The Conversation*, 26 Marxh 2012. Available at http://theconversation.com/thriving-villages-are-key-to-indias-success-5023.

19 'India's Farmed Shrimp Sector in 2020: A White Paper', *Aqua Culture, Asia Pacific*, 31 July 2021. Available at https://aquaasiapac.com/2021/07/31/indias-farmed-shrimp-sector-in-2020-a-white-paper/; A. Victor Suresh, 'How India Became the World's Top Shrimp Producer', *Global Seafood Alliance*, 5 October 2020. Available at https://www.globalseafood.org/advocate/how-india-became-the-worlds-top-shrimp-producer/

20 'India's Seafood Exports Pegged at 12,89,651 MT in FY 2019-20', *Economic Times*, 17 August 2020. Available at https://economictimes.indiatimes.com/news/economy/foreign-trade/indias-seafood-exports-pegged-at-1289651-mt-in-fy-2019.

21 M. Kumaran, R. Geetha, Jose Antony, et al., 'Prospective Impact of Corona Virus Disease (COVID-19) Related Lockdown on Shrimp Aquaculture Sector in India – A Sectoral Assessment', *Aquaculture* 531 (2021). DOI: https://doi.org/10.1016/j.aquaculture.2020.735922.

22 Emerson Kagoo and N. Rajalakshmi, 'Environmental and Social Conflicts of Aquaculture in Tamilnadu and Andhra Pradesh', *Journal of Social and Economic Development* 4, no. 1 (2002):13–26. DOI: http://www.isec.ac.in/JSED/JSED_V4_I1_13-26.pdf; http://www.indiaenvironmentportal.org.in/files/file/aquaculture%20East%20Godavari.pdf

23 Rajamanohar Somasundaram, 'Why Covid Should Fast-track Tech Adoption in Indian Aquaculture', *The Fish Site*, 4 November 2020. Available at https://thefishsite.com/articles/why-covid-should-fast-track-tech-adoption-in-indian-aquaculture-1.

24 The Gujarat capital is expected to reach megacity status by 2030.

25 P. Sane, 'Dudhsagar Dairy at Mehsana, India (1970–73): Achyut Kanvinde and the Architecture of White Revolution', in *Proceedings of the Society of Architectural Historians, Australia and New Zealand: 30, Open*, ed. Alexandra Brown and Andrew Leach 1 (2013): 355–364.

26 'Gateway to Dairy Production and Products', *Food and Agricultural Organization of the United Nations*. Available at https://www.fao.org/dairy-production-products/production/en/.

27 Karl Kruszelnicki, 'Dr Karl Explains the Difference between A1 and A2 Milk', *ABC News*, 19 June 2018. Available at https://www.abc.net.au/news/science/2018-06-19/dr-karl-a1-vs-a2-milk/9879800.

28 Rakesh K. Tandon, Y. K. Joshi, D. S. Singh, M. Narendranathan, V. Balakrishnan, and K Lal, 'Lactose Intolerance in North and

South Indians', *The American Journal of Nutrition* 34 (1981): 943–946.

29 Annette McGivney, 'Almonds Are Out. Dairy Is a Disaster. So What Milk Should We Drink?', *Guardian*, 29 January 2020. Available at https://www.theguardian.com/environment/2020/jan/28/what-plant-milk-should-i-drink-almond-killing-bees-aoe.

30 Shantanu Nandan Sharma, 'Great Indian Cattle Count: An Inside Story', *Economic Times*, 27 January 2019. Available at https://economictimes.indiatimes.com/news/politics-and-nation/how-a-team-of-experts-are-conducting-indias-first-tech-aided-livestock-census/articleshow/67704952.cms?from=mdr.

31 There is production of buffalo milk mozzarella in Haryana; Amul describes its mozzarella product as 'genuine'. Thus, it should be made with buffalo milk.

32 Adding 'value' to food products typically means making foods more convenient by reducing the labour required, adding flavourings or other ingredients, and packaging these to make them more attractive.

33 Arzoo Dina, 'These Brands Will Deliver Amazing Artisanal Cheeses to Your Doorstep', *Lifestyle Asia*. Available at https://www.lifestyleasia.com/ind/food-drink/dining/best-cheese-delivery-services-in-india/.

34 The milk for this is expected to come from increasing the size of the cow herd.

35 https://www.darimafarms.com/

36 Avantika Bhuyan, 'Experiments with Himalayan Cheese in Kalimpong', *Live Mint*, 26 October 2020. Available at https://lifestyle.livemint.com/food/discover/experiments-with-himalayan-cheese-in-kalimpong-111603682811849.html

37 Manu Joseph, 'Falling for the Village Romantics', in *India Now and In Transition*, ed. A. K Thakur (New Delhi: Niyogi Books, 2017), p. 254.

38 '40 Under 40: India's Most Exciting Young Chefs', *CN Traveller*, 10 February 2020. Available at https://www.cntraveller.in/magazine-story/best-indian-chefs-under-40-bangalore-delhi-mumbai-goa-pune/.

39 Possibly not a concept that bodes well for urban farming as I don't think the flavour of Delhi smog or Mumbai's Thane Creek would be appealing!

40 Anjana Pasricha, 'Pandemic Triggers Reverse Migration from India Cities to Villages', *VOA News*, 24 July 2020. Available at https://www.voanews.com/covid-19-pandemic/pandemic-triggers-reverse-migration-india-cities-villages.

41 Ibid.

Conclusion: The Future of Indian Food

1 Suman Tarafdar, 'AD Singh: The Man who Changed the Way India Eats Out', *Punch Magazine*, 30 March 2017. Available at https://thepunchmagazine.com/culture/hospitality/ad-singh-the-man-who-changed-the-way-india-eats-out.

2 A. Appadurai, 'How to Make a National Cuisine: Cookbooks in Contemporary India', *Comparative Studies in Society and History* 30 (1988): 3–24.

3 The Australian Government, for example, is actively focused on supporting Australian food and wine producers to gain access to the Indian market.

4 Tulasi Srinivas, 'Exploring Indian Culture through Food', *Education About Asia* (2022): 39.

5 Moin Qazi, 'India's Failed Food System', *Asian Age*, 27 December 2017. Available at https://www.asianage.com/india/all-india/271217/indias-failed-food-system; Vikash Mohan, 'Agricultural Wastage is India's Problem No 1 – Here is Why', *Times of India*, 4 September 2019. Available at

https://timesofindia.indiatimes.com/business/india-business/agricultural-wastage-is-indias-problem-no-1-here-is-why

6   Sanira Mediratta, 'Chicken Tikka Masala is Britain's National Dish', *InShorts*, 10 November 2016. Available at https://inshorts.com/en/news/chicken-tikka-masala-is-britains-national-dish-1478771928909.

7   Charmaine O'Brien, *The Colonial Kitchen: Australia 1788–1901* (New York: Rowman & Littlefield, New York, 2016), pp. 1–27.

8   Nayantara Dutta, 'Reclaiming Indian Food from the White Gaze', *Eater,* 30 June 2020. Available at https://www.eater.com/2020/6/30/21307238/taking-back-indian-food-from-the-white-gaze-cookbook-recipes; Julia Sherman, 'What One Writer Eats After a Slew of Rich Restaurant Meals', *The New York Times,* 9 July 2018. Available at https://www.nytimes.com/2018/07/09/t-magazine/stephanie-danler-kitchari-recipe.html.

9   Nayantara Dutta, 'Reclaiming Indian Food from the White Gaze', *Eater,* 30 June 2020. Available at https://www.eater.com/2020/6/30/21307238/taking-back-indian-food-from-the-white-gaze-cookbook-recipes.

Select Bibliography

If you are interested in learning more about India in world food history or understanding how economic, technological, and social development has impacted changes in the foodways in India and other societies in the past, I recommend the food history section of this bibliography as a syllabus for that undertaking.

Food History

Achaya, K. T. *Indian Food: A Historical Companion*. Delhi: Oxford University Press, 1994

Appadurai, Arjun. 'How to Make a National Cuisine: Cookbooks in Contemporary India'. *Comparative Studies in Society and History*, 30 (1988): 3–24.

Coe, Sophie, and Michael Coe. *The True History of Chocolate*. London: Thames & Hudson, 1996.

Collingham, L. *Curry: A Biography*. London: Chatto & Windus, 2005.

Farb, P., and G. Armelagos. *Consuming Passions: The Anthropology of Eating*. Boston: Houghton Mifflin Company, 1980.

Finn, M. *Discriminating Taste: How Class Anxiety Created the American Food Revolution*. Camden, NJ: Rutgers University Press, 2017.

Goody, Jack. *Cooking, Cuisine and Class: A Study in Comparative Sociology*. Cambridge: Cambridge University Press, 1982.

Kaufman, Jean-Claude. *The Meaning of Cooking*. Cambridge, U.K.: Polity Press, 2010.

Laudan, Rachel. *Cuisine & Empire: Cooking in World History*. Los Angeles: University of California Press, 2013.

Mason, Laura. *Sugar-plums and Sherbet: The Prehistory of Sweets*. UK: Prospect Books, 2003.

Mennell, Stephen. *All Manners of Food: Eating and Taste in England and France from the Middle Ages to the Present*. United Kingdom: Blackwell, 1985.

Mintz, Sidney. *Sweetness and Power: The Place of Sugar in Modern History*. New York: Penguin Books, 1985.

Mintz, S. W., and C. M. Du Bois. 'The Anthropology of Food and Eating'. *Annual Review of Anthropology*, 31 (2002): 99–119.

Naccarto, Peter, and Kathleen Lebesco. *Culinary Capital*. London: Berg, 2012.

Tannahill, R. *Food in History*. London: Penguin, 1973.

Contemporary Food

Diwekar, R. *Indian Superfoods*. New Delhi: Juggernaut, 2016.

Harris, Solomon. *Metabolic Living: Food, Fat, and the Absorption of Illness in India*. Durham: Duke University Press, 2016.

Karanth, G. K. 'Foodscapes in Bengaluru—Changing Patterns of Family Eating Out and Waste Generation'. *International Development Policy | Revue internationale de politique de développement* [Online], 8.2. 2017.

Katrak, K. 'Food and Belonging: At "Home" in "Alien-Kitchens". In *Through the Kitchen Window: Women Explore the Intimate Meanings of Food and Cooking*, edited by Arlene Voski Avakian. Boston: Beacon Press, 1997.

Khara, T., and M. B. Ruby. 'Meat Eating and the Transition from Plant-Based Diets among Urban Indians'. *M/C Journal*, 22: 2. 2019. https://doi.org/10.5204/mcj.1509

Khare, R. S. 'Postscript – Globalizing South Asian Food Cultures: Earlier Stops to New Horizons'. In *Curried Cultures: Globalization, Food, and South Asia*, edited by Krishnendu Ray and Tulasi Srinivas, pp. 237–254. Berkeley: University of California Press, 2012.

Little. A. *The Fate of Food: What We'll Eat in a Bigger, Hotter, Smarter World*. London: One World Publications, 2019.

Mahadevan, M., Blair, D., and Raines, E. R. 'Changing Food Habits in a South Indian Hindu Brahmin Community: A Case of Transitioning Gender Roles and Family Dynamics'. *Ecology of Food and Nutrition*, 53 (2014): 596–617.

Mooji, Jos. 'Food Policy and Politics. The Political Economy of the Public Distribution System in India'. *The Journal of Peasant Studies*, 25 (1998): 77–101.

Nestle, Marion. *Food Politics: How the Food Industry Influences Nutrition and Health / Marion Nestle*. California: University of California Press Berkeley, 2007.

Nestle, Marion. *Unsavoury Truth: How Food Companies Skew the Science of What We Eat*. New York: Basic Books, 2018.

Ray, Krishnendu, and Srinivas, Tulasi, eds. *Curried Cultures: Globalization, Food, and South Asia*. Berkeley: University of California Press, 2012.

Reshii, M. H. *The Flavour of Spice: Journeys, Recipes, Stories*. Gurugram: Hachette Publishing, 2017.

Rangwala, Shenaz, Chanaka Jayawardhena, Chanaka, and Saxena, Gunjan. 'From Caged Birds to Women with Wings: A Perspective on Consumption Practices of New Middle-Class Indian Women'. *European Journal of Marketing*, 54, no. 1 (2020): 2803–2824.

Spector, Tim. *Why Almost Everything We Have Been Told About Food is Wrong*. London: Jonathan Cape, 2020.

Srinivas, Tulasi. 'Masala Matters: Globalization, Female Food Entrepreneurs and the Changing Politics of Provisioning'. In *Curried Cultures: Globalization, Food, and South Asia* edited by Krishnendu Ray and Tulasi Srinivas, pp. 219–236. Berkeley: University of California Press, 2012.

Wansink, Brian. *Mindless Eating: Why we eat more than we think.* California, United States: Hay House, 2010.

General

Chandrasekaran, N., and Purushothaman, Roopa. *Bridgital Nation: Solving Technology's People Problem.* New Delhi: Penguin, 2019.

Sanghvi, V. *The Game Changers: Transforming India.* New Delhi: Westland Publications, 2019.

Thakur, A.K., ed. *India Now and In Transition.* New Delhi: Niyogi Books, 2017.

Podcasts

Rabobank. Consumer Foods to Go
https://research.rabobank.com/far/en/sectors/consumer-foods/consumer-foods-to-go.html

Maintenance Phase: Wellness and Weightloss Dubunked and Decoded
https://www.maintenancephase.com

Other Selected Works by the Author

'The Devil at Work? The Cook in Colonial Australian literature'. In *The Routledge Companion to Food in Literature*, Routledge Publishing Ltd, Abingdon, United Kingdom, 2018.

The Colonial Kitchen: Australia 1788–1901. New York: Rowman & Littlefield, 2016.

The Penguin Food Guide to India. India: Penguin Books, 2013.

Flavours of Melbourne: A Culinary Biography. Adelaide: Wakefield Press, 2008.

Recipes from an Urban Village: A Cookbook from Hazrat Nizamuddin Basti. New Delhi: The Hope Project Charitable Trust, 2003.

Flavours of Delhi: A Food Lover's Guide. India: Penguin Books, 2003.